The Union of Tanganyika and Zanzibar: Formation of Tanzania and its Challenges

Godfrey Mwakikagile

Copyright © 2016 Godfrey Mwakikagile
All rights reserved.

The Union of Tanganyika and Zanzibar:
Formation of Tanzania and its Challenges

First Edition

ISBN 978-9987-16-046-4

New Africa Press
Dar es Salaam, Tanzania

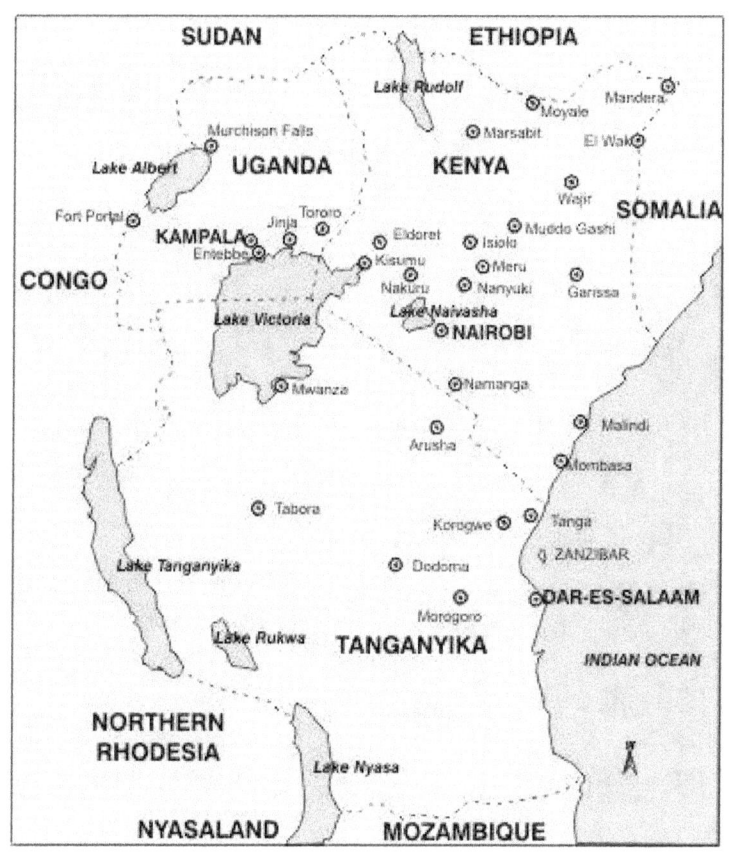

Acknowledgements

I WISH to express my profound gratitude to the sources I have used to document my work.

All the sources I have cited are given full attribution. I am very grateful to all of them without a single exception. My work would not be what it is in terms of documentation without them except for the analysis which is entirely mine including its shortcomings.

I must express my profound gratitude to Professor Ethan Sanders for using his paper, "Conceiving the Tanganyika-Zanzibar Union in the Midst of the Cold War: Internal and International Factors," in my analysis.

His paper is especially significant for this second edition because it helps fortify the central argument I advanced in my first edition in which I argued that the union of Tanganyika and Zanzibar was a product of an African initiative by President Julius Nyerere and his colleagues in Tanganyika and Zanzibar.

My special gratitude also goes to Professor Paul Bjerk for using his work, *Building a Peaceful Nation: Julius Nyerere and The Establishment of Sovereignty in Tanzania, 1960 – 1964*, in complementing my analysis of the consummation of the union of Tanganyika and Zanzibar and the factors which led to the merger of the two countries – although some people, such as Robert Hennemeyer, the deputy American ambassador to Tanzania in the mid-sixties, did not consider it to be a merger but a very loose union of the former independent states in spite of the fact that both lost their sovereignties after they submerged their identities in the macro-nation of Tanzania under one strong central government.

There is evidence to show that the union was not a product of American and British efforts to unite the two countries; although its formation may have served the geopolitical interests of the Western powers as well, warding off "communist penetration" of the region, by weakening communist elements in Zanzibar, especially Abdulrahman Mohamed Babu who was said to be the mastermind of this onslaught. Abdallah Kassim Hanga was another target but not feared as much as Babu was.

Also, special thanks must go to the American diplomats who were accredited to Tanzania and whose interviews, reproduced here, provide some insights into a number of areas including the subjects I have addressed, although what they discussed goes beyond the central thesis of my work. They are vital references, nonetheless.

I am also profoundly grateful to those who conducted the interviews and to the Foreign Affairs Oral History Collection, Association for Diplomatic Studies and Training (ADST) in Arlington, Virginia, USA, www.adst.org, the copyright holder, for permission to use their material in this book.

The material has been very helpful in many ways including providing inspiration to other people who may want to go beyond my work to learn more about my home country, Tanzania, and how things were in those days when Tanganyika united with Zanzibar during the Cold War – to form Tanzania – and what happened in the following years which were some of the most critical in the history of post-colonial Africa.

Introduction

THE unification of Tanganyika and Zanzibar in April 1964 was the first political union between independent countries ever to take place on the African continent in the post-colonial era. And it continues to be a subject of interest among many people more than 50 years after its consummation.

It was preceded by the Zanzibar revolution which took place on 12 January 1964. Three months later, the new nation of Tanzania was formed after the two former independent states of Tanganyika and Zanzibar surrendered their sovereignties to a supra-national entity which came to be officially known as the United Republic of Tanzania. There is no question that the revolution played a major role in encouraging or pushing the leaders towards unification.

The union of Tanganyika and Zanzibar may still have been consummated had the revolution not taken place in the island nation. We will never know. But given the Pan-Africanist inclinations of the leaders involved in the consummation of the union, there was a high probability that the two countries would have united sometime at a later date.

The union was a milestone in the history of post-colonial Africa and in the continent's quest for unity and had an impact that is still felt today, decades after it was formed. It influenced political and diplomatic relations between and among countries and changed the course of history.

It was even a factor in the super-power rivalry between the United States and the Soviet Union during the Cold War. It also became a major subject of intellectual and ideological debates in and outside Africa for many years. And it continues to stimulate debate even today among many Tanzanians and other people.

There are some people in Tanzania including a number of leaders who think uniting the two countries was a mistake. Some people say the union was formed in hurry without seriously considering all the issues involved. Then there are those who say the union should not have been formed at all and that the two countries of Tanganyika and Zanzibar should have remained separate entities with full sovereign status they attained when they won independence from Britain on separate dates.

Tanganyika won independence on 9 December 1961 and Zanzibar on 10 December 1963, although the legitimacy of Zanzibar's government which assumed power on independence day was highly questionable since the black African majority in the island nation were excluded from power by their Arab rulers; one of the factors which played a major role in igniting the Zanzibar revolution.

It has been a bumpy road since independence. And many problems still lie ahead as the two partners continue to find ways to resolve their differences and strengthen the union. In fact, a significant number of Zanzibaris, especially on Pemba island, would like to see the union dissolved and return to the status quo ante.

Only time will tell where the union is headed.

Problems faced by the union of Tanganyika and Zanzibar have also served as a warning to other African countries which may contemplate uniting under one government, although that is a remote possibility on a continent where nationalism transcends Pan-Africanism despite professions to the contrary.

Even within Tanzania itself, Zanzibari "nationalism" is still strong, although Zanzibar is no longer a separate country with sovereign status. It is an integral part of the United Republic of Tanzania. But that has not stopped many Zanzibaris from demanding independence and dissolution of the union.

Some of the union's strongest opponents are members of the Civic United Front (CUF), one of Tanzania's major opposition parties, which has its biggest support in the former island nation, mainly on Pemba Island, and has ties to Oman and other Gulf states.

Opposition to the union also comes from a significant number of people who were supporters of the old Arab regime and are mostly Arab themselves.

The union was a major achievement. But it also has many problems, some of which may not have been anticipated by the architects of this macro-nation.

Why was the union formed, when it was, besides the desire that already existed among the leaders to unite the two countries? Were others forces at work?

Did the United States and Britain exert pressure on Nyerere to unite the two countries as Professor Ali Mazrui and others contend? As Mazrui stated in his article, "Nyerere and I," October 1999, in which he eulogised the former Tanzanian leader:

"My strongest disagreement with Nyerere concerned Zanzibar and Nigeria (when Tanzania recognised the secessionist region of Eastern Nigeria as the independent Republic of Biafra).

Did Tanganyika unite with Zanzibar to form Tanzania under pressure from President Lyndon Johnson of the United States and Prime Minister Sir Alec Douglas-Home of Britain who did not want Zanzibar to become another communist Cuba?"

Was the merger of the countries a Pan-African initiative by Nyerere and the leader of Zanzibar after the revolution, Abeid Karume and some of his colleagues, to form one country?

Were the two leaders, Nyerere and Karume, equally motivated to unite their countries?

Was it Nyerere who was behind it all? Or was it Karume who first suggested to Nyerere that their countries should unite? As Tanzania's former First Vice President Aboud Jumbe, who had fallen out with Nyerere, bluntly stated at a press conference in Dar es Salaam on 12 January 1998 on the 34th anniversary of the Zanzibar revolution which, among other things, provided an impetus towards unification of the two countries:

"Ask Nyerere, because he is the one who went to Zanzibar. He is the one who wanted the union. He must have had goals. Has he achieved them? I can not speak for mainlanders on the achievement of the union."

Was there an interplay of forces at work when the union was formed? Cold War intrigues and rivalries; Pan-African solidarity and commitment to regional and continental unity under one government by President Julius Nyerere of Tanganyika and his colleagues such as Tanganyika's minister defence and foreign affairs, Oscar Kambona, among other factors.

Was it driven by the imperatives of geography and historical dictates including the "natural" desire by weak countries to work together and even unite and the "inevitability" of regional integration in the East African context, considering the history of the region?

What role, if any, did the Cold War play in inspiring and facilitating the merger of the two East African countries?

Was the union an African initiative by the nationalist leaders of Tanganyika and Zanzibar without any need for encouragement from the United States and Britain? Did Pan-Africanism and pan-African solidarity play a primary or a minor role? Or was it the prime determinant?

Other factors included a passionate appeal by Zanzibari prime minister and vice president, Kassim Hanga, to his colleagues in the Zanzibar Revolutionary Council to support the merger of the two countries; fear of a communist regime which could have been established in Zanzibar after the revolution, turning the island nation into what the United States and other Western powers feared would be another Cuba or "the Cuba of Africa"; security concerns by Tanganyika if Zanzibar, so close to the mainland, were to have a hostile regime or became unstable, thus posing a threat to the mainland; fear by Zanzibari leaders especially President Abeid Karume who was worried that his political enemies, especially the Marxist-Leninist Abdulrahman Mohamed Babu, could oust him and the only way he could survive and be secure would be by uniting his country with Tanganyika for protection by a bigger and more powerful neighbour.

What role did all those factors play in the unification process which led to the establishment of of the United Republic of Tanzania after Tanganyika and Zanzibar united to form one country?

Why did Zanzibari leaders such as Kassim Hanga and even Abdulrahman Babu, well-known Marxist-Leninists, support the union with Tanganyika, knowing full well that it would cost them – weaken them politically and deprive them of their power base in Zanzibar and thus make them "allies" of their enemies, the United States and other Western powers, who encouraged the merger of the two countries to neutralise them in order to prevent them from establishing a communist regime in Zanzibar that would pose a threat to Western geopolitical and strategic interests in the region and in Africa as a whole? Why did they support such a union, which amounted to political suicide for them in their native land, Zanzibar, as Marxist-Leninists who ended up being powerless there? And why do the leaders of Tanzania mainland want to maintain the union at any cost although Zanzibar is an economic burden on the mainland?

The union remains a highly contentious subject among many Tanzanians. Many questions are still being asked. And most of them have not been fully answered.

It is not the purpose of this book to answer those questions, whether or not the union should have been formed, or whether or not it was the right thing to do.

The focus of this work is on whether or not Nyerere and his colleagues on the mainland – Tanganyika – and those in Zanzibar initiated the move towards unification.

Cold War considerations are also an integral part of this analysis as a counter thesis to Pan-African initiatives as the driving force behind the consummation of the union.

This work complements my previous one, *The Union of Tanganyika and Zanzibar: Product of the Cold War?*

The Union of Tanganyika and Zanzibar

THE UNION of Tanganyika and Zanzibar was the first merger of independent states on the entire continent and the only one that has ever been consummated.

The Ghana-Guinea union formed on 23 November 1958 between the first black African country to win independence from Britain and the first to achieve it from France, and joined by Mali in 1961 to form the Ghana-Guinea-Mali union, was more symbolic than functional.[1]

In the case of Tanzania, both Tanganyika and Zanzibar renounced their sovereignties and submerged their separate national identities in the new macro-nation. The establishment of Tanzania from this merger is also one of the most memorable achievements of the late President Julius Nyerere.

Tanganyika united with Zanzibar on 26 April 1964. For six months, the new country was simply known as the Union of Tanganyika and Zanzibar. It was also officially known by its much longer name as the United Republic of Tanganyika and Zanzibar, and was renamed the United Republic of Tanzania on October 29th in the same year. Dar es Salaam, the capital of Tanganyika, which means 'haven of peace" or "the abode of peace" in Arabic and was founded by the Arab rulers, became the seat of the union government.

The union was preceded by the revolution in Zanzibar which ended Arab hegemonic control of the islands that lasted for hundreds of years since the latter part of the 1600s.

The violent uprising was led by John Okello, a Ugandan who had settled on Pemba Island and who saw himself as a messianic figure on a mission to free his people – blacks in Zanzibar – from Arab domination. And the role this self-styled field marshal played in the redemption of his race on the isles became a sub-text in the unfolding drama that eventually led to the consummation of the union. As Professor Haroub Othman, a Tanzanian of Zanzibari origin teaching at the University of Dar es Salaam in Tanzania, explained:

"Nyerere states that he casually proposed the idea of Union to Karume when the latter visited him to discuss the fate of John Okello. According to Nyerere, Karume immediately agreed to the idea and suggested that Nyerere should be the president of such a union. In a New Year's message to the nation on 1 January 1965, Nyerere implied that even if the ASP (Afro-Sirazi Party led by Karume in Zanzibar) had come into power by constitutional means and not as a result of revolution, the Union would still have taken place."[2]

Even though a convergence of interests – Western (especially American and British) concern that Zanzibar was about to become "the Cuba of Africa," and Nyerere's Pan-African desire to unite with Zanzibar – may seem to have helped create a climate conducive to unification of the two independent African states, the union would probably still have been established on Nyerere's own initiative, even if there was no "communist" threat on the isles and independent Zanzibar – under black majority rule – was a capitalist haven, provided the leaders of Zanzibar also, like Nyerere, had the political will to do so.

Nyerere had just failed, in 1963, to convince the leaders of Kenya and Uganda to unite with Tanganyika and form an East African federation. Now, Zanzibar provided him with an opportunity to realise his Pan-African ambition although on a smaller scale.

American officials themselves who were in government service under President Lyndon B. Johnson during that time did not even claim credit for engineering the union. As Frank Carlucci, who was US consul in Zanzibar and who later became CIA director and then American secretary of defence, stated in an interview in 1986:

"Nyerere had to do something about the Zanzibar problem. I don't know for a fact whether he came up with the idea himself, or whether we gave him the prescription. Whether our urging him to do something about Zanzibar had an effect on him....I do know that the situation in Zanzibar was one of continuing deterioration. In the absence of action from Tanganyika, the place would have been completely controlled by the communists."[3]

The highly volatile situation in Zanzibar during that critical period provided momentum towards unification, but at a tempo influenced even if not dictated by Nyerere – the main architect of the union – and his colleagues in Tanganyika and Zanzibar, since it was they who stipulated the terms for unification. That the events in Zanzibar dictated the pace of this consensus building between the leaders of the two countries which led to the establishment of the union is clearly demonstrated by the short time span in which the entire process was completed.

The two countries united within three-and-a-half months: the proposal, negotiations and consummation of the union all took place within that short period. And tough negotiations took place because some Zanzibari leaders were opposed to the merger. As Professor Haroub

Othman stated:

"Discussions on the Union were conducted very secretively. From the archives, and the statements of those who were in the corridors of power at the time, it would appear that not many people in the Tanganyika Government, or the Zanzibar Revolutionary Council, knew what was happening.

Apart from Nyerere and Karume, the only other people who might have been privy to these discussions were Rashidi Kawawa, Oscar Kambona, Abdallah Kassim Hanga and Salim Rashid.

What is important is that the Articles of Union, signed by Karume and Nyerere on 22 April 1964, were subsequently ratified by both the Tanganyika National Assembly and the Zanzibar Revolutionary Council.

Both Abdulrahman Babu and Khamis Abdallah-Ameir, the two former Umma Party leaders who were in the Revolutionary Council at the time, have confirmed that the matter was discussed in the Council and that, while there were reservations on the part of some members, these were overcome by Abdallah Kassim Hanga who made an emotional appeal in support of the Union.

Presenting the proposal for a Union to the Tanganyika National Assembly on 25 April 1964, Nyerere based his argument on the proximity of the Islands to the Mainland, a common language, friendship between TANU and the ASP (Afro-Shirazi Party in Zanzibar), and common cultural traditions. But the ultimate ground for the Union was, he said, a commitment to the cause of African unity. Nyerere saw the Union with Zanzibar as a step towards federation in East Africa."[4]

With that step, Nyerere made a lasting contribution towards African unity and, after he died, left behind a very peaceful and stable nation; one of the very few on this turbulent continent. That Nyerere left behind such a cohesive entity he skillfully built – first as Tanganyika – and nurtured for more than 40 years is probably his most enduring legacy; yet the least appreciated among his most ardent critics who talk and write about his failed socialist policies more than anything else while ignoring his achievements. But in spite of all that, his influence continued to grow and he remained a towering figure on the national scene and in the international arena throughout his political life.

Even after he voluntarily stepped down from the presidency in November 1985, he remained such a formidable figure on the national scene that he not only provided guidance when needed but influenced the course of events in Tanzania until his death. His choice of his successors, Ali Hassan Mwinyi and Benjamin Mkapa, was easily approved by the ruling party, Chama Cha Mapinduzi (CCM), a Kiswahili name that literally means the Party of the Revolution, or Revolutionary Party.

His opposition to the establishment of a separate government for Tanganyika as demanded in the early 1990s by some members of parliament from Tanzania mainland, and even by some Zanzibaris such as the former first vice president, Aboud Jumbe, was equally supported by the ruling party – against prevailing sentiment within the party itself in favour of a separate government for Tanganyika – and probably saved the union which may not have survived with three governments: one for Zanzibar as has always been the case since the union formed; one for Tanganyika as proposed by some members of parliament in 1993 but rejected outright by Nyerere; and one union government for the whole country which has at the same time served as the government of Tanzania mainland, hence Tanganyika, although the latter no longer exists as a political entity the way Zanzibar still does.

In fact, it is also politically unacceptable in a nationalist context for the people on the mainland to call themselves Tanganyikans, unlike the people of Zanzibar who still call themselves Zanzibaris probably more than anything else when they assert and affirm their identity, express their grievances against the union, and are nostalgic about the halcyon days when they were a separate independent nation.

That Nyerere was able to prevail in these and many other cases was vindication of his status as the most powerful leader in Tanzania even after his retirement. He remained the final arbiter on the national scene until his death. And because of his formidable influence, there was some concern that the union of Tanganyika and Zanzibar would not survive without him. As President Benjamin Mkapa said when he announced the death of Nyerere on national radio in Kiswahili:

"I know the death of the father of the nation will shock and dismay many. There are many who fear that national unity will disintegrate, the union will falter and our relations with our neighbours will deteriorate following the passing of Nyerere. But Nyerere has built a sustainable foundation for national unity, the union and relations with our neighbours."[5]

President Mkapa also issued a stern warning to those who may try to break up the union of Tanganyika and Zanzibar. He said they would be dealt with severely: "(Anyone) dreaming about breaking the unity of Tanzania, generating insecurity or stirring up tensions...will be dealt with ruthlessly and their activities curtailed."[6]

Obviously, the warning was taken seriously despite attempts by the Civic United Front (CUF) – which was then the largest opposition party in Tanzania and whose biggest support still comes from Zanzibar, especially Pemba Island, its stronghold – and by maverick politicians such as Christopher Mtikila, a Christian fundamentalist minister from the mainland and leader of a small opposition group, the Democratic Party, to destabilise and break up the union.

The union was consummated at the height of the Cold War, and there have been all kinds of speculations, allegations and innuendoes that the merger was externally engineered. The implication of these arguments is that Nyerere would not have formed the union had he not been prompted, prodded, exhorted and manipulated by these external forces to do so. As Professor Ali Mazrui stated in "Nyerere and I":

"Did Tanganyika unite with Zanzibar to form Tanzania under pressure from President Lyndon Johnson of the United States and Prime Minister Sir Alec Douglas Home of Britain who did not want Zanzibar to become another communist Cuba?

Nyerere bristled when it was suggested that the union with Zanzibar was part of the Cold War and not a case of Pan-Africanism."[7]

The argument that Nyerere was coerced by the United States and Britain into uniting Tanganyika with Zanzibar to deprive communists of a base on the island nation is not validated by Nyerere's track record. And as we learned earlier, the American consul in Zanzibar during that time, Frank Carlucci, did not even claim that the United States – or any other Western power including Britain – engineered the union.

Looking at Nyerere's record, we see that throughout his political career, he demonstrated a degree of independence in pursuit of his goals which irritated and sometimes even infuriated both ideological camps, East and West, during the Cold War.

As far back as 1959, before he led Tanganyika to independence from Britain, he called for a boycott of apartheid South Africa because of her racist policies at a time when both the United States and Britain and other Western powers were giving full and unconditional support to the apartheid regime which was oppressing black people and other non-whites. He was not intimidated by the West and maintained his principled stand against apartheid and other white minority regimes on the continent as was clearly demonstrated when he invited the freedom fighters to establish their bases in Tanganyika soon after the country won independence from Britain on 9 December 1961. He did all that contrary to Western wishes and interests, and in defiance of the West.

He also defied the West when he established strong ties with the People's Republic of China, the Soviet Union and other Eastern-bloc countries soon after independence. But he also annoyed communist nations when he continued to maintain equally strong ties with the West in pursuit of his policy of positive non-alignment. As he sharply responded to critics from the East and the West as far back as 1961: "We have no desire to have a friendly country choosing our enemies for us."[8]

He even publicly chastised the Soviet Union when Warsaw Pact troops, led by the Soviets, invaded Czechoslovakia in August 1968.

Nyerere's commitment to African unity, like Nkrumah's, was well-known. And he lived up to that commitment; which had nothing to do with getting encouragement from the West to advance Pan-African goals.

Those were the very same countries which were intent on perpetuating their domination of Africa and were therefore opposed to any move which would threaten or undermine their hegemonic control of the continent.

A strong, united Africa would naturally not be in their best interest since it would seek to end such domination. And Nyerere was one of the most implacable foes of imperial domination of Africa by both the East and the West. As he stated in August 1961, about four months before he led Tanganyika to independence:

"I believe the danger to African unity is going to come from...external forces.... The rich countries of the world – both capitalist and socialist – are using their wealth to dominate the poor countries. And they are ready to weaken and divide the poor countries for that purpose of domination....

Whenever we try to talk in terms of larger units on the African continent, we are told that it can't be done; we are told that the units we would create would be 'artificial.' As if they could be any more artificial than the 'national' units on which we are now building!.... Many of them are deliberately emphasizing the difficulties on our continent for the express purpose of maintaining them and sabotaging any move to unite Africa.

The technique is very simple. One power bloc labels a move for unity a 'Communist plot' – not because it is Communist, but because they don't like it. Another power bloc labels another move for unity an 'imperialist plot' – not because it is so, but because they don't like it.

What annoys me is not the use of these slogans by power-hungry nations, for this is something we do expect; but what does infuriate me is that they should expect us to allow ourselves to be treated as if we were a bunch of idiots!"[9]

In pursuit of his Pan-African goals, Nyerere had earlier, in 1960, offered to delay Tanganyika's independence due in 1961 so that the three East African countries of Kenya, Uganda, and Tanganyika would emerge from colonial rule on the same day and form a federation. Yet, no one would seriously suggest – if at all – that Nyerere offered to do so at the behest of the departing colonial masters in order to establish a federation.

Nyerere sought to unite African countries even as far back as the fifties. Therefore, it was not surprising that he wanted to unite Tanganyika with Zanzibar, an island nation that already had long historical and cultural ties with his country.

During the struggle for independence, Nyerere already had a strong desire to unite the East African countries under one government. He had the support of some of his colleagues in Tanganyika and even in the other East African countries. Therefore, there was already a movement towards unity in the region.

In fact, Kenya, Uganda and Tanganyika already had common services which united them as a regional bloc on economic matters even during colonial rule. They even had a common currency and a common market.

The other entities were the East African Posts and Telecommunications Corporation, the East African Harbours and Railways Corporation, the East African Airways and research facilities, all under the umbrella of the East African Common Services Organisation (EACSO) based in Nairobi, Kenya, which virtually functioned as the colonial capital of East Africa. All three countries – Kenya, Uganda and Tanganyika – were under British rule.

Nyerere saw all that as a basis for regional unity and sought, together with the other East African leaders, to transform and strengthen the common bonds shared by the three countries into a vehicle that would form a strong foundation for a political union under one government.

The union of Tanganyika and Zanzibar formed under his leadership was therefore only a part of the Pan-African quest for regional federation and eventually for continental unity; which is what prompted him to say, if two countries (Tanganyika and Zanzibar) can unite, three can; if three can, thirty can.

It was also Nyerere who brought together the political parties in the countries of East and Central Africa which were fighting for independence in order to coordinate the struggle against imperial rule. He invited the leaders of the parties to a conference in Mwanza, Tanganyika, held from

16 – 18 September 1958, which led to the establishment of an organisation, the Pan-African Freedom Movement for East and Central Africa (PAFMECA), under his leadership.

The organisation was expanded, again under his leadership, in 1962 to include the countries of southern Africa and was renamed the Pan-African Freedom Movement for East, Central and Southern Africa (PAFMECSA). PAFMECSA played a major role in the establishment of the Organisation of African Unity (OAU) in Addis Ababa, Ethiopia, in May 1963.

A few years earlier in 1960 after a PAFMECA meeting in Addis Ababa, Nyerere said the following concerning the imperative need for unity:

"Many of us agree without pretences or inhibitions that the East African Federation will be a good thing. We have stated this, and it remains true, that the borders separating our countries were put in place not by ourselves but by imperialists.

Therefore, we should not allow them to be used against our unity....We must persistently knock at the offices of the colonialists not to demand the independence of Tanganyika, then Kenya and Uganda and finally Zanzibar, but we must do it to demand the independence of East Africa as one political federation."[10]

He pursued the goal relentlessly more than any other leader in the region. Years later, he said failure to form an East African federation was his biggest disappointment. He said that in an interview with James McKinley of *The New York Times* in his home village of Butiama in August 1996 after he stepped down from the presidency and more than 30 years after the failure to form an East African federation before the end of 1963 as the the three East African leaders – Nyerere, Jomo Kenyatta of Kenya and Milton Obote of Uganda – had agreed to do at a conference in Nairobi in June 1963. They also said Zanzibar was invited to join the federation and could do so after it won independence. Therefore it would have been a federation of four countries: Kenya, Uganda, Tanganyika and Zanzibar.

But it was never formed. Instead, only two countries out of four, Tanganyika and Zanzibar, were able to unite under one government under the leadership of Nyerere.

Looking back at his political career, in an interview in 1966, Nyerere said his greatest failure was that although he managed to form a union between Tanganyika and Zanzibar in 1964 to create Tanzania, he never succeeded in persuading the leaders of the other countries – Kenya and Uganda – to form a larger entity in 1963, a move that would have made the region a powerhouse. As he put it:

"I felt that these little countries in Africa were really too small, they would not be viable – the Tanganyikas, the Rwandas, the Burundis, the Kenyas. My ambition in East Africa was really never to build a Tanganyika. I wanted an East African federation.

So what did I succeed in doing? My success is building a nation out of this collection of tribes."[11]

When he tried to convince the other East African leaders to form an East African federation, before Kenya, Uganda and Tanganyika won independence, Nyerere stated in June 1960:

"In the struggle against colonialism the fundamental unity of the people of Africa is evident and is deeply felt. It is, however, a unity forged in diversity in a battle against an outside Government. If the triumph in this battle is to be followed by an equal triumph against the forces of neo-imperialism and also against poverty, ignorance and disease, then this unity must be strengthened and maintained.

The feeling of unity which now exists could, however, be whittled away if each country gets its independence separately and becomes open to the temptations of nationhood and the intrigues of those who find their strength in the weakness of small nations.

There is one way to ensure in East Africa that the present unity of opposition should become a unity of construction. The unity and freedom movements should be combined, and the East African territories achieve independence as one unit at the earliest possible moment. This means a Federation of the Territories now administered separately.

But a federation of Kenya, Tanganyika, Uganda and Zanzibar can not and must not be imposed upon the people of these territories. It must be a decision of the people expressed through their elected representatives. Only by this method will the present sentiment of unity become an actuality capable of transforming the economic and social position of our territories. This means that discussions on the question of the establishment of a Federation of East Africa can only come after all the countries concerned have governments which are responsive to the wishes of the people, elected by the people and which have full internal power. This position can be reached early in 1961. I believe it must be reached then so that the four governments have an opportunity to put into political effect the unity now felt throughout our countries.

At the moment Tanganyika is more advanced on the road to independence than any of the other territories; the British government could not refuse a demand from us for independence in 1961. I believe, however, that it is in the best interests of Tanganyika as well as of the other territories that we should unite into a federation. I also believe that the attainment of complete independence by Tanganyika alone would complicate the establishment of a new political unit. If the British government is willing to amend their timetable for the constitutional changes of the other territories and then those territories expressed a desire for federation, I would be willing to ask the people of Tanganyika to join that federation with the others.

Ever since we started discussing this question of a Federation of East Africa, I have not found anybody yet either in East Africa or outside East Africa who is against the principle of federation. Indeed, when the leaders of the PAFMECA Conference met recently in Mbale, they unanimously agreed that the proposed federation was worth supporting and that we should work out the details and how to bring it about. I think it is the details of this federation and how to bring it about on which we are likely to have differences of opinion.

I would like to express my own views, not on the details of ultimately what form of federation we are going to have; those we must leave to the leaders, if and when they decide to frame in more detail the form of federation they would like to see. The views I want to express are how to bring it about.

I believe that if it is desired to bring about this federation, the right moment to do this is not after each country has separately achieved its own independence but before. Already there are people in East Africa who have expressed differences of opinion about this approach. There are people who believe, no doubt sincerely, that in order that the decision to bring about the federation may be, and may appear to be, a free expression of the people of East Africa themselves, we must wait until the separate countries are completely independent. If is argued that if we were to achieve this federation before the countries were completely independent, there is a danger that it might appear that the federation was imposed on us by the colonial power and that it was not a free expression of wishes of the people of East Africa.

It has also been argued that if we do not prepare for the separate independence of the East African territories but were to merge them into a federation before they had separately achieved their independence, the merger might delay the independence of East Africa.

It is true that in order that this federation may be a reality, it must be willed, designed and put into effect by the peoples of East Africa themselves. An imposed federation like the Central African Federation has no chance of succeeding and is completely out of the question. I believe, however, that the expression of the wishes of the people of East Africa does not have to wait until these countries are completely independent.

We in Tanganyika, for instance, have now a form of government which we call Responsible Government. If the Legislative Council of Tanganyika were to seek the independence of Tanganyika, and this is what we are going to do in March, nobody, by any stretch of the imagination, can say that the expression of the Legislative Council of Tanganyika seeking the independence of Tanganyika is not an expression of the people of Tanganyika.

Similarly, if the Legislative Council was to express a view that Tanganyika wanted to to come out of colonial status to independence as part of East Africa, that expression would be an expression of the views of the people of Tanganyika – unless, of course, the people of Tanganyika were opposed to such views.

I realise that at present no other East African country has the same kind of government. It is for this reason that I have suggested that if the people of East Africa want a federation, the right moment to bring it about is after each country in East Africa has reached the same kind of constitutional change as has now been reached by Tanganyika, and that we should insist that the elections which are due to take place in all those countries should result in governments truly responsible to the people.

If after these countries have achieved elected government they decided to achieve their independence separately, that decision would be a true expression of the views of the peoples of those countries. If, on the other hand, they all decided that they wanted to achieve their independence as one political unit and they have the backing of their people, they would equally be expressing the wishes of their countries.

I do not see, therefore, that for the purpose of making sure that the desire to join a federation is the wish of the peoples of those countries, we have to wait until those countries have achieved complete independence.

It has been argued, largely by some of our friends in Uganda, that we must put our separate houses in order first, before we can contemplate federation. I do accept this argument. If we were all in chaos, it would be silly to add chaos to chaos – although one can ask the difference it would make. But when does one satisfy oneself that our house has been put in order? I say after Responsible Government. Some of my friends say after independence. I find it difficult to accept this. Surely, the argument of 'let's put our house in order first' will be made stronger after independence than before independence. As I'll try to show later, federation before independence can help to put each house in order. Federation after independence will not even have this attraction which appears to be so dear to our friends.

If people resist a move now which has every chance of hastening the complete independence of East Africa, during a period when the struggle for independence is our unifying force, how can they help to resist federation after independence has been achieved separately? Surely our friends who argue separate independence first can not have considered the matter seriously.

The argument of 'bado kidogo,' 'you are not ready,' is the same argument the imperialists have always used to delay our independence. Is it not going to be the most curious piece of irony if we, African nationalists, who have always wanted unity, were to inherit and use this argument in order to perpetuate colonial divisions?

There are obvious disadvantages if we wait until all the

countries of East Africa have reached complete independence before we begin to bring them together in one federal unit. If each nation achieves independence separately, any move by one of them in the direction of federation is likely to be misunderstood and will certainly be subjected to a campaign alleging imperialistic designs and a search for personal power. For this reason the most honest and least selfish of the leaders will be strongly tempted to avoid the issue. Further, the leaders of each state will become so preoccupied with the immediate problems of their own government that the long-term disadvantages which can come from the establishment of a federation will be crowded out of consideration.

We have to accept, too, that if each of the East African territories is independent, we shall each have to open embassies in the main overseas territories, accept diplomatic offices in each of our capitals, and, because of our close ties, we shall even have to exchange diplomatic representation. All these things are a waste of scarce resources.

But the main danger to the prospects of federation comes from the proliferation of foreign embassies in our respective territories. These embassies will be interested in the strength of their our countries and not in our unity. We shall find ourselves being flattered and filled with false nationalistic pride by reference to our virtues in contrast with the evil habits of our neighbours – or vice versa. We shall find in the fact that the present sentiment of unity gets weaker and weaker.

Further, ones the four nations each have their own representative at the United Nations, have their own flags and foreign representatives, we shall have established centres of vested interests against unity. This is not because we shall be increasing the number of human beings who have a personal interest in disunity; because they are human beings, most of them will be more conscious of the advantages of the present situation and the difficulties of change than of the long-term benefits which could come.

Furthermore, federation after complete independence means the surrender of sovereignty and all the prestige and symbols of such sovereignty. Surely, if it is difficult now to convince some of our friends that federation is desirable, when it does not involve surrendering any sovereignty, it is going to be a million times more difficult to convince them later. As I'll try to show later, federation now has the possibility, even probability, of hastening the independence of our countries, a prospect very dear to all our hearts. Federation after independence does not have this obvious binding force. The appeal of unity is much stronger now than it will be after independence. And yet the need for that strength-in-unity, which will enable us to preserve our hard-won independence, will be at least as great after independence as before. But, and this is very important, unless we emerge out of colonialism as one political unit, separate independence will have made us less united than we are at present, and will at the same time have reduced both the desire for unity and the chances of bringing it about.

We need no visas to cross our boundaries now. Separate independence will almost inevitably impose visas on us. Those unfortunate tribes who now find themselves divided by the present boundaries find it very awkward now. But they will find it more awkward, if awkward is the word, in future, for separate independence will, internationally, make Tanganyika as foreign to Kenya or Uganda, as China or America is. Their cousins on the other side of the border will be foreigners. We trade now without tariff barriers; separate independence may necessitate such barriers.

We have a common currency which could easily lead to a common Central Bank. Separate independence will almost inevitably lead to separate currencies and the establishment of national central banks to make separate independence a reality. One could go on almost ad infinitum to show that separate independence will encourage disunity, not unity. Separate independence means in effect that we shall find ourselves less united after colonialism than before colonialism. Independence will have resulted in greater disunity and the more or less permanent balkanisation of our region. The irony of separate independence is as stark as that.

THE BALKANISATION OF AFRICA

The balkanisation of Africa is a source of weakness to our continent. The forces of imperialism and of neo-imperialism will find their own strength in this basic weakness of our continent. Surely, one would have expected that if we have a chance to undo part of the harm that has already been done by this balkanisation of our continent, we would not hesitate in taking that chance. My contention is that our best chance of removing this balaknisation of East Africa is a few months from now, after all countries have got elected governments.

African nationalists who resist this will find themselves in the same bed with the oddest of companions. There is the intelligent imperialist who knows without a doubt that the moment the East African countries have joined forces after reaching responsible government separately, non-one can stop them from naming the date for independence of East Africa. He will resist this obvious strengthening of the forces of nationalism. The same imperialist will know that since the advocates of federation are linking it with the Responsible Government in all the East African countries, the gathering momentum in favour of federation is bound to hasten the achievement of Responsible Government in the remaining two territories of East Africa. This is what happened in the case of British Somaliland. Those who would not like this to happen will resist it and help Africans too to resist it.

The imperialist who knows that the gathering momentum for a voluntary federation will destroy any chance of maintaining an imposed federation in Central Africa, will resist the establishment of a popular Federation in East Africa. This is no conjecture.

When I was in London recently, many intelligent people remarked that the success of an East African Federation voluntarily created by the African leaders themselves would spell the end of the unpopular Central African Federation. It was even bluntly said that I had gone to London to sabotage the Central African Federation. This was not true, but there is not the slightest doubt in my mind that a popular federation can not but hasten the collapse of an unpopular federation next door.

The British Government itself is placed in a most awkward position by this talk of an East African Federation. If several years back we were mad enough to advocate a Federation for East Africa, Britain would have backed it up without any hesitation. Today matters have changed. The Rip van Winkles are not aware of the change.

The United Kingdom Government can not back up a popular federation without destroying or encouraging the destruction of an unpopular one. If we establish a voluntary federation in East Africa, no argument, not even force, could prevent our colleagues in both Nyasaland and Northern Rhodesia from claiming the freedom to join that federation.

This is so obvious, and for that reason alone, the friends of the unpopular federation will resist the establishment of the popular one. But there is an even stronger reason. They, and their friends in South Africa and in Portuguese East Africa, would rather have Tanganyika alone as their neighbour than than a free and united East and Central Africa with nearly 30 million people. They would encourage us 'to put our separate houses in order first,' not only before, but also after our separate independence. Why should they want a united Eastern Africa? They, together with the many others who would join them in encouraging the balkanisation, would have a better chance of manipulating an East Africa so divided. They will flatter and bribe us and produce even greater arguments for the perpetuation of the balkanisation of East Africa, and exploit our need for technical and financial assistance to keep us divided.

The flattery and corruption of African leaders in order to keep them separated has already started. As I said earlier, it will be intensified a million times when each of our capitals has the embassies of all those countries in the world which find power and prestige in the weakness and disunity of others. Those of us who so innocently produce this sweet argument of delay will find themselves in company with the greatest enemies of the true independence and dignity of our continent.

It has been suggested by some stupid people that I advocate federation because I am a stooge of the British and I want to impose on East Africa a form of government acceptable to my British masters. I believe in the unity of Africa. I do not mind, therefore, what appellations stupid people give me as a result of that belief. But let us examine the true position.

We have always been advocates of unity. In our nationalist organisations, we have constantly warned ourselves against the snares of the imperialists whose policy is 'divide and rule.' Whenever we have asked for our right to govern ourselves, it has been the imperialist who has told us that we are not ready because we still have tribal, religious, communal and other differences. At the same time, it has been the imperialist who has encouraged these divisions in order to continue to rule a weak and divided people. It is the fellow who fell into this snare of the 'divide and rule' apostles whom we rightly regarded as a stooge of the imperialists.

When did this rule change? Are we now going to

regard as true African nationalists those who say we are not ready to unite? Are we now to regard them as our true heroes those who join the imperialists and the neo-imperialists in perpetuating the balkanisation of East Africa? Are we going to regard as stooges those who are now carrying the battle for unity beyond those artificial boundaries created by the imperialists to more natural boundaries of our own creation?

The answers to these questions are obvious. It is the apostles of 'bado kidogo' – when they really mean 'never' – and the apostles of balkanisation whom we must ask to produce their membership cards in the imperialist clubs. Those of us who want to see a united East Africa as soon as a free choice can be made are being absolutely consistent. We have nothing to explain or apologise for. If we want to look for stooges and tribalists, we must look into the camp of the 'bados.'

Surely if the advocates of separate independence were consistent, they would, for instance, allow the dismemberment of Uganda now and try to put it together later. The suggestion is as illogical in the case of East Africa as in the case of Uganda.

I know that the advocates of delay will reply that Uganda is different. It is one country already, whereas East Africa consists of different units. Admitted. But we are adjacent countries, governed by the same colonial power, doing many things in common already. The difference is one of degree and not of kind.

Besides, in our pure nationalistic moments, we shout that we do not recognise these artificial boundaries which were drawn by the imperialists without consulting us. Either, we mean what we say or we are a bunch of hypocrites. If we mean it, we should refuse to recognise those boundaries now and demand our independence from the imperialists as one federal unit. I am sure that the moment we do that the forces of imperialism will crumble in no time. If unity can also hasten our independence, what more can we want as African nationalists determined to free our continent from the humiliation of colonial rule? If we have a chance to bequeath to our children a free and united East Africa, should we treat that chance lightly, or take it seriously as all true patriots should?

REASONS FOR FEDERATION

It would be naïve to claim or leave the impression that all those who want federation now want it for purely patriotic motives. Such a claim would be unfounded. Different people join great movements for different motives. In our own separate nationalist movements, we have all sorts of people. Indeed, the imperialists often try to exploit this fact to discredit our nationalist movements. But the case for independence from colonial rule stands on its own merit. It does not derive its sanction from the sanctity of its advocates. If all the advocates of freedom from colonial rule were selfish and evil-minded people, that fact would not destroy the right of every people to govern themselves. Similarly with federation. Among the advocates of federation could be found people motivated by different considerations.

There will be businessmen, capitalist businessmen, imperialistic businessmen, who will see federation offering a large opportunity for profit making, or neo-imperialism on a grand scale. There will be self-seekers who, having failed to make a mark on territorial politics, will want to try their luck on the federal plane. There will be people who will advocate federation because a personal enemy opposes federation; just as there will be people who will oppose federation because an enemy advocates it. There will be all sorts of people on the side of federation and they have all sorts of motives. They can form as strange a mixture as the mixture I have tried to describe of the 'bado kidogo' group.

But, I repeat, the case for a federation freely willed,

designed and effected by our own people stands on its own merit. It can not be marred or helped by the motives, the character, the status or colour of its advocates. The value of diamonds does not depend upon the character or motives of those who mine them. A mineral is a diamond or it is not.

If the devil himself appeared in person to support this scheme for federation, that fact would not change my views on the federation or the devil himself. If the devil is not a fool, it is easy to see how his mind would work. He knows exactly what federation means. If he opposes it, he will make it popular. If he supports it, people will begin to have doubts. If he does not want the federal scheme, his choice is quite simple: he will try to give it the kiss of death. Those who would otherwise have supported the scheme but for the 'support' it received from the devil would have fallen into a very simple trap, and the devil would rejoice.

The suggestion that federation can delay the independence of East Africa is almost absurd. I can not see such a possibility. The only country is East Africa at present which is fairly certain of its approximate date of independence is Tanganyika: it is reasonable to assume that if the East African countries are going to achieve their independence separately, Tanganyika is is very likely to be the first country to achieve independence. If, therefore, independence for East Africa was to come much later than the likely date for Tanganyika's independence, it would be Tanganyika which would have to be delayed.

But I can not see how the very fact of the East African countries joining forces in demanding their independence would lead to the possibility of their achieving their independence later than if they had not joined forces in demanding their independence. I can foresee exactly the opposite.

In March, Tanganyika is holding a conference with Her Majesty's Government in the United Kingdom to determine a date for Tanganyika's independence. After that date for Tanganyika's independence has been fixed, all of us in East African countries have three choices. If we decided to demand our independence together, we can demand a date earlier than the Tanganyika date. In all those three choices, no choice is likely to be later than any of the other countries would have achieved its independence separately if we had not joined forces. It appears obvious, therefore, that the decision to demand independence together is likely to hasten and not to delay the independence of any part of East Africa.

We have precedent before us: Somalia was a Trust Territory like Tanganyika: her date for independence had not been fixed, Somaliland was a protectorate under the British: her date for independence had not been fixed. The two countries decided that they should emerge out of colonialism as one unit. This did not necessitate the delay of independence for Somalia whose date had already been fixed; it did not necessitate the delay of independence for British Somaliland. The result in fact was exactly the opposite.

The British Government, in order to meet the desire of the two countries to become one, deliberately hastened the independence of Somaliland which in fact achieved her independence five days before Somalia!

With that precedent before us, surely the East African countries would be in a very strong position to demand that Tanganyika's date for independence should be the date for independence for the rest of East Africa. The argument, therefore, that there is any possibility of the decision to form a federation delaying the independence of any part of East Africa appears to me to be unfounded.

But I believe in the unity of our countries. I do not want to leave the impression that no price need be paid for such unity. If I go into a shop and I want a packet of cigarettes, I pay the price for it. If we believe that the balkanisation of East Africa is an evil thing; if a price is necessary to remove this evil, then in all honesty to ourselves, we must say that we are prepared to pay the price, if it appears to be a fair price.

Supposing, therefore, that the people of Tanganyika fixed their independence for 1961. Supposing all the people of East Africa wanted a federation. Supposing some devil made it impossible for the federation to achieve its independence in 1961 but fixed a federal independence date for 1962. Supposing my claim is correct, that separate independence would tend to perpetuate the balkanisation of our region, and therefore Tanganyika's separate independence would contribute to this perpetuation of a balkanised East Africa. I, for one, would be prepared to postpone the celebration of Tanganyika's independence for a few months and celebrate East Africa's independence in 1962 rather than take the risk of perpetuating the balkanisation of East Africa.

Nigeria paid a similar price. The two Southern regions of Nigeria could, if they had so desired, have achieved their separate independence much earlier. They did not do so. After achieving internal self-government, they decided to work for a greater Nigeria. Thanks to their vision, we have now on the continent a country that has the potential of protecting its hard-won independence through strength.

But, as I have already indicated, this price on the part of Tanganyika is likely to be a theoretical one and I have tried to answer it theoretically. In actual fact, we do not have to pay it at all.

There are those who argue that an independent Tanganyika will be in a much better position to hasten the independence of both Kenya and Uganda. Thus, it is argued, even if federation before independence is not deliberately designed to delay East Africa's independence, such delay is bound to be its result, if, because of federation, Tanganyika does not take her separate independence now.

This view is very flattering to Tanganyika. But it

exaggerates the power of an independent Tanganyika and minimises the forces of nationalism within both Kenya and Uganda. Tanganyika or no Tanganyika, the independence of both Kenya and Uganda is a foregone conclusion.

If we achieved our independence separately, and Kenya and Uganda followed a few months later, I'd certainly be one of the last people to claim that Kenya's and Uganda's independence was due to the influence of an independent Tanganyika. In a very short time, both Kenya and Uganda are bound to become independent. Thus, independence of East Africa is no longer in any doubt except in the minds of nincompoops. What is in doubt, and in the minds of very intelligent people, is our unity, after achieving independence.

One need only to look at what happened in other parts of Africa and the world to see the truth of this. Separate independence did not help the unity of the subcontinent of India. Western Europe has a greater scope for unity than we have in East Africa. But the fact that Western Europe is already balkanised into different sovereign states rules out any prospects of political union.

Western Africa has smaller units than we have in East and Central Africa. But the fact that those units are now sovereign independent states makes the problem of unity much greater than it is for us. This is true not only of the English speaking West African units, but also of the French speaking units.

One could go on multiplying these examples which show that unity is very difficult after sovereign independence has been achieved separately.

One could equally go on giving numerous examples to show that it is easier to achieve such unity simultaneously with the achievement of independence. I have already mentioned the example of the two parts which form the present Republic of Somalia. There are numerous other examples.

The U.S.A. is a federation. But the struggle for freedom from colonial rule and the struggle for unity were combined into one and the same thing. The thirteen original colonies came out of colonialism as a federation. Canada is a federation, but is not a federation which was brought about by merging different sovereign and independent states. Freedom and unity were brought about in the same way.

The Republic of India is a federation which was brought about at the same time as India achieved her independence. The negative lesson of India and Pakistan I have already mentioned. Nigeria, Africa's biggest nation, is a federation brought about in the same way. The Nigerians wisely and deliberately avoided an India/Pakistan situation.

In Africa we have only one exception to this rule. But it is one of those rare exceptions which *truly* prove the rule. There is unity between Guinea and Ghana. This unity was brought about after each country was a sovereign independent state. But it is not the kind of unity which has been achieved by the countries I have cited. It is in fact a strong friendship between two sovereign states. A very desirable thing indeed. Yet these countries are led by two of the most brilliant and far-sighted of the sons of Africa. No-one but a fool could say that their desire for African unity is either half-hearted or selfish. It is neither.

The fact is that there is the right moment for everything, and the right moment for unity is certainly not after the achievement of separate sovereign independence. If separate independence is inevitable, we should certainly not give up trying, but it is going to be a much harder task to unite our countries. But in the case of East Africa, separate independence is not inevitable.

The United Arab Republic is the only true exception I can think of. But if we really want to remedy the balkanisation of our part of Africa, we would be most unwise to act contrarily to the clear lessons of history and assume that we will be another exception to this rule.

I have no doubt in my mind that history has given us East Africans a unique opportunity. Let us use it now and earn the gratitude of future generations. If we really mean business, here's the challenge:

LET US MAKE 1961 EAST AFRICA'S YEAR OF INDEPENDENCE IN UNITY.

'It has been frequently remarked that it seems to have been reserved to the people of this country, by their conduct and example, to decide the important question of whether societies of men are really capable or not of establishing good governments from reflection and choice, or whether they are forever destined to depend for their political constitutions on accident and force.' – Alexander Hamilton in *The Federalist*.

'Men at some times are masters of their own fates. The fault...is not in our stars but in ourselves that we are underlings.'

'There is a tide in the affairs of men, which, taken at the flood, leads on to fortune: omitted, all the voyage of their life is bound in shallows and in miseries. On such a full sea are we now afloat; and we must take the current when it serves, or lose our our ventures.' – William Shakespeare.

People of East Africa, Unite! You have nothing to lose but your chains!

'Behold how good and pleasant it is for brethren to dwell together in unity.' – Psalmist."[12]

As in the case of Kenya, Uganda and Tanganyika, inclusion of Zanzibar in the envisaged East African federation was an integral part of Nyerere's agenda to unite the region under one government. Therefore, it should not surprise anyone who is familiar with his political career as a staunch advocate of African unity determined to unite countries on regional and continental basis that he pursued unity with Zanzibar and achieved part of his goal, although on a smaller scale, when he united his country with the island nation.

That was not Cold War politics. That was African politics. When as far back as 1960 he talked about forming an East African federation which would include Zanzibar, the Zanzibar revolution which brought the Cold War to the island nation – and to Tanganyika – had not even taken place. It was not even in the planning stage; it was three-and-a-half years away when he wrote the article above in June 1960.

Did the Cold War back then, before the Zanzibar revolution, also push him to pursue federation of the East African countries which would include Zanzibar? Or was it his Pan-African commitment when he said it would be a great achievement if all the countries in the region, including Zanzibar, united before they won independence?

In his article above, he said 1961 would be the best year for the East African countries to win independence together on the same day and emerge from colonial rule as a single political entity and form a federation. That was the year Tanganyika was scheduled to get independence; and it became the first in the region to attain sovereign status.

Although he did not achieve his ultimate goal of uniting the four East African countries – Kenya, Uganda, Tanganyika and Zanzibar – under one government, he achieved something that was unprecedented in the history of post-colonial Africa and that has not been achieved elsewhere on the continent since then: uniting two independent states.

It was not the Americans or the British who succeeded in uniting Tanganyika with Zanzibar to form the new nation of Tanzania under one government. Formation of the union can not be attributed to pressure exerted on Nyerere by the United States and Britain to do something he already wanted to do. With or without the United States and Britain, he would have pursued the same goal to unite Tanganyika and Zanzibar, as he did in the past, and he succeeded in doing so in 1964.

The CIA itself conceded the union was initiated by Nyerere, not by the United States or Great Great Britain, and took place under his guidance:

"The idea of a union was not a new one. Nyerere probably had it in the back of his mind when he first became involved in Zanzibar politics, beginning around 1956. For years, he had looked forward to the time when an African government would come to power in Zanzibar, at which time he planned to merge the two countries....

The important point is that the union of Tanganyika and Zanzibar *was a Tanganyikan initiative* (italics added by Godfrey Mwakikagile).

Although the idea had occurred to Western officials as the obvious solution to the Zanzibar problem, the subject was never officially discussed with the Tanganyikans. Thus, it appears that the move to form the union was strictly African in origin, without British or American inspiration; the news of the event caught all of the major world powers by surprise.

For more than a month, Nyerere and his representatives had been conducting secret negotiations with Karume and other Zanzibari leaders."[13]

Decades later, in an interview in 2000, Donald Petterson who once served as the American ambassador to Tanzania and who before then was the head of the American consulate in Zanzibar during the revolution, said the same thing the CIA wrote in its report – that the major powers were caught by surprise when the announcement was made that Tanganyika had united with Zanzibar. As Ambassador Petterson stated:

"Their decision (by Nyerere and Karume), when announced, came as a complete surprise."

The United States and Britain would not have been caught by surprise when formation of the union was announced if they were the ones who engineered it.

Also, Helen-Luoise Hunter stated in her book, *Zanzibar: The Hundred Days Revolution*:

"Even before the revolution, the affiliation of Zanzibar with Tanganyika had been under discussion in the context of a larger East African federation. Nyerere, Karume, and Hanga were on record as favoring such a federation; Babu was opposed. It had never been a question of a union between Tanganyika and Zanzibar alone, however; that possibility arose as a direct result of the revolution.

As noted earlier, it was Nyerere who initiated the negotiations leading to the union. Much has been written about his reasons for wanting a Tanganyika-Zanzibar union. Press comment in the United States and other Western countries tended to emphasize the cold war aspects of the situation....

The tendency of the United States and other Western press to emphasize the cold war aspects of Tanganyikan-Zanzibar relations complicated Nyerere's efforts to work out a solution within the framework of non-alignment. He said on a number of occasions that he was personally furious with the way the American and British press treated the union....

Among Zanzibari leaders, Hanga was probably the most receptive to the Tanganyikan initiave. He stated privately that he and Kambona agreed that Tanganyika and Zanzibar should unite when they were students together in London. Nyerere also commented that Hanga favored the union even more than Karume.

In July, Tanzanian Foreign Affairs Parliamentary Secretary Tambwe claimed that Nyerere was 'particularly pleased with Hanga because he is, above all, an African nationalist who really supports the union.' "[14]

Nyerere himself – without American or British inspiration – wanted to neutralise radical elements in Zanzibar, especially Babu and his followers of the Umma (people's) party. The most effective way to do that was to deprive Babu of his political base in Zanzibar by uniting the island nation with Tanganyika. Therefore, he did not need encouragement from the West to do that.

He did get such encouragement. But it was unnecessary. And it was not unique. Even fellow African leaders – except Nkrumah – encouraged Nyerere in his quest for regional unity which included uniting Tanganyika with Zanzibar, not just with Kenya and Uganda. They were not asked, encouraged or pressured by the United States and Britain to support Nyerere in his Pan-African quest.

And like Nyerere himself, the biggest supporters of the Zanzibar revolution were Africans themselves – leaders such as Nkrumah, Abubakar Tafawa Balewa, the prime minister of Nigeria, and Jaja Wachuku who was Nigeria's minister of foreign affairs and a friend of Babu.

Nyerere's desire to unite Tanganyika with Zanzibar came from within – Africa itself – without external inspiration even if such inspiration may have been "fuelled," somewhat, by external interest, American and British, in the geopolitical dynamics generated by the Zanzibar revolution.

Therefore, even if the United States and Britain and the rest of the West did not exist at all, he would have pursued the same goal. Just because they encouraged the merger does not mean they initiated it; nor does it mean they were the driving force behind it; Nyerere initiated the merger and was the driving force behind it.

It just happened that the West and Nyerere shared the same concern about the island nation's radical shift towards the communist bloc under Babu's influence and had nothing to do with pressure being exerted by Western powers – the United States and Britain – on Nyerere to "absorb" Zanzibar, something he himself wanted to do, and was going to do, anyway, compounded with his Pan-African desire to unite East African countries even if it had to be on a smaller scale first, uniting Tanganyika with Zanzibar, which is what he did.

The West does not deserve any credit for that. Credit goes to Nyerere for initiating and successfully completing the merger of the two countries.

The interests of the West only coincided with Nyerere's interest over Zanzibar and were *not* the primary motive for unification of the two independent states. The driving force was Nyerere as the CIA itself conceded in its classified reports which were later declassified.

But it is true that the revolution did provide an impetus for unification which probably took place sooner than even Nyerere himself had expected or anticipated. The fundamental issue here is that the desire to unite the two countries was in his mind all the time even before the revolution, an interest that did *not* come from the West.

Even if Western powers, the United States and Britain, played a role in facilitating the union because Tanganyika's interests coincided with theirs in terms of neutralising communist influence in Zanzibar, it was only peripheral. Internal dynamics played a far more important role and were the determining factor in the formation of the union. As Mohammed Ali Bakari, a lecturer at the University of Dar es Salaam, stated in his book, *The Democratisation Process in Zanzibar: A Retarded Transition*:

"There has been an extensive discussion on the process leading to the Union between Tanganyika and Zanzibar with varying emphasis on either domestic factors or external factors. The book by Amrit Wilson (*US Foreign Policy and Revolution: The Creation of Tanzania*, Pluto Press, 1989) has well documented the process leading to the Union. In this book with a lot of documentary evidence, the United States has been portrayed to have played a key role. The main concern of the United States then was geopolitical and strategic; that Zanzibar immediately after the revolution was seemingly heading towards a radical leftist direction to the extent that, it was thought by Washington, it could become a 'Cuba of East Africa.'

Although the influence of foreign forces on the founding of the Union, cannot be underestimated, domestic factors seemed decisive. Had Karume not felt highly insecure, and had Nyerere believed or at least had not been made to believe that strategically he would be insecure in the event of Zanzibar becoming a radical leftist regime, the attempt by Western powers and the US in particular to manipulate them into accepting the Union would have been futile."[15]

Nyerere knew on his own, without being told or manipulated by the United States, that an unstable Zanzibar would be a threat to the security of Tanganyika because of its close proximity to the mainland – only about 20 miles away. That is why he once said if he could move the island nation farther into the ocean, he would. He said that not only before the Zanzibar revolution but even before he led Tanganyika to independence. He said it in 1960. Therefore, he did not need to be convinced – four years later – by the Americans and the British about the danger of an unstable or radical Zanzibar.

Bakari also quotes Nyerere who said at a mass rally in Dar es Salaam on 15 November 1964, about seven months after the union was formed:

"We sent our police to Zanzibar. After overcoming various problems we united. We ourselves voluntarily agreed on union. Karume and I met. *Only the two of us met.* When I mentioned the question of the union. Karume did not give a second thought. He instantly asked me to call a meeting of the press to announce our intention. I advised him to wait a bit as it was too early for the press to be informed. (Emphasis added by Bakari)."[16]

Western interest in Zanzibar tended to overshadow Nyerere, especially in the Western media, as the architect of the union and its driving force from the beginning. The focus was on Cold War intrigues and rivalries in the island nation between the two ideological camps, East and West. But, as Donald (Don) Petterson who was the American consul in Zanzibar when the revolution took place (after Frank Carlucci was expelled) and who later served as ambassador to Tanzania, stated in an interview years later on 30 November 2000:

"Nyerere and Karume decided that they would unify their two countries to undercut Babu. This they did, telling only a very few trusted advisors. Their decision, when announced, came as a complete surprise....Nyerere wanted it and Karume wanted it."[17]

The deputy American ambassador to Tanzania, Robert Hennemeyer who (as DCM – Deputy Chief of Mission) served under Ambassador William Leonhart, was also in Tanganyika when Tanganyika united with Zanzibar. He said the union "was not a merger" but a federation. Leonhart was the first American ambassador to be accredited to Tanganyika, later Tanzania.

Hennemeyer also talked about other subjects concerning Tanganyika, later Tanzania, and reflected on the years he was there:

"**Q:** When you came out (of the University of Oxford), you were really put into a very critical position, weren't you? You went to Tanganyika. How did you get the appointment?

Hennemeyer: I don't know how it happened. I received orders while I was at Oxford that I would be going to Dar es Salaam, which then was still a U.N. trust territory under British trusteeship. Therefore, our post was a consul general. Red Duggan was our consul general, and I was to go there as his number two.

There was one very fortunate thing that happened and one very sad thing that happened. The fortunate thing was that while at Oxford, I met four Tanganyikans who were studying there. All four, within a couple of years, became Cabinet members when they returned, and this gave me a set of contacts that was almost unique, because while at Oxford, we were very close. That was a very positive thing and gave me a leg up in starting at Dar es Salaam.

The sad thing was that Red's eyesight was failing very rapidly, and just after (Tanganyika's) independence in December of 1961, within days, Red's eyesight failed completely. He had glaucoma. He had to be Medevaced. Then I was chargé for an extended period. It would have been better had Red been able to stay on, because he had a wealth of knowledge of the post. He had been there for several years, a very able man. But it didn't work out that way.

Q: Could you describe the situation when you first arrived? This was still colonial in 1961.

Hennemeyer: I got there in July of 1961, and independence came that December. So it was an atypical colonial situation in that it was a honeymoon period. The agreement on the date for independence had been reached. The British were doing their best in a short period of time and in an orderly fashion to phase out. The Tanganyikans were very, very upbeat and happy about the coming independence state. It was a real honeymoon. Nobody was complaining about anything.

The only complaints I heard were from the British, who were grousing a bit about how many positions they would have to continue to staff at the Tanganyikans' request, because they didn't have enough people to take over. So it was not an atmosphere where they would be pushed out at all.

Q: Also, Tanganyika was somewhat different in that it had been a German colony. The British roots, I assume, weren't as deep there as they would have been in Kenya and other places.

Hennemeyer: That's true. The British settler community was minuscule, unlike Kenya. So they were not really a political factor at all. Well, that's an overstatement. They were a minor political factor.

There were times during the inter-war period when British governments in London sought to merge Tanganyika with Kenya and Uganda into a greater East Africa entity on the Kenya model. Some governments wanted to encourage large-scale British settlement in Tanganyika. But interestingly enough, there were British governors-general during that period in Tanganyika who reminded London that this was initially a League of Nations mandate, and subsequently a U.N. trustee territory, and that didn't accord with the conditions of the mandate, and resisted the idea of British settlement.

So there's some unsung heroes there, because rather than a Mau Mau epoch as Kenya experienced, Tanganyika had none of that. The very few British settlers who were there, Derek Bryceson was one who became Minister of Agriculture in the first government, and Lady Marion Chesham, another settler, an American by birth, married to a British subject, who remained after independence and became a member of Parliament. So it was a very amicable transition.

Q: How did the story develop as you saw it and may have experienced it?

Hennemeyer: The first couple of years of independence, I stayed until July of 1964, exactly three years. The first two years went fairly smoothly, the transition where more and more Tanganyikans took over senior positions.

One noticed that it didn't always work as well as it had in the past, but on the other hand, they were trying to do more difficult things and they were trying to do it with relatively inexperienced people. But it went along fairly well, and relations with the remaining British were quite good, and our relations with the government were excellent.

Q: They didn't have the feeling that the United States was being a bit starry-eyed about this new independence, whereas the British were saying, 'Well, you know, this isn't going to work,' sort of dog in the manger?

Hennemeyer: No. I'm sure that was an attitude in some other places, but I think because of the fact that the colonial civil service (servants) who went to Tanganyika always knew that it was a different set of ground rules, a mandate or a trust territory, and that this did not have a colonial future, I think that was understood.

They were a different breed of cat from colonial civil servants that I had met elsewhere. I admire(d) them. For the most part, they were very good people with a clear understanding that their role was a temporary one, and that their task was really to work themselves out of a job. So I found very little of that. I'm sure some of them thought that the Americans were starry-eyed, but I didn't find the dog-in-the-manger attitude.

Q: Ambassador Leonhart was there.

Hennemeyer: Right.....

Q: Going back to the situation in Tanganyika, it is now Tanzania.

Hennemeyer: It became Tanzania after the federation with Zanzibar. It never was a merger.

Q: Could you talk about your relations and your observations of Julius Nyerere, who is, of course, a seminal figure in the African scene?

Hennemeyer: First of all, on a very personal level, an extremely likeable man, not pretentious, not full of himself at all, enjoyed a joke, a person who was pleasant to be with. He was also a great political theorist and, unfortunately, economical theorist. I think as a manager he left much to be desired. He was a charismatic figure on the stump, a great leader of his people. I don't believe for a moment that he meant anything but to do the best he could for the wellbeing of his people.

But I guess the best way I could put it is that during early 1962, Nyerere decided that the party, TANU, Tanganyika African National Union, was not functioning the way it was supposed to. It wasn't really mobilizing the masses for new initiatives and so on. So he decided he would give up the premiership and go out in the boonies, revitalize the Party, and he would turn to Rashidi Kawawa to be acting premier. He (Kawawa) was a minister--I've forgotten of what, a very small man but well-known because he had been an actor in Swahili-language films. So everybody in the country knew him.

At any rate, Rashidi Kawawa was no great political figure at all, but within days of Julius' departure for the boonies, one noticed a difference in the way government functioned. You got answers to questions, decisions were made, and it was simply because Kawawa was not [a] theorist, didn't spend hours and hours talking about the future of the world with visitors from other parts of the world, but instead came to his desk promptly early in the morning, looked at his 'in' box, took things out of his 'in' box, made decisions, and put them in his 'out' box. It made a world of difference.

Q: Bob, what was the situation with Nyerere? How did you see him?

Hennemeyer: As I mentioned, one could not help but

like and respect him as a leader. **Clearly he was a world leader, not just an African leader.** But he was not really one who enjoyed the nitty-gritty of government, and he was not very good at it. He tended not to empty his 'in' box, and that was a complaint I heard from his ministers and so on. That was not his strong suit. The result was, of course, that since this became a one-party state and became highly centralized in his person, when he didn't empty his 'in' box, a lot of things didn't happen.

Q: You saw him as the leader who was going to be around for some time.

Hennemeyer: Oh, yes, no doubt. He was unchallenged.

Q: As the United States representatives there, did you find yourselves being concerned about the fact that he seemed to be off, you might say, on the left-wing socialist side, both for our own political interests, but also for concern about the economy?

Hennemeyer: That wasn't so apparent during the time that I was there. We did have some concern about the speed with which he was trying to develop cooperatives as an alternative to the Indian middle class, which had a monopoly of commerce. Obviously there was a political imperative for him to involve his own people, to involve the local people in the economy. That had to be done. But some of us had some concern about the pace and the method. But that didn't really become an acute problem until after I left, until the Lusaka Manifesto (the Arusha Declaration?) and things like that.

Q: We had no real commercial interests there, did we?

Hennemeyer: Almost none. There was a time some years earlier when the U.S. automobile industry had some major exports to Africa, but by that time we had been displaced largely by Peugeot in East Africa, and I suspect they've been replaced by the Japanese since then.

Q: There are schools that say that American policy

is driven by economics and trade and all that, but in many cases there just isn't that much at stake there. You didn't feel anybody breathing down your shoulder on that?

Hennemeyer: No, not at all. No, that was not a major factor at all. I think we started out with a lot of genuine goodwill towards Tanganyika and Nyerere as a leader. I think as time went on, our concern was that the Soviet bloc or the Chinese not acquire undue influence there. We wanted to keep Nyerere basically Western oriented; that was our objective. I think, with minor glitches, that was successful.

He never really went over to the other camp. He flirted, but I suspect some of that was tactical, and some of that, of course, was dictated by the fact that he saw one of his major roles to be a haven for those who were trying to free from colonialism the rest of Southern Africa

So one of the more interesting aspects of my time in Dar es Salaam was the presence there of major Southern African liberation organizations or political parties. ANC was there, PAC, Frelimo. In fact, I knew Eduardo Mondlane quite well. That gave the place certain spice that it would not otherwise have had.

Q: What was our attitude? What were your instructions on how to deal with Frelimo? We're talking about the early sixties.

Hennemeyer: That's right. We maintained close and friendly relations with them. By this time we had on our staff a very, very able first-tour officer, John Blacken, who is now our ambassador in Guinea-Bissau. John and I worked very hard to maintain close personal relations with Sam Nujoma (of SWAPO, Namibia), who was there at that time, and with a great many others. We would invite them to our homes, we would see them in their offices. What some of them wanted very much--they realized soon that that was not in the cards--was military assistance from us. It just wasn't going to happen.

Q: You made that quite clear?

Hennemeyer: Well, that had to be made clear right away that we weren't going to do that. What we did try to provide them were educational opportunities, believing that while eventually they would succeed in governing their own countries, in the interim it might be very worthwhile for some of their better young people to acquire skills that would be useful in an independent non-apartheid South Africa.

So through AID, we contracted with the African American Institute. Pat Murphy was then the director of the program in Dar es Salaam, and we ran an active program of providing scholarship opportunities in the States and elsewhere in the West for exiled Africans, if you will, and we established a small school, also under African American Institute auspices, funded by AID, for Mozambican government. However, at the same time, we were aware, of course, that they were receiving military assistance.

I remember one case where a ship from Algeria came in with a great deal of military equipment for Frelimo and other organizations. So others were doing that, but clearly that was something we could not do, but we felt it was important to maintain contact with these people and, in the area of education, to do something constructive for them for their future. I think even though some of them are rather high-powered in their rhetoric of criticizing us, I think some of them are really aware that what we did at that time was helpful.

Q: How about Nyerere? Back to him for a minute. What was his attitude toward the United States?

Hennemeyer: I think it was very friendly. I thought his attitude toward the United States was generally positive. I think there were times when he felt that we were neglecting Africa, other times that he felt that we were excessively preoccupied with the Cold War, but I felt that, too.

Q: How about the situation in Zanzibar? That became rather volatile while you were there.

Hennemeyer: Yes, it did. That happened in January of 1964. To me it came as a surprise, although, in retrospect, Fritz Picard, who was our consular there at the time, was aware of growing unrest. I don't think any of us predicted what finally happened. Yes, I remember very well.

Then the press descended on Dar es Salaam to try to find out what was going on in Zanzibar. But we had no special brief for the Sultan's Government in Zanzibar. In fact, as you recall, the election, which had confirmed the Sultan's Government in power, was one that was a very dubious affair, and nobody was really happy with the result. It was clear, I think, to most observers that if it was going to survive, it was going to have a lot more representatives, and it didn't have a chance to do that.

A lot of people have forgotten what a bloody affair that was--there were several thousand people killed, Arabs driven down to the beaches and slaughtered at the beaches by the insurgents.

There was an Italian photographer who chartered a plane from Mombasa, flew down there and got some extraordinary footage of the slaughter on the beach.

At any rate, our concern was exactly the same as the Tanganyikan Government's concern, and that was to contain the rebellion on Zanzibar and direct it to a more constructive end. That is, it accomplished its immediate purpose--that is, it brought a black African majority group into power. But then the question arose for Tanganyika's own security: What kinds of relationships would that new government have? As you know, very early on there was a fairly strong East Bloc presence, and that concerned us and the Tanganyikans.

So very quietly and discreetly we worked with the Tanganyikans to help them establish a police presence initially on Zanzibar, and we encouraged Nyerere in his efforts to develop a cooperative federal arrangement with the Zanzibar Government. That succeeded to some extent, although it never worked the way it was supposed to. But in time, the red house on Zanzibar, for whatever reason, calmed down and it never became what **some sensationalists** predicted, the 'Cuba of Africa.'

Q: Did you have any part in dealing with it? At one point, Picard and the others were actually under arrest and they had a problem extracting.

Hennemeyer: That's right. I was involved in the call. There was a U.S. Navy ship in the city. At that time the Navy ran periodic cruises around Africa. I think they were called SoLant Amity at the time. The ship was the USS Manley, I remember very well, was visiting Mombasa at the time of the Zanzibar revolt. Picard and the other Americans there, particularly the Project Mercury people, which was a NASA project, a tracking station for NASA's satellite program, most of them were contract employees of Bendix, as I recall, they were literally trapped on the island. There came the question of trying to get them out. Fritz Picard, with great courage, persuaded Karume and the revolutionary council to agree that the Americans would leave.

Ambassador Leonhart and Jim Rookte, who came down from Nairobi to help us out, and I, we succeeded in getting in tough with the Manley and got approval for the Manley to come down. I believe Jim flew back to Mombasa, boarded the Manley, then went with the Manley into Zanzibar.

Fritz, at great personal risk, succeeded in getting everybody on the ship. He and maybe Dale Povenmire, stayed behind. I can't swear to that. But Fritz stayed behind. I remember Fritz's wife, Shona, and their son came and stayed with us. Fritz came out later, but I've forgotten how. He also came to live with us.

As you know, he was quite ill at the time. He had what seemed to be a kind of nervous breakdown. No sooner did he arrive with us than the Tanganyika Army mutinied.

Fritz thought he was back on Zanzibar, and this was Zanzibar happening again. So he was very difficult to control for a few days.

Unfortunately, during some of that time, I was under arrest by the mutineers, and after that, trapped in our embassy, in the chancellory, for a while. So I was unable to assist my wife in trying to manage Fritz. It was a very difficult time for her. Shona and Hoge, the boy, we had gotten out earlier before the mutiny, and they had gone to Nairobi.

At any rate, the mutiny burst on us completely unprepared. We didn't know that was going to happen. I realize now what the immediate causes of it were, and it was one of these unfortunate management glitches which occurred on Nyerere's watch. There was a program for Africanizing the Tanganyika rifles officer corps. The non-commissioned officers and the enlisted personnel were all Africans. This was supposed to be phased in over a period of time; I've forgotten how long it was. It was a three- or four-year period.

In the meantime, Tanganyikan African officer candidates were being sent to Sandhurst, the British military academy, for the short course, and as they returned, one more British officer would return to his regular regiment. In the process, however, not all billets were slated for Africanization in the near future. In a few of those cases, some British officers were being replaced by British officers. This was misunderstood by many of the Tanganyikan non-commissioned officers who thought that meant that Africanization was being abandoned.

The reason they thought that was that Nyerere had made a speech that because they had moved too quickly in Africanization, there were a number of economic activities and other government activities that had suffered in the process, and therefore they were going to have to reschedule this and draw this out. This coincided with three new British officers arriving. Mind you, we're dealing with a fairly small universe. A number of senior non-coms decided this meant that Africanization of the officer corps was being abandoned, and they had pay demands, as well, and so on. Within a couple of nights, the mutiny was plotted.

The first inkling we had of it was when I got a call in the middle of the night from an African officer, Alex Nyirenda, one of the first commissioned officers, later became commanding general, saying that the troops had mutinied, that many of the officers had fled, and that some of the British officers had been captured up at Colito Barracks, north of Dar es Salaam, were being held prisoner, and he was saying, 'You should keep your people off the streets.' That's what his message was.

So I called Ambassador Leonhart. We had a warden system, and he agreed to implement the warden system and tell people to stay home. I agreed I would go down to the chancellory and get a message out. So I started driving down. It must have been about 1:00 or 2:00 in the morning. I decided I would drive by State House to see if anything was going on, or if Nyerere was up, I'd talk to him.

I got there just in time to see a group of soldiers breaking down the front gate, while being resisted by a group of police. So I decided not to stop there, and drove down to Azania Front, which was the street right on the harbor in the center of town, where the old German bungalows were, which housed some of the ministers.

I saw, on the street corner, my British colleague. He was the number two, but was then serving as chargé, Steven Miles, and the Minister of the Interior, Job Lusinde. So I stopped. We were chatting, trying to put together what was happening. Just then an Army jeep Landrover pulled up with a group of soldiers on it, and they grabbed the three of us and threw us in the back of the Landrover and drove off with us, not far, a few blocks away to the post and telegraph building, where they put us up against the wall and held us there.

This group was rather disorderly. Some had been drinking, and some, I think, had been smoking bang, a type of hemp. Some were sort of in bits of pieces of uniforms. All of them had their new British-issued rifles that they had gotten to replace the old Lee Enfield 303s. They had their new SLR NATO-type rifles.

Periodically, several of them would say they were going to shoot us, and they'd level their rifles at us. One, the only who I think was not drinking, a corporal, kept saying, 'No, no, they're not British officers.' Well, they knew who Lusinde was, but they thought Miles and I were new British officers who had come. The others kept saying we were, and we should be shot.

I remember one imaginative young soldier taking the clip out of his rifle, taking the cartridges out of the clip, sharpening them on the sidewalk (in front) of us, reloading, pulling the bolt, and putting the muzzle right up against my nose, and saying, in what English he knew, 'Time is finish. Now is time to kill.'

At any rate, this went on all night. I remember I turned to Job Lusinde and I said, 'What are we going to do about this, Job?' He turned to me and said, 'It's better if we don't know each other.' So we three tried to stay as quiet as we could while this internal debate went on.

I remember sometime during the course of the night, a truckload of soldiers came by and said that they wanted to take us along. Our guys said, 'Go find your own prisoners.' At any rate, it was a long and difficult night.

Q: In a situation like that, all the diplomatic niceties and everything else go by the boards, because there's nowhere to go or to protest or anything else.

Hennemeyer: No, and I tried a diplomatic nicety, but it didn't work. I didn't know how to say I was deputy to the ambassador in Swahili, but I knew how to say 'ambassador.' So I told them I was the ambassador and I was going to my office. One said, 'No, I've seen the ambassador, and you're not the ambassador.' So I just made my case more difficult.

At any rate, this went on in this vein, with them being ugly and calm at intervals, until about 7:00 in the morning, I guess, when they suddenly said to me, 'Kwenda.' 'Go.'

I started to walk down the street, making myself walk very slowly. I turned around and I saw that they had their rifles leveled at me. I don't know if that was to see if I would run or what, but at any rate, I walked down the street, and when I got to the first corner, I ducked around it, only to find two more standing there saying I couldn't go that way, I had to go back out in the same street.

At any rate, I walked down the length of the street, turned the corner, and got over to the chancellory, where Bill Leonhart was waiting and very anxious about what had happened. He asked, and I said, 'Well, the mutineers took me prisoner.' I remember he said, 'Good. You can try to finish this cable.' He handed it to me. He was trying to describe what had happened, and thought that since I had been with them, I could finish it.

I sat down to try to write it. Just then, the reaction set in. I couldn't write, my hand was shaking so. That lasted only about a half-hour or so, but at any rate, we got the word out. That was my little adventure.

Then came the problem of what to do, because some of the mutineers were getting out of hand, there was a little looting. Although in retrospect, I have to say, given what I've heard of since, it was a relatively orderly mutiny.

Q: It wasn't of the scale, say, of the Force Publique, which was full of killing and looting?

Hennemeyer: No, no. There was a little killing and a little looting, but by and large, as I say, in retrospect I have to say that it was a fairly orderly mutiny.

As soon as we could move around a little bit, which took a day or so, in the meantime, the mutineers decided that there might be a landing and that they would take my house as a stronghold to defend against the expected landing. My wife and our two very small children were surrounded by these soldiers, who didn't harm them, but it was frightening for them.

Then came a rather confused several days when we were consulting with our British allies, trying to figure out what to do. Basically, this was Bill Leonhart's responsibility, with the British chargé, to persuade Nyerere to ask for British assistance. That proved to be rather difficult, but eventually he did agree.

At that time, the British aircraft carrier, the HMS Centaur, came in from Adana with the Royal Marine commandos. There were some extraordinary events, some of which I heard about, some of which I saw, of getting Brigadier Patrick Shelton Douglas, who was the deposed commander of the Tanganyika Rifles, out to the Centaur to lead the Royal Marine commandos. That was accomplished largely, I think, by the NI-5 man at the British High Commission, a gentleman by the name of Jacobson.

There were a few of us who knew that the Royal Marine commandos were going to come in to Colito Barracks the next morning very early, and as I recall, those of us who knew agreed to stay in the chancellory or at the High Commission that night so there would be no leak.

They did come in. They had a bombardment of blanks first, artillery blanks, over the barracks, then came in with helicopters. Douglas landed first and told them to surrender, identified himself. There were a few shots fired. The Marine commandos then fired a bazooka, shot through the orderly room, killed a few of the mutineers, and then the others ran. They ran to the bush, and the helicopters rounded them up. Most of them were taken prisoner. They were picked up over a period of days.

I think the following day, the Royal Marines flew to the other garrisons. I think there was one down at Iringa (Nachingwea), one up in Moshi or Arusha, I can't remember where, and one in Tabora. They took their surrender, so that ended it.

Then subsequently there was a Commonwealth arrangement whereby the Nigerians came in and replaced the British. The Nigerians maintained order until Tanganyikans were able to reorganize another force.

Q: Did Nyerere come to you or to our embassy, or did you go to them as being a party off to one side?

Hennemeyer: Nyerere was in hiding during this week. Subsequently, I learned that he was held very closely, and I was not involved with the negotiation with Nyerere, so I didn't have to know. But I've learned later that he was in a convent on the south end of the harbor, the other side of town. But he was reachable. It was, I think, mostly Steven Miles who conducted the negotiations.

There was some criticism of Nyerere at the time for being in hiding. I guess one has to respect his judgment. It was Oscar Kambona, the Minister of Defense, who went out on the streets and tried to get the disorderly elements of the troops to go back to their barracks, and who then went out to the barracks to try to free the British officers who were being held prisoner, for which he was beaten and pretty roughed up by the soldiers.

At the time we thought Kambona showed great courage, and it contrasted with Nyerere's being in hiding. But there may have been more important reasons for that. I'm not suggesting Nyerere should have gotten out on the streets. He might have been killed, and the sole rallying point for the country would have been lost. But I think it hurt him somewhat politically and probably led later to the quarrel with Kambona, which resulted in Kambona being exiled. I believe he's still in exile in London. I think from that time, there was ill feeling, but I'm speculating here. That was the conventional wisdom.

There was considerable disorder and considerable confusion. I remember the chief of protocol was also chief of the secret police. We were friendly. He came to my house to warn my wife that he feared the next day there would be kind of a 'night of the long knives' against the wives. This allegedly because the dock workers' union, the leadership of which had been East German-trained, had made common cause with the police, and they had decided that they would also mutiny.

The police, by the way, had more or less disappeared when the Army came, with the exception of the prison wardens out at Morogoro, who decided to march on Dar es Salaam to combat the Army, which would have been very foolish because they didn't have the weaponry at all. Fortunately, somebody stopped them before they got there. At any rate, these are random bits and pieces.

Q: What was our embassy role at the time? Was it basically one of reporting?

Hennemeyer: It was basically one of reporting, and supporting our British colleagues, who were the ones directly involved in trying to bring some order out of the chaos. We supported their effort to get Nyerere to agree to ask the British to come in, because the alternative was anarchy. So our role was a support role, not a lead role.

Q: That was just before you left?

Hennemeyer: This was January 24th, within a week of the Zanzibar events.

Q: When did you leave?

Hennemeyer: I left in July. The rest of the time following the post-mutiny events in Tanganyika and the negotiations that Nyerere was having with Karume to establish Tanzania, one of the concerns of the Tanganyikan Government, which was initially allowed to send a small police contingent over to help maintain order in Zanzibar, was allowed by the Zanzibari Revolutionary Council, was that compared to the Zanzibar rebels, they did not have the same fire power at all.

So we were of some assistance in getting the place some hardware which they could then give to their force in Zanzibar. That may or may not have played a role, but ultimately, as you know, the negotiations were successful.

I think April was the date when Tanzania was announced.

It was a very, very loose federation, indeed, with a good bit of friction between mainland and island. But it did, I think, mark the high point of what could have been potential disorder from the island to the mainland. From then on, things gradually got under some degree of control."[18]

Hennemeyer was later appointed ambassador to The Gambia.

One of the American diplomats who was in Zanzibar before and after the revolution and when Tanganyika united with Zanzibar was Donald Petterson. He was in Zanzibar from 1963 to 1965. Years later, he served as the United States ambassador to Tanzania from December 1986 to December 1989. He said the following in an interview years later about those days:

Petterson: I had applied for hard language training, specifically for Swahili. That summer of '62, I would say about July, I received notice that I had been accepted for Swahili language training and that my onward assignment after language training would be Zanzibar. Now this was a rare thing, when you had advance notice a year ahead of time –

Q: Yes.

Petterson: Not only of your training, but also of the following assignment.

Swahili language training was to start in November. We left several weeks earlier, Julie and I with our baby, Susan, who had been born in late July and was about two months old when we departed Mexico. We drove to California to see friends and relatives. From there, wee drove across the United States, still in the same VW (Volkswagen) Bug. We arrived just at the height of the Cuban Missile Crisis. I began Swahili training, the second class in Swahili given by the Foreign Service Institute. Julie enrolled in an

English course in downtown Washington.

In my class, there were five of us going to various places, including Uganda, Kenya, and, of course, Zanzibar. In time two people peeled off early for their assignments, and we ended with three of us in the class. I slogged through the Swahili and got a three, three. I had been reading all I could about East Africa and Zanzibar. And Julie and I did what a Foreign Service junior officer and his spouse would do in those days to get ready for a Third-World assignment. We had to buy supplies of things we wouldn't find where we were going, and we bought them as cheaply as possible. For example, with another couple, we bought glassware from a restaurant supply store in Washington, D.C....

We didn't get princely salaries, but it was great when I first started working to have a paycheck coming in regularly for the first time since I left the navy. I started out at $5,500 or $5,600 a year. By this time, at the beginning of 1963, I was making about $6,500.

We got reservations on the USS *Constitution*. In those days you could journey by sea if you were going to a place where U.S. lines were traveling. We had a ten-day trip to Genoa, which was wonderful, a wonderful way to travel....

We went to Genoa and visited with our friend Carolyn Kingsley, who was assigned to the consulate there. After two days, we took a train to Rome, where we boarded a propeller aircraft for the trip to Nairobi. It was a long flight, and it was late in the day when landed at Nairobi's airport. We transferred to a DC-3 and flew to Mombasa, Tanga, and finally Zanzibar, arriving in the darkness of night.

Getting out of the airplane, we were enveloped by warm, humid tropical air. We were met by Frederick "Fritz" Picard, the consul, and Dale Povenmire, the vice-consul, and driven over to Fritz's house for dinner. From there we passed through checkpoints manned by British soldiers. The pre-independence elections had just been held, and there was tension on the island. We were taken to our house, a thatch-roofed, whitewashed coral and lime structure that originally was a stable. It would be our temporary home until Povenmire, whom I was replacing, was transferred.

Our life in Africa had begun.

Q: You were in Zanzibar from when to when?

Petterson: From July 1963 until November 1965, over two years.

Q: I wonder, could you explain what the situation was when you arrived, not what happened after, but when you arrived, and what our consulate was doing or expected?

Petterson: The American consulate, the first consulate in Zanzibar, was established in 1837. As a cost-saving measure, it was closed in 1915, but reopened in 1961. The reopening was occasioned by the establishment of a Project Mercury tracking station on Zanzibar Island.

Q: Yes, our space program.

Petterson: Project Mercury was the first manned space effort of the United States, and tracking stations were set up at various places around the world. Zanzibar was one of them. At that time, Zanzibar was moving toward independence. It was a British protectorate under the guidance of British colonial authorities, led by the resident. His title was "resident," not "governor," because Zanzibar was a protectorate, not a colony as such. The protectorate consisted of Zanzibar Island and the island of Pemba, which lay about 45 miles northeast of Zanzibar, and a few very small islands. Arabs had dominated Zanzibar since the end of the seventeenth century, when Omani Arabs seized control of it.

The Sultan of Oman moved his sultanate to Zanzibar in 1832. It became a British possession in 1890, when the Germans, who had gained control of Tanganyika and were on the verge of occupying Zanzibar, agreed to let the British have it in exchange for Heligoland. The British ruled through the Sultan of Zanzibar but retained ultimate power and administered the protectorate.

There had been some turmoil in the years immediately leading up to independence, because of deep antagonism between the black African majority and the Arab minority who continued to dominate Zanzibar politically and, with the Asians, people of Indian and Pakistani origin, economically. The Arabs were a minority, with about 50,000 inhabitants, whereas the Africans numbered some 250,000. The Asians, a community of about 20,000 divided into various religious sects, were mainly businessmen, shopkeepers, and professional people, most of them living in Zanzibar Town. The European community numbered about 500 – the British colonial administrators, some business people, and spouses and children. The sixty or so Americans in Zanzibar were counted as members of the European community.

The elections in 1961 had been accompanied by riots and some killings. So the British, concerned about the '63 elections, brought in troops, Scots Guards, to maintain the peace. The election went off with no violence.

Q: The election had taken place before you arrived?

Petterson: Yes, just before our arrival in July 1963. A coalition of the Arab-led Zanzibar Nationalist Party and a smaller party consisting mainly of people of mixed blood, won the elections. There were accusations that the British had gerrymandered the electoral constituencies so that the African majority would not win. In the event though, it was the divisions among the Africans, their inexperience in politics, and the organizing skills of the Arabs that won the prize for the Arabs and their allies. An Arab named Ali Muhsin led the coalition government.

From the elections until independence, which came on December 12, 1963, although the African politicians voiced strong opposition to the acts of the pre-independence government, there were few overt signs of serious unrest among the Africans. Yet, many worried that after independence there could be some trouble, for the Africans were deeply upset by what had occurred. I remember that a Special Branch police officer, a Briton who was about to leave Zanzibar, told Fritz Picard that there would be trouble, but not until well into the year.

With the arrival of Zanzibar's independence, our small consulate became an embassy. Picard, the consul, was to became the chargé d'affaires. I was the other State Department embassy officer, and Stuart Lillico was the U.S. Information Service officer. Imelda Johnson, was Fritz's secretary. The four of us made up the American diplomatic establishment in Zanzibar. The other Americans on the island, in addition to our families, were associated with the tracking station.

Q: Let me ask you what you have to say about Zanzibar independence.

Petterson: Neither the British nor the Americans knew that for months, almost a year, before independence, a shadowy figure by the name of John Okello was making preparations for an armed revolt. The African majority party, the Afro-Shirazi Party, which had lost the election, had determined that, if necessary, they might resort to arms to take over the country, whose government they believed rightfully belonged to them. Okello, who was from Uganda, had come to Pemba in 1959. Four years later, in early 1963, he came to Zanzibar and began plotting revolution. The handful of people in the Afro-Shirazi Party who became aware of this did not include the party's leaders.

During the independence ceremony, there was an ominous incident that foreshadowed trouble. At midnight, when the British flag was lowered, the lights went out, and when they went back on, the new Zanzibar government flag was raised. There were cheers from among the gathered dignitaries, but the Africans, including the hundreds who were off to the side of the cricket pitch where the independence ceremony was held, were ominously quiet.

On January 12, 1964, a month after independence, the revolution took place. During that month, the Arab-dominated government had done just about everything they should not have done to anger the Africans. They passed legislation that was unfavorable to the African population. In addition, they made it clear that Zanzibar was going to align itself with Egypt and the Arab world, rather than with the sub-Saharan, black African world, as the Africans wanted.

On the night of January 11, I had come home in the evening. There was a well attended dance going on in the African quarter, Ng'ambo, where I had taken the children's nanny home, but I saw no sign of anything untoward. At about 2:30 in the morning, the phone rang. I went to the hall and answered it. While I was walking to the phone, I could hear popping sounds. Fritz Picard, my boss, the American chargé d'affaires, was on the line. He told me that something was up and that I should begin to notify Americans to stay home. The firing became more intense. I could hear it quite distinctly.

Our next-door neighbor was Ali Muhsin, the leader of the government (not the prime minister, but the de facto leader), and armed revolutionaries had come to get him. So we were very close to the action at the time. As the morning wore on, Fritz, Stu Lillico, and I managed to get in touch with most or all the Americans. They hunkered down.

It became apparent that the government was no longer in control. At about seven o'clock, Okello got on the radio for the first time and began a series of broadcasts in which he announced that the radio station had been seized, the government had been toppled, and a new government was taking over under the leadership, Okello said, of Abeid Amani Karume, the head of the Afro-Shirazi Party.

Karume was actually, at that time, in Tanganyika, in Dar es Salaam. Young revolutionaries who had came to his house on the night of the 11th had told him that he should leave the island because it might be dangerous for him. He was taken to Dar on a boat. Two other leading Zanzibari opposition politicians had also gone to Dar. One of those was Abdulrahman Mohammed, "Babu."

The Americans and the British viewed Babu as a Communist who was exerting a dangerous pro-Communist influence. Just before the 1963 elections, he had broken with the Zanzibar Nationalist Party, of which he had been the Organizing Secretary. Much more radical than the party's other leaders, he founded his own political party, the Umma Party. In the first week of January, the government banned the Umma Party, searched its offices and Babu's house. As a warrant for his arrest was being prepared, he fled the island and went to Dar es Salaam.

So the big actors of the opposition were in Dar es Salaam when the revolution took place, which further indicates that they really were not in charge of its inception, as was said later. Okello was. Nevertheless, he announced that Karume would head the government. Karume came back to Zanzibar the day after the revolution, along with Babu and Abdul Kassim Hanga, who would become Karume's vice president.

To get back to the action that morning, about midmorning Fritz said we should all gather near the airport in case we needed to evacuate. He had been trying to get in touch with the government and with the British authorities, who were still there. Although the British had ceded control to the new government, many British civil servants remained, some of them occupying high administrative positions. Fritz did reach some of these officials, but none was well informed about what was happening. He also tried to communicate with Afro-Shirazi Party leaders, but without success. Thus he did not know the degree to which Americans and other foreigners might be in danger. However, he did not determine at that point that we should evacuate.

The firing around our house had subsided by the time that Fritz had called me. So when he said we should go to Stu and Helen Lillico's house, which was not far from the airport, I figured it was no safe enough to do so.

I had gone into town on my bicycle about seven or eight o'clock to see what was going on. I didn't tell Fritz I was going to do this, but I thought it would be interesting. As I approached Ng'ambo, Africans told me I should get out of there because it was dangerous, and indeed, people had been killed in that area earlier that morning. Most of the violence was taking place outside of Zanzibar Town by that time, but it was still dangerous in town.

Julie and I bundled up the two little girls. I guess I neglected to mention that in September, Julie gave birth to our second daughter, Julianne, at the Karimjee Jivanjee Hospital (soon to become the V.I. Lenin hospital). Julianne was the second American ever to be born in Zanzibar.

We put the two little girls in the Volkswagen, and I drove from our house, past Ali Muhsin's, to the road that led to the airport. The prison was close to the left side of the road a couple hundred yards farther down. As we approached, a rebel attack on it was taking place. Suddenly we saw just ahead on the right side of the road a group of twenty or thirty men armed with various weapons. When they saw us coming, they turned and pointed their weapons at us. But when they saw who we were, they yelled at us to get out of there and removed the roadblock they had placed across the road. We chugged by.

Q: You did not turn around?
Petterson: No.
Q: You continued on?
Petterson: I continued driving on, thinking, "Well, that's that," I suppose, if I thought anything! [Laughter]

We came around a corner less than 200 yards after that, and there behind some palm trees was another group of Africans, another log across the road, and another firefight going on. Once again we were confronted by people with weapons, everything from spears to old rifles. Bullets were actually whizzing over the car, as I stopped it. I could hear them smacking into trees. The rebels, as before, saw that we were foreigners. They told me to drive around the roadblock and get out of there, which I did. [Laughter]

We went on our way. Once we were clear of that area, I had to stop the car for a moment and steady myself, because it dawned on me how close we had come to losing our lives. Julie was extremely scared. Poor little Susie, who was a year and a half old, was very, very frightened. The baby [laughter] didn't have any problems. She was in her basket at Julie's feet. Susie was on Julie's lap.

We proceeded, and drove out to the Lillicos' house. There we gathered with the other Americans who had come together to wait and see what happened. Picard, who lived a little further out, had not arrived yet. I talked to him on the phone, and he said to come over, which I did. It was quiet in that area. He and his wife, Shoana, had been packing. After we had talked for a bit, I took Shoana and their three children to the Lillicos'. Fritz followed later. Once at the Lillicos', Fritz, who had been in contact with the embassy in Dar es Salaam by telephone, called again to inform them of the state of play. Even though the rebels controlled everything by that time, they had not cut international telephone service.

Peering through gaps in the shutters – we had closed the door and shuttered the windows – we watched revolutionaries as they went into nearby Arab houses. We could hear people screaming and saw some killing. It was frightening. The Americans who were gathered with us were very, very apprehensive.

At some point in the early afternoon, Fritz decided that he and I should go to the airport to see if we could arrange for an evacuation. We drove the less than one mile to the airport. As we approached it, a car filled with Africans headed towards us, and as it went by us, the long barrel of a large weapon emerged from one of the windows and blasted a cloud of black smoke and I don't know what else.

They apparently were trying to give us a fright, not harm us. They succeeded, but nevertheless we went on to the airport control tower, where we talked with the two British air traffic controllers. They pointed out some groups of armed rebels who were standing about in the tall grass just beyond the periphery of the airfield. They told that it was too risky for any aircraft to try to land. Fritz and I left and returned to the Lillico's.

Q: Hang on a second.

Petterson: Yes.

Q: Who was in control of the airport at this point, Arabs or Europeans?

Petterson: Europeans.

Q: Europeans.

Petterson: The airport was managed by an Arab professional, Ali Khalifa, and it had a mixed-race staff. The air traffic controllers were British. At this time, when Fritz and I were at the airport, nobody else was around, just the two controllers.

Q: Were there any either East African Airways, the small East African Airways planes, or charter planes around?

Petterson: No, there were no aircraft there. The East African Airways flight that normally would have come in that morning had been diverted. The prime minister of Zanzibar had been trying to get a shipment of weapons in. He had communicated his request through the controllers, who were in radio contact with the mainland. But the weapons never arrived. Shortly after Fritz and I left the airport, the Africans took it over.

Our decision then was whether to evacuate or not. Fritz decided that an evacuation was called for. Because it would have to be done by sea, we would need to go into Zanzibar Town and congregate there with the Americans who lived to the north of the city. Once together, we would prepare for an evacuation.

Fritz asked me and a fellow named Irv Zolo, who worked for the tracking station, to drive into town to see if the road was safe. We got into my car and headed into town. I was sweating profusely, and not just because it was hot and humid! We both were nervous because we didn't know what would be around each curve in the road. As it happened, we encountered no problem. We saw some results of the revolution. Cars shot up. We saw no bodies. They had been removed already. We went all the way into town. Conditions seemed to be safe enough for the rest of the Americans to make the trip. After we went back, everyone got their things together, and in a convoy of several cars, we drove into town to the English Club, which was right on the beach.

In the meantime, the Americans who lived on the other side of town had gathered together in one of their houses. After hearing from us about the decision to evacuate from the English Club, they drove toward town in several cars. Unlike us, they did encounter rebels, who stopped them, threatened them, and might have harmed them. But someone with authority interceded, and they were allowed to proceed. On their way in, they saw some grisly sights of Arabs who had been killed and had been mutilated in a very gruesome fashion. So they had first-hand experience with some consequences of the revolution's first day, consequences to –

Q: The Africans that threatened those people in those cars, did they know that they were Americans?

Petterson: Yes, well, they knew that the people were Europeans, as all whites were termed.

Q: Europeans? Why would they be sort of angry with Europeans?

Petterson: Well, there was no love on the part of many of these people for foreigners, who led comfortable lives and had all the things that most Africans didn't have. But this was not the problem, for there really was no deep hatred. The rebels carrying weapons were, for the most part, simply ragtag fellows who had no discipline, who had been drinking, or were on something, and they were out of control. They were trying to shake down the Americans.

At one point, a baby began to cry, and one of the rebels said to the mother to shut the baby up, or he would kill it. They were pretty nasty. But then someone more reasonable arrived, someone in authority, and he changed the climate of what was going on there. The Americans were allowed to proceed, and reached the English Club without further incident. There were 60 or 65 Americans at the club, and later some Europeans tourists in town joined us.

Q: So that includes the people from the tracking station as well?

Petterson: That's right. The official American community - the small embassy and USIS staff - along with the tracking station people, and our respective families. With the tourists, there must have been some seventy to eighty people in the hotel as the sun went down. We decided that we would man a command post downstairs. Upstairs, men, women and children got set for the night. Fortunately there was some food in the establishment, and people were able to get something to eat that night. I stayed downstairs and manned the command post all night long, as it turned out, because of an incident that took place in the middle of the night.

Fritz Picard became very concerned about the fate of Stu Lillico's secretary, a young Zanzibari woman whose name was Fathiya. She was an incredibly beautiful woman, and Fritz was having an affair with her, which I mention because it turned out to be quite germane to what could have happened to the Americans.

The revolutionaries were looking for members of the government. One of her relatives was a cabinet minister, a man named Mshangama. She was at his house, which was not very far from the English Club. Fritz had been talking to her on the telephone, and she told him that rebels were coming.

Fritz came down from upstairs and without telling me and the other fellow who was with me at the command post what he was going to do, he went out into the street and began to make a racket. I didn't know what he was doing. I went out and told him to come back into the English Club, but he persisted. What he was trying to do was to divert the attention of the rebels who might be endangering Fathiya and her family. He wanted to get them to stop what they were doing and come to the English Club instead. He succeeded in doing this because very soon a group of armed men came by and tried to ascertain what he was doing. He bantered with them for a while. Finally they told him to shut up and go back inside, which he did.

At that point, I was simply worried about Fritz. I didn't know what he was doing. He then explained, and I was very angry because he had put all of the people in the English Club at risk. Whether or not his diversion saved Fathiya, I'll never know, but at any rate, the rebels did not go into that house. Later that night Fathiya, her mother, and her two children came into the club. Fritz had telephoned her and told her to come there. He met them at the door and took them inside. She was downstairs, and his wife was upstairs.

Q: Oh, really?

Petterson: Yes. He arranged for her to stay in a place downstairs away from the Americans who were upstairs, including Shoana. In fact, nobody knew about Fathiya until the end of the following day.

In the morning, the embassy in Dar es Salaam informed us that approval of the evacuation had been given, and that an American destroyer, the USS Manley, would be coming in to take the Americans off the island. The Manley had been in Kenya at the port of Mombasa on a ship visit when the revolution occurred. The ship was ordered to steam back and forth off the coast of Zanzibar over the horizon until the decision was made that an evacuation could be carried out.

During the course of that day, Fritz continued to act in a way that disturbed me. For example, when we went out of the English Club onto the beach to talk to rebels, Fritz, at one point, brought his five-year-old son with him. Throughout the day he carried a mug of beer with him, whether he was in the club or outside. It caused a lot of people to raise their eyebrows. It was bizarre behavior. Nevertheless, he showed some very fine qualities later in the day. Certainly his judgment as to the need for the evacuation was not questioned by anyone. The Americans, all of them, were thoroughly frightened and wanted off the island.

The Manley picked its way into the harbor very slowly about mid-afternoon. A small boat came ashore with Jim Ruchti, who was the deputy chief of mission at the American embassy in Nairobi. He had been in Mombasa for the ship visit. The captain had asked him to accompany the ship to Zanzibar and to give him political advice. Jim received permission to do that. He brought with him a Kenyan cab driver, so there would be somebody who could speak Swahili, listen to the radio to hear local broadcasts, and thereby help keep Ruchti and the captain abreast of what was happening in Zanzibar Town.

After the ship had anchored, Ruchti came ashore in the ship's whaleboat with the executive officer and several sailors. They were not permitted, initially, to land until Fritz prevailed upon a group of armed rebels on the beach to permit Ruchti and the executive officer ashore. The sailors had to remain in the boat. Fritz and I took Jim and the exec to the English Club, where we continued to try to contact the revolutionary government.

Q: Let me just ask you a quick question there, interrupt you. Picard and the captain of the ship had

not themselves just decided to evacuate the personnel who were at the English Club? Just go ahead and do it?

Petterson: No. The State Department, Defense Department, and White House had approved Fritz's request for the evacuation. But when the executive officer of the ship came ashore with Jim Ruchti, we had not yet received permission from the rebels. It was only through negotiating with the rebels on the beach that were we able to get those two people off the whaleboat, so that they could wait with us to see whether or not permission for the evacuation would be granted.

Q: Permission from the?

Petterson: From the rebels.

Q: Revolutionaries?

Petterson: That's right....

We returned to the English Club. Fritz went off to the hotels to pick up those tourists who were still there. While Ruchti and the executive officer went down to the boat to get the crew ready for the operation and to notify the captain what had happened at Raha Leo, Lillico and I met with the Americans, who waiting for us on the club's upper porch, which overlooked the beach. Earlier, we had stipulated that women and children, regardless of nationality, would go first. However, now a couple of the Americans, tracking station employees, said, "Uh-uh, Americans first, foreigners second." Stu and I
said [laughter], 'Not on your life! Women and children first.' And we made that stick. With Fritz now back, everyone who wanted to go was at the club, and the whaleboat and another boat, the captain's gig, began taking the evacuees out to the destroyer. The sun had gone down and it soon grew very dark. I took Julie and the babies down to the boat with the few possessions that she had brought, mainly things for the children and some clothes. We said goodbye, and I kissed her and the two little girls.

She was fearful, as she said later in letters to her parents and to mine, that she would never see me again. I had no such thoughts, myself! [Laughter] I was having too much of an interesting time! Off she and the children went into the gloom. We had set up some portable lights from the ship on the beach, but their beams didn't carry much beyond 30 or 40 yards out to sea. The boats would disappear into the darkness as they went out to the ship. After all the evacuees were aboard, the Manley sailed to Dar es Salaam.

Q: Let me interrupt you again for a second.

Petterson: Yes.

Q: Were personnel from any other consulates taken off, the British for example?

Petterson: No. There were no other diplomatic establishments, just the British and the Americans at that time. The British had not made a decision to evacuate. They considered it, but had not yet decided. There was some criticism of the American decision to evacuate, but Fritz had sound reasons for doing what he did. (1) We had no idea that the word was out not to harm foreigners. (2) We were unable to get in touch with the revolutionaries. We didn't know whether the violence would get worse, or whether it would subside. (3) There had been animosity shown toward the Americans by some of the very people who carried out the revolution. They had protested the presence in Zanzibar of what they termed the American rocket base and demanded its removal. There was a lot of hostile propaganda directed against America in that month after independence.

The Manley arrived in Dar es Salaam harbor that night, but couldn't go in through the channel, which was very narrow.

Q: Including yourself?

Petterson: Oh, no, no! Pardon me! I forgot to mention that Fritz and I stayed. We had agreed that somebody should stay behind to look after the embassy and the property of Americans. Washington said that if we wanted to stay we could, so that left the two of us on the island. The next day, in Dar es Salaam the Americans disembarked from the destroyer. My family and Fritz's family remained in Dar until a week later.

Q: How about Fritz's girlfriend?
Petterson: She was there. Everybody [laughter] saw her on the Manley.

Q: She went over to Dar as well?
Petterson: Yes.

Fritz and I then went home that night and drank a lot of beer. I had a beer or two, but by that time I'd been up for over 48 hours and was very tired. I went home to my now lonely house. By the way, we were no longer in the stable. We had moved two months earlier to my predecessor's house in another part of town, a much nicer home.

The next day, Fritz and I were told by the revolutionaries not to leave our respective houses, but later in the day we were given permission to go about our business. My Swahili came in to very good use, either that day or the next. We were driving from Fritz's place to the embassy when we came upon a group of armed men, who yelled in Swahili, '*Simana*,' which meant, 'Stop!'

Fritz didn't speak Swahili; I did. I said, "Fritz, stop the car" which he did. [Laughter] Otherwise, he would have kept going and we might have been shot at.

By the way, my Swahili (and I'm talking to Nick who studied Swahili with me) –

Q: A classmate.
Petterson: That's right…was very useful....

On the morning of January 16, four days after the revolution, we were at the embassy. Fritz received a telephone call from the British high commissioner, who somewhat testily said, 'Some of your people are causing a problem down at the port, reporters, your people, Americans.' He said they were a matter of 'grave embarrassment.'

So Fritz told me to go there, which I did. At the boat landing, I encountered several armed men who were gathered at the top of a concrete sea wall from which steps led down to the water. A couple of British colonial port officials also were there. I could see the top of a dhow's mast. After explaining who I was and why I had come, I was allowed go to the edge of the sea wall. I saw that there were seven men in the boat.

We talked, and I learned that they were American, British, and Canadian newspapermen – reporters for *Time*, *Newsweek*, *The New York Herald Tribune*, a Canadian paper, and a British paper – and an Indian photographer for *Life* magazine. So they weren't just Americans, were not, in the words of the High Commissioner, 'your people' only. They had sailed in the dhow from the mainland, arriving in Zanzibar the previous night.

They started asking me questions. Foolishly I answered. At that point a rifle was pointed right at my face, and I was told to "Shut up!" So I stopped talking, [laughter] the better part of valor! Some authorities from the revolutionary government joined these armed people at dockside. They said that the men in the boat were spies and we were going to be taken to revolutionary headquarters. Off we went. I tried to explain to the rebels who I was. They couldn't care less, nor did they accept that these were just newspaper people.

We had been held at Raha Leo for several hours when Fritz showed up. He finally had found out where we were and what the problem was, and had talked to a minister in the government. Karume was away. He had gone to Dar es Salaam that day. The minister said, 'Well, sure. Let these people go.' Fritz told us the good news, and he and I drove the journalists to the Zanzibar Hotel, where they got rooms and then went off about their business.

But suspicions were high about these people. Some of them had U.S. Defense Department press cards, and they showed them when asked for an ID (identification) card.

The name of one of the reporters was Conley, Robert Conley. That sounded like "colonel." So the rebels had this Colonel Robert, and they had Defense Department ID cards. Spies, you know! It really rang a bell with some of these less-than-sophisticated rebels.

When Karume returned late that afternoon, or early that evening, he was told about the reporters and the suspicious about them. He was also given some of their notes, which had been taken from them and which were not too complimentary about the revolution. Karume was angry, and he went to the Zanzibar Hotel to confront them. Picard was with them.

The minister who had allowed these fellows to go about their business happened to be a political enemy of Karume, even though he was in the cabinet. When Karume saw Picard with his political enemy and the correspondents, he was furious. Babu, who was with him, and another government official, who had no love for Fritz, egged Karume on. In essence they said, 'You know, these people are up to no good. Picard has interfered.' Karume bought that and angrily ordered Picard, at gunpoint, to be taken to his house.

I was over at the embassy at that time, composing a long classified cable, using a primitive system of those days called a 'one-time pad,' and as, Nick [laughter], you'd know, it was a very laborious task! It took me a couple of hours to encrypt the message. It was dark outside when I locked up, left the embassy, and started across the square – Kelele Square – to Cable and Wireless to deliver my telegram for transmission. In the darkness, in the middle of the square, I came upon Karume and a gaggle of fellows with weapons. Karume asked me what I was doing.

I said, 'I'm taking a message over to be sent.'

He said, 'No, I can't allow that!' He told me what had happened. He said that he had arrested Picard, that Picard had done something bad and would be expelled from the island, and that I would have to be placed under arrest, too.

He ordered four of the armed men to get in my car, the VW, and accompany me. I drove toward my house with the barrel of a rifle in the back of my neck, not intentionally, but it was a bit disconcerting! They didn't stop at my house, but instead took me to Picard's. There I spent the night with Fritz, who was drinking heavily.

The next day, a chartered plane came over from Dar. Fritz was placed on the airplane, along with some of his possessions and the Lillico's dog, which had been left behind, and off he went. I was at the airport with him and breathed a sigh of relief when the plane left, because I had been worried that his behavior since the onset of revolution might lead to his harm. There were some Chinese at the airport taking pictures of Fritz's expulsion. Babu and some of his people were also present....

I had a number of adventures in trying to protect American property, failing in some cases because looters had come, encountering looters at one property and chasing after them, foolishly, on my bicycle, and capturing one of them, only to find that he was just a kid. If I turned him in he would be executed, so I let him go, and warned him not to do that anymore.

I managed to communicate by telephone with the embassy in Dar es Salaam. I was not given diplomatic privileges. I could send nothing out by diplomatic pouch and could send cables only if they were not encrypted and were approved by a government censor at Cable and Wireless. Now and then, the censor didn't like my choice of words and refused to all the message to be transmitted....

Occasionally I got a classified message out by taking it over to the British, who had been given the permission to use their classified pouch. Twice, at the airport I met American officials who were on a flight from Dar to Nairobi via Zanzibar. I was allowed to go out and talk to them. I slipped each of them an envelope with a message in it.

My time was largely taken up with looking after the American property, trying to find out what was going on, dealing with the revolutionary government, and reporting as well as I could.

By mid-February, it was clear that the revolutionary government was getting fed up with the lack of recognition from the British and the Americans. Concern about Zanzibar in the American government reached the highest level, President Johnson, and in the British government at its highest level, Prime Minister Alec Douglas-Home. This was extraordinary when you think about it. Zanzibar was seen as a precursor of revolution for Africa, as a Communist foothold could spread into the continent. The Chinese communists, the Soviets, and East Germans had established embassies (which grew to be quite large) and had begun arranging for military and economic aid. Communist diplomats, technicians, and military trainers began to come to Zanzibar in relatively large numbers.

The British were dithering. They didn't want to recognize a government that had come to power by force of arms. Moreover, they didn't like this government's pro-Communist or apparent pro-Communist leanings. So the British waited despite the urgings of Tanganyikan Prime Minister Julius Nyerere that they grant recognition to the new government of Zanzibar. Washington followed the British lead. By a month or so after the revolution, the Zanzibaris were out of patience.

On the 19th of February, I was summoned to revolutionary headquarters, where the British high commissioner had arrived just before me. Karume told us that because the U.S. and UK (United Kingdom) had not recognized his government, we would have to go; otherwise, the people might rise up and do harm to us or to the government. Well, that was an exaggeration, but we were given 24 hours to leave.

From the embassy, I called the American ambassador to Tanganyika, William Leonhart, in Dar es Salaam and informed him of what had happened. Then I went back to burning classified documents, which I had been doing for several days, using a small potbellied stove. Leonhart tried that day to convince Nyerere to influence Karume to postpone my expulsion, but without success. That evening, the ambassador called me. Passing a message from Washington, he said I should see Karume if I could and ask him to delay the expulsion for at least twenty-four hours. I should tell him that a U.S. official from Washington had just arrived in Dar and could come over the next day to talk to him about recognition.

I managed to get through to Karume, who said I could come see him. He didn't agree to the proposal but left the door open. After another exchange between Leonhart and me, and a message from Washington for Karume, which arrived at seven o'clock the following morning, Karume agreed to receive Leonhart and the man from Washington.

At midmorning, Ambassador Leonhart and Frank Carlucci, a Foreign Service officer, came to Zanzibar in a small chartered aircraft. I met them and went with them to see Karume.

Q: What was Carlucci doing in Dar?

Petterson: Frank had been in the Congo, where he had acquired a reputation as an exceptionally able Foreign Service officer. He was the embassy's troubleshooter in the Congo. After the Congo and before coming to Zanzibar, he had a job in the State Department –

Q: Well, when I saw him, he was assistant desk officer for the Congo under Charlie Whitehouse.

Petterson: OK.

Q: That was '63.

Petterson: Yes. Frank was well-regarded by Joe Palmer, the Assistant Secretary of State for African Affairs and by Charlie Whitehouse, and by everybody else. It had been decided that Frank would be the new chargé d'affaires in Zanzibar. He came with a letter from President Johnson that indicated recognition would be coming soon. Frank and Leonhart tried to convince Karume that with recognition just around the corner, it would be much better if he didn't throw me off the island. By the way, the whole Revolutionary Council, which included all the wild men along with some of the more able and moderate Zanzibari Africans who were in the cabinet, were at this meeting.

The discussion went on for a couple of hours, but in the end Karume and the Council rejected the American proposal. Karume, when he said goodbye, said, 'If you come back, if recognition takes place, and you come back, Mr. Carlucci, we'll have a parade in your honor.' So with that, Frank and Ambassador Leonhart returned to Dar es Salaam.

I went back to the embassy to finish burning the classified materials. I had just started when there was a pounding on the front door. Ali Mafoudh, the head of the newly created special police force, demanded to come into the embassy. When I refused him entry, he said he would have to take me in custody. He drove me to State House, the seat of the government. An official there told Mafoudh to take me back to the embassy and not interfere with me.

After I did some burning, I went home for a quick lunch. When I returned, the officer in charge of the soldiers who had surrounded the building said I could not reenter it. When I argued with him, he told me a government official wanted to see me and he drove me to a government office.

I was taken to the office of Abdul Azziz Twala, one of the more militant members of the cabinet. Unbeknownst to me, an argument had preceded my arrival. Some of the people there wanted to kill me. At least that's what a man named Mohammed Ali Foum, who was there at the time and later became a diplomat in Tanzanian diplomatic service, told me years afterward. We met at the United

Nations one day, and he told me this. I don't know if it's true, but he swore it was. He said that after some argument, it was decided that killing me would cause too many problems. At any rate, when I got there, Twala simply told me to return to the embassy, then go home and get ready to leave later that day. This was –

Q: You had been summoned over to the Revolutionary Council headquarters?

Petterson: No, to an administrative office –

Q: They'd asked you to come over?

Petterson: Yes, right.

Q: But once you got there, nothing much happened?

Petterson: That's correct.

Q: And then you went back home?

Petterson: No, to the embassy. After using an ax to demolish the code machine, which didn't work and we'd never used, I started burning papers again. I soon realized that I couldn't destroy all the classified papers using just the stove, so I got one of the two or three destruction kits that were stored on the same floor as the walk-in vault, where we kept the classified files. Each kit was a heavy cardboard cylindrical drum, about three and a half feet high and two feet in diameter, the size of a large garbage can. It contained a bag, or bags, I can't remember, of inflammable chemicals in granular form and a magnesium igniter.

I put in papers, threw some of the chemical stuff on them, put in more papers, more chemicals, until all the papers were in the container. With everything now ready, I then dropped in the igniter. It worked like a hand grenade. You pull the pin, drop it in, and whoosh! A sheet of fire shot up. The heat of the fire was so intense that had I not kept the vault door open, I would have been incinerated. The pressure that resulted was so strong that to close the vault door, which I left open, I had to put my feet against of the opposite wall of the narrow hallway outside the vault and use my leg muscles to get the door closed. I began to wonder, 'What the hell have I done?'

Knowing that the troops outside would see smoke coming through the small open barred space in the vault, I went outside and talked to the guy in charge. Sure enough, black smoke could be seen pouring through the opening. He asked me what I was doing. I said, 'Oh, I'm just burning a few papers. It's normal for us to do that, you know.' And he accepted it, and I went back inside. I really thought, 'How am I going to explain [laughter] to Washington that I burned down the embassy?'

Luckily the vault was built of steel-reinforced concrete. Had it not been, the walls would have buckled, and the fire might well have spread. But it was contained in the vault, and I didn't burn down the embassy.

Q: This is all very interesting because your evacuation certainly wasn't the last and won't be the last. But one of the lessons learned perhaps is that when you use these destruction kits, you should use them outdoors?

Petterson: Absolutely!

Q: Or on a roof, or something?

Petterson: Absolutely! They didn't have directions on them. A couple of weeks or so later, I sent what we called an "operations memorandum" to Washington describing in detail what had happened and urging the Department to put a label on the destruction kits, "Do not use indoors under any circumstances!" I'm told that that memorandum made the rounds in the department and [laughter] got a lot of laughs.

I went home, packed a suitcase, and waited to be taken to the airport for the flight to Dar es Salaam.

Q: On an East African Airways flight?

Petterson: Yes, a regularly scheduled flight. I was met at the airport in Dar, taken to the embassy where I was debriefed. I wrote a report before I left the next day for Nairobi, where Julie and the children were. They had been in Dar es Salaam but had been evacuated from there after a mutiny by the Tanganyikan army had almost toppled the government of Julius Nyerere and had brought considerable violence to Dar es Salaam. During that violence, Fritz began to relive the Zanzibar revolution, and he had to be medically evacuated. He'd been under great stress and was as tight as a drum. After medical treatment in the States, he was medically cleared and resumed his career. It had been damaged, however, and ended after his next overseas assignment had not given him the kind of efficiency report he needed for a promotion.

I flew to Nairobi and spent two or three days there. I had the flu, but didn't feel too bad. I got a call from Frank Carlucci in Dar telling me to come back, that recognition had been granted. He and I would be going over to Zanzibar right away. So I flew to Dar, and, with Ambassador Leonhart, Frank and I flew over to the island. There was no parade to welcome us. Karume, who was visibly pleased, received us at State House, and Frank read to him the formal note of recognition. Leonhart returned to Dar es Salaam. Frank and I opened the embassy.

The first thing we did was clean up the vault, which was covered by a thick coating of slimy dark brown [laughter] soot. While Frank, his secretary, Lynne Derzo, and I were doing that, I almost passed out. I was done in by a bad case of flu, fatigue, and maybe weight loss. I had lost a lot of weight when I was alone on the island, cooking for myself or being fed by friends. Anyway, I was simply....

Q: Exhausted!

Petterson: Yes. So I went back to Nairobi, spent about a week with Julie and the children before going back to Zanzibar to resume my job working with my new boss, the chargé d'affaires of the American embassy, Frank Carlucci.

I began a very good year with Frank Carlucci, one of the most able, dedicated people I've known anywhere, certainly an outstanding Foreign Service Officer. Frank was very generous in giving me free rein to do whatever I wanted to do in the way of political reporting. Under Fritz I had been confined to lower-level officials and labor reporting. But Frank gave me, as I said, free rein.

I learned a lot from him by his example. He was an excellent reporter. He got out, beat the bushes, met people. He was charming. He got people to trust him. He dealt with people who were essentially hostile to us at that time, befriended them, and got a lot out of it. He knew what was going on in Zanzibar before he'd been there very long. A measure of his dedication is shown by the fact that whereas he spoke no Swahili when he got there, one year later, by taking tutoring from an Anglican nun and listening to tapes, Frank got a three-three in Swahili when he was tested at the Foreign Service Institute.

Q: Let me just interrupt you there to say, you know, obviously, you have a lot of respect and admiration for Carlucci. But I think it might be interesting for researchers, as well as journalists and other people who are going to use this interview, for you to describe briefly what the characteristics are, in your opinion, of an outstanding American diplomat. What is it that Carlucci represented, in your opinion?

Petterson: First of all, he had extraordinary intelligence, coupled with very good common sense, and an outgoing nature. He knew how to get along with Africans. He wassensitive to their culture. He had no false pretensions. He was an excellent writer, had superior analytical skills, and was a superb manager. He knew how to delegate.

Q: What makes a good reporting officer, Don?

Petterson: Somebody who's willing to get out of the office, travel around the country, to do whatever is necessary to get information, to establish a rapport with people so they will talk to you. You collect intelligence from people whom you meet and process it through whatever abilities you have. You learn to sift out good information from bad.

I believe, too, that, like Frank, the best officers are very industrious and dedicated. Frank worked long, hard hours and gave a great deal of thought to his work. He also (maybe this isn't a quality of a great reporter or necessarily a successful Foreign Service officer, but to me it's something very important) cared about people, the people who worked with him, and he showed that. He got their loyalty, and he got a lot out of them. He had all the qualities that would later propel him to high offices in the U.S. government, including secretary of defense.

Q: Okay, so there you are in Zanzibar?

Petterson: That's right. We are behind the bamboo curtain, as we said in those days, or the clove curtain, as some joked, cloves being Zanzibar's principal export. Frank set out to meet and establish a relationship with as many people as possible in the government and other areas.

Q: Yes, but this story is about you and not about Frank.

Petterson: [Laughter] Yes, but –

Q: So you were doing the same thing?

Petterson: Yes, I was very happy to be able to start becoming a political reporter because it was what I had wanted to do, and I had not been able to do it either in Mexico or much in Zanzibar before the revolution. I now got out and about, established whatever contacts I could. It was very difficult because we were under suspicion. Sometimes we were under surveillance. People were afraid to see us. We could not entertain Zanzibaris; nobody would come to our house. So we didn't have the usual kind of social opportunities to meet people and get information.

But we could wander around and go to people's offices and other places where we could meet people who might give us information of the kind we needed in order to inform Washington what was happening in Zanzibar, which had become (in the eyes of Washington and London) a bastion of Communism. The Chinese brought in more people - military trainers, agriculturists, and embassy staff - as did the Soviets and the East Germans. The East Germans were delighted to have a diplomatic establishment in Zanzibar. Before getting Zanzibar's recognition, they had not been recognized by any other countries except communist countries.

Q: But those three countries are among the three most difficult countries for a Western diplomat to observe and gather information about.

Petterson: True. We were we trying to report not only on what was happening in Zanzibar among the Zanzibaris, but, more important from Washington's standpoint, on what the Chinese, East Germans, and Soviets were doing. Other communist countries were also represented in Zanzibar. Cuba, for example, the Czechs, the Poles, North Vietnamese, Bulgarians, you name them; they were all there. It was a great place to be as a young reporting officer in the Cold War days.

We set about our work. As I said, I learned a lot from Frank and began doing political reporting. I was also the administrative officer and the consular officer. Our embassy began to grow. Suddenly we were in the front lines of the East-West struggle and a place, at least for some more months to come, considered to be very important in the eyes of the State Department and others in Washington.

Q: When you say that you began to grow, for example, did the USIA (United States Information Agency), USIS send any people? Were there any CIA (Central Intelligence Agency) people there?

Petterson: USIS reestablished their office, and an officer came to run it. The CIA did come in. This was the major factor in the growth of the embassy, as you can imagine. Zanzibar was very fertile ground for the CIA, the KGB (Komitet Gosudarstvennoy Bezopasnosti,

Committee for State Security, USSR), and other counterparts of these intelligence services.

So yes, we now have a CIA presence. We had a station chief and his staff, which included communications personnel, an administrative person, and a secretary. The State Department side began to grow a little, too, as we got another secretary and an administrative assistant, who took the admin burden off of me. So from a four-person U.S. mission, we expanded to about a dozen.

Q: Did the NASA tracking station people come back?

Petterson: Momentarily. The Karume government decided in April that the tracking station would have to close down. The decision came despite a report that had been issued just before the revolution by a Swedish diplomat whom the previous government had asked to assess the station. He attested to the peaceful purposes of the manned space program (which indeed they were). Pressure to close the station decision had been building. It was being exerted by Communist diplomats, as well as by people within the government, including but not limited to Babu and other leftists.

Whether they believed it or not, I don't know, but some continued to call the tracking station an American rocket base. Karume summoned Frank and told him the tracking station would have to be dismantled. So a few of the Project Mercury people and the NASA representative came back and very quickly dismantled the station, much faster than Karume had thought it would take. He was pleased by the professional way they did this.

Q: This would be about mid '64?

Petterson: No, we're still in the early part of '64....

Q: Let me ask you, Don. In Tanganyika at the time of independence, there was a small Indian minority as well as a few Arabs. If there were also these minorities in Zanzibar, what happened to them?

Petterson: The population, as I mentioned earlier,

included about 250,000 Africans. A high percentage of them were them people from the mainland who had come over to pick cloves and then had stayed and had established their families in Zanzibar. Some of the Africans were longer-term inhabitants, many of whom, especially those living in Pemba, called themselves Shirazis, claiming that they were descended from the Shiraz people of Iran. In addition to the Africans, Zanzibar had 50,000 Arabs, and about 20,000 Asians of Pakistani and Indian origin.

During the revolution, some 5,000 people were killed. Almost all of these were Arabs. That's one tenth of the Arab population. By the time I left the island near the end of 1965, the number of Arabs was less than 25,000. Those who remained had no place in the power structure whatsoever. The Asian population was also down by half or more by that time. As the government of Zanzibar became more and more repressive, Asians wanted out, and those who could, left.

Karume, despite a lot of good qualities, became increasingly dictatorial. I didn't see the worst of it during my time and I got along very well with him, as did Frank. But subsequent to our time there, he became more and more erratic, more and more dictatorial. Eventually he was assassinated, and a more moderate man, Aboud Jumbe, whom I mentioned earlier, became Zanzibar's president.

Frank and I settled down for a long siege of working in the Cold War trenches. Julie and the children came back in March. In April, because of anti-American demonstrations, they went back to Dar for a short time, returning after the demonstrations were ended and any possible threat was over.

We had a wonderful life in Zanzibar when all the hullabaloo was over. We had a small circle of friends – small because we couldn't mix with Zanzibaris. The Revolutionary Council had become very anti-Western and prohibited Zanzibaris from having anything to do with the

Americans and British. Even cabinet members were afraid to associate with us. So our social circle was limited to the small British community that remained, members of the British high commission, the Americans, and a few other foreigners, including some Africans. We had a tight-knit little community. We did a lot of socializing. The beaches were lovely. A number of us took our children to a beach just about every Sunday.

Zanzibar was a nice place to be, from that standpoint, and a very fascinating place to be because of what was occurring there, as we watched the influx of Communists and observed how things were playing out. We tried to influence Karume and others in the government to take a more moderate stance, and to be more truly nonaligned. We finally succeeded in that. Frank made a lot of inroads and a lot of progress before he had to leave the island.

Q: I wanted to ask. This is a good time. Were there any AID (United States Agency for International Development) or Peace Corps people on the island when you were there?

Petterson: No Peace Corps or AID. But we had an AID project, and AID officers from Dar es Salaam came over occasionally, or I would go over there to confer with them. The project was the construction and equipping of a secondary manual arts school that would turn out artisans, technicians, which the island very much needed. Karume looked upon the project with great favor.

A Zanzibari resident, a South African architect, designed the school to our specifications. The project, which cost about a million dollars, was appropriate to Zanzibar's needs and was not at all grandiose or ill conceived. Within a decade, however, it failed. After the school was turned over to the Zanzibari authorities to run by themselves, they didn't handle it well at all, and it deteriorated physically as well as academically.

Q: While you were there, then, this AID project was one of the tools of American diplomacy. Were there any

other tools that you had to try to influence the Zanzibari government?

Petterson: Well, the tool of rational discourse with the Zanzibaris. The agency has its own way of making friends, and some money was passed around. Whether that that produced any lasting positive results, I don't know. Our USIS library was very popular with Zanzibaris, especially young people. But its very success as a tool of our diplomacy was its undoing. At different times in the coming year and a half, our opponents succeeded in bringing trumped up charges against two USIS officers and getting them expelled.

Another thing we had going for us was the mistakes made by the communists themselves. The East Germans promised to build a massive housing projects, enough housing for all the Africans in Ng'ambo. We're talking about 40,000 or 50,000 people. In the end the Germans built some apartments that were unsuitable to the culture of the Zanzibari people, who didn't want to live in large blocks of flats. They wanted a house that would be their own. The Chinese imported a lot of commercial goods, some of which were shoddy. For example, they brought in some talcum powder, which sat in a warehouse and congealed in the heat and humidity. The Soviets didn't come through with the kind of aid they promised.

I don't want to give a picture that the Communists really blew it. Because of their mistakes, they may have lost some of the luster they had gained right after the revolution, but overall their aid was welcomed. The Chinese gave a cash grant of one million pounds, which the Zanzibar government sorely needed. Although the Chinese rice production of the communal farms was hardly bountiful, Zanzibar's leaders seemed favorably impressed by it. And the Chinese brought in medical personnel to work in the hospital. Soviet military advisors, as well as Chinese, continued to train Zanzibari soldiers. Both countries provided more arms, equipment and ammunition. And the East Germans brought in technicians of various kinds, and teachers as well. They also delivered an armed patrol boat and some fishing boats.

As for our AID project, we never promised what we couldn't deliver, and I think that set well with Karume. He was impressed by what we did. He wanted to have a balanced relationship with East and West - very hard to do in those days. He seemed to come to the conclusion that we were there not to do him in, but to work with him. Even though he had been very much angered and upset because of the delay of our recognition, in time we developed a good working relationship with him during those years before he became so erratic, eccentric, and dictatorial.

Q: It sounds to me as though Karume, at least for a while, had the same sort of balance among foreigners and foreign interests as Julius Nyerere had in Tanzania with the Russians –

Petterson: To a degree, yes.

Q: And the Chinese that were in Tanzania, as well as the Scandinavians and the Germans and the Canadians.

Petterson: Yes, but the West didn't have as many countries represented in Zanzibar, just the British, a one-man French consulate, and ourselves. So we were really outnumbered by the communist countries, and more so by the number of people they brought into Zanzibar. In the long run, it would not matter, as Zanzibar's importance in the Cold War diminished and both East and West lost interest in it. But that did not happen while I was there.

Q: Okay. So now we're up to '65?

Petterson: Yes, let's put it at the very beginning of 1965. Frank was well in stride running the embassy. All of us were pretty productive. U.S. relations with Zanzibar had improved. So, things were definitely going well when, suddenly, there was an unexpected reverse. On January 15, Frank went to Dar es Salaam. While he was there, Bill

Leonhart was summoned to Nyerere, who said that Frank and Leonhart's deputy chief of mission, Bob Gordon, had been involved in a plot to overthrow the government of Zanzibar.

Now this was totally idiotic. It stemmed from a telephone conversation that Frank and Bob had had earlier in the month, a telephone conversation in which they were trying to work out a way to get a high-level American official to attend the celebration of the first anniversary of the revolution. Ambassador Leonhart was against the idea, and there was opposition to it in the State Department. Frank and Bob were developing arguments in its favor. They were speaking guardedly, using code words, because they figured the phones were tapped. Among other things, one of them said something like, 'This will give us ammunition to get the big gun,' the big gun meaning [laughter] Assistant Secretary of State Soapy Williams, G. Mennen Williams, who they hoped would come for the celebration.

Whether the tape was doctored or not, it and some spurious intelligence reports that he had seen convinced Nyerere that Frank and Bob Gordon were concocting a plan to bring down the Zanzibar government. Nyerere foolishly believed it.

His rush to judgement is all the more incredible considering that only two months earlier he had been burned by an equally unlikely fabrication that the American government, in league with Portugal, was plotting to overthrow the Tanzanian government.

The allegation was based on documents that had been sent to Nyerere's foreign minister by the Tanzanian ambassador to the Congo Republic. The foreign minister, Oscar Kambona, had made them public and denounced the United States. This gave rise to a surge of anti-Americanism in the country.

Subsequently, a document-authentication expert proved to the Tanzanians that the documents were crude forgeries.

Kambona's and Nyerere's readiness to believe the worst of the United States had made them look foolish and must have been embarrassing to Nyerere. But here he was, once again acting precipitately.

Ambassador Leonhart urged him to reconsider, but Nyerere was adamant. Frank and Bob Gordon had to go. Frank was allowed to come back to Zanzibar to be able to pack before leaving. He went to Karume and told him the whole story. Karume was sympathetic, and said that he had no role in the affair. He and Frank parted on cordial terms. The next day, we said goodbye, and off he went. His wife, Jean, stayed on long enough to pack their household effects.

Nyerere, incidentally, finally came to realize, after receiving messages from President Johnson and from Secretary Rusk in which the entire story had been laid out to him, that he had made a mistake. He was contrite, but nothing could be done.

Q: But obviously it had no bad effect on Frank's career. So there you are in Zanzibar, again in charge?

Petterson: Yes. There I was, once again, in charge of the embassy. I was acting consul. By the way, we were no longer an embassy because when Zanzibar and Tanganyika joined to become Tanzania, Zanzibar no longer was the capital, so we were reverted back to consular status. I was acting consul for a larger establishment than when I was acting chargé d'affaires, when I was the only one there. I now had, in some ways, a more challenging kind of a job, certainly from a management point of view.

Before long, Washington, perhaps figuring that if once again they sent someone to be my boss again, he might get thrown out [laughter], decided to let me be consul for the rest of my tour of duty. This was done even though Frank's replacement would come out while I was still there and would be an officer who outranked me. The officer was Tom Pickering, and we worked together for the rest of my tour, which ended in November 1965.

Q: Tom Pickering, another one of the shining stars of the United States Foreign Service!

Petterson: Absolutely.

Q: Yes, you worked with both Frank Carlucci and Tom Pickering.

Petterson: Yes, I tell people that I made Tom's career.

Q: [Laughter]

Petterson: I wrote an efficiency report [laughter] on him. I hope it was a good one! He was an extraordinary guy and a lot of fun to work with. He and Alice, and Julie and I had good times in the months that we were together in Zanzibar continuing to do the kind of work that Frank and I had done. We had some new difficulties. For example, the Zanzibaris accused Harry Radday, who was the USIS officer, of being up to no good. According to the charges against him, he was seeing the wrong kind of people, plotting, doing this or that. It was total nonsense. I went to Karume, and said, in effect, "This is not true; don't do this! He is a good officer, who has done nothing wrong."

But Karume was inflexible. He said the decision had been made by the Revolutionary Council and could not be changed. Harry, who was popular among the Zanzibaris, and, because he was so tall – at least six foot five – was called "Bwana Twiga" (Mister Giraffe), had gotten around town a lot, meeting a wide range of people in the course of doing his job as our cultural affairs and information officer. I'm convinced that either a hostile intelligence service or extreme radicals in the government, or the two working together, had fabricated the reports about Harry. And they had chosen him because he was being effective in countering the anti-American propaganda that was so prevalent and was providing Zanzibaris with information about the United States and the outside world that otherwise was not available to them.

Q: So he was good at his job?

Petterson: He was good at his job.

Q: And making friends for America?

Petterson: Yes. Harry was expelled quietly, which was how Karume had proposed to handle the matter. Another USIS officer, a man named Barney Coleman, whose most recent assignment had been in Nigeria, replaced Harry. Barney eventually ran into the same problem. He was out seeing people and doing his job. Our enemies didn't like it, stories were circulated about him, nasty stories, and Karume said he had to go. Again, I remonstrated with him. Karume could be reasonable on some things, but he dug his heels in, and Barney Coleman had to go. So we didn't have complete easy sailing, to say the least. There was always some kind of battle going on.

Q: So what it sounds then, Don, a little bit sort of like Stalin, you know. Karume is a man with great strengths, but also very deep suspicions, because this makes, I think, three American diplomats who have been quietly or otherwise pushed out of Zanzibar in a year!

Petterson: That's right, and before that, of course, Fritz Picard. Karume did have definite weaknesses. He was a very suspicious man, and with reason as time went on because he had enemies within his own establishment. Some of those people came to grief later on and were executed. Othman Sharif was. He was the minister I mentioned when Fritz Picard got expelled, the one who had authorized the release of the American reporters and before the revolution had been a political enemy of Karume.

After the union of Tanganyika and Zanzibar, he became a minister in the Tanzanian government, serving in Dar es Salaam. Later, he went to Washington as ambassador. On a return trip to Zanzibar, Karume imprisoned him. Nyerere got him out, and he went back to the mainland. But later on, the government of Zanzibar accused him treason. He was brought back to the island and was executed. Abdul

Kassim Hanga, the vice president of Zanzibar, was also executed, along with some others.

Q: More and more like Stalin?

Petterson: Yes, he became, unfortunately, more and more –

Q: Paranoid?

Petterson: Paranoid, erratic and dictatorial as time went on. My own relationship with him, and again, this was before he really got bad, was quite good because of the friendship we had established when I was a vice consul, and because I continued to deal with him in his own language, and, of course, treated him with a proper measure of respect.

Q: So, Don, in terms of the career Foreign Service, this is another really good argument for language training?

Petterson: Oh, absolutely.

Q: Would you say, in retrospect, that the Foreign Service should be doing more in terms of training officers in languages?

Petterson: Yes! The Foreign Service at different times placed greater emphasis on foreign language training, but in general the focus was on training as many people as possible, but not training enough in depth. Many officers, as a result, would gain a superficial working knowledge of a language, but far short of excellence. The Service did not, and still does not, have enough officers possessing a grasp of languages approaching bilinguality, especially in difficult, important languages such as Arabic, Chinese, and Japanese. We have some, but not nearly enough.

Q: So that sort of wraps up Zanzibar?

Petterson: Zanzibar, almost. Our second and third children, Julianne and John, were born while we were in Zanzibar. Julianne was born on the island in 1963 and John in Dar es Salaam in 1965. Julie had gone to the mainland to have John because the hospital in Zanzibar had deteriorated so much by 1965. In September we had our first and only vacation while we were in Zanzibar. We spent four days in game parks at Ngorongoro Crater and Lake Manyara and had a wonderful time. She and the children left Zanzibar near the end of September, and I followed in November, ending my assignment in Zanzibar and turning the reins over to Tom Pickering.

Let me interject here, that if whoever reads this account would like more details on what happened in Zanzibar, I have written a book entitled *Revolution in Zanzibar* that will be published by Westview Press in April 2002.

Q: Okay, so that's then –

Petterson: The end of 1965. Julie had gone before me so she could spend several weeks with her parents and family in Mexico. After I rejoined her and the children there, we went to California. I had a lot of home leave, and we spent December in San Luis Obispo.

Q: Sixty-five.

Petterson: After New Year's Day, we went to Washington before going off on our next assignment. En route to Mexico from Zanzibar, I had stopped in Washington for consultations and to see about an assignment.

My personnel officer was Charlie Whitehouse. He didn't think much of my request to go to the Congo or Vietnam, or some such interesting place. He said, 'You know, Frank's example shows that if you stay with your neck out on the block long enough, it's going to get chopped off.'

He thought a less volatile country would be in order and that I needed a political officer job in a large embassy, since I had had a consular job in Mexico and had just come from a tiny post. He said, 'Nigeria would be a good assignment for you – Lagos, Nigeria.'

So I was assigned as the number two officer in a three-person political section in Lagos. We left Washington in January 1966 and flew on a Pan Am flight to Lagos. Pan Am then had a flight from the U.S. to Africa.

As we approached the airport in Lagos, announced, 'Ladies and gentlemen, I'm sorry to tell you that there's been some trouble. The airport has been seized by army troops. The government has just been taken over by the military.'

Let me give a little background. Nigeria had been independent for a several years. Its coalition government was led by Abubakar Tafawa Balewa, a northerner and a very remarkable man. There was political friction in Nigeria, especially between the larger tribes, the Yoruba in the west, the Ibos in the south, and the Hausa-Fulani in the north. The northerners, the more numerous people in the country, were somewhat dominant. The frictions were causing unrest, and some violence had broken out.

Before I arrived in Nigeria, I knew there was some political turmoil, but I didn't know how bad it was. The embassy was not sending political officers out of town enough to comprehend the full scope of the violence that was taking place not all that far from Lagos. They really did not have a handle on the full extent of the dissension and violence."[19]

Another American diplomat who was in Tanzania during the Zanzibar revolution and when Tanganyika united with Zanzibar was Robert Gordon. He was in Tanzania from 1964 – 1965 and left after being declared *persona non grata*. As he stated years later in this interview on a number of subjects:

"**Q: You left Khartoum in 1961 and then went to the War College in 1964.**

Gordon: Personnel in 1961 to '63, two years. Head of European Personnel.

Q: I would like to move to your appointment as Deputy Chief of Mission, the DCM in Dar es Salaam. Was it called Tanzania in those days?

Gordon: It became Tanzania while I was there.

Q: In the first place, what was the country called at the time?

Gordon: It was Tanganyika and Zanzibar. Tanganyika had been its name clear back in the 19th century. I agree with you, we're way over the time, but probably the most fascinating, important work I did was in Personnel, the three or four tours I had in it. But it's nothing, basically, for overseas.

Q: I thought we would come back to Personnel a little later.

Gordon: Fine. Anyway, I went to the War College. And like all the FSOs at the War College, we all knew that we were going to have to have new assignments at the end of the War College.

While I was at the War College, I was promoted to class two and so I became eligible for a DCM job by the criteria then existing. When Dar es Salaam came open they asked me if I was interested. I said I was, very much so, because it sounded like an interesting post. Although I had been in the Sudan and while they are both in Africa, they are quite different countries. Just like Morocco and Zambia are in Africa, but there's no comparison. And so I said I would be interested in that job and I got it. And within a month after the War College I was in Dar es Salaam as DCM.

Q: Who was the ambassador?

Gordon: It was William Leonhart.

Q: How would you describe him as an ambassador?

Gordon: He was a very hard driving man who felt that if the embassy hours were 7:30 to 2:30, but if he wasn't there until 7 o'clock at night, he felt he hadn't put in a full day. And he liked people around writing reports, and recommendations, and analyses. He was very demanding on himself and his staff and, at times, he was a difficult man to work for. He probably didn't think so.

Yet, I can remember one time later I was being inspected. And the inspector was a very senior inspector. I can't remember his name. He asked me, 'Well, how was it working for Bill Leonhart? I've understood from several sources he's a very difficult guy to work for, very demanding.' I said, 'Well, after all, I only worked for him six months.' Because I was declared *persona non grata*, I only had a six-months tour with him there.

As I say, every time anybody would take anything to him, he would have to completely rewrite it. I didn't mind that, that's the prerogative of the ambassador. But the fact that eight out of ten times he improved what I did, I didn't like that at all.

Q: What was the situation in Tanganyika at the time?

Gordon: As I say, in the spring of 1964 it had become Tanzania and had united with Zanzibar. And we had an office in Zanzibar comprised of two officers, Frank Carlucci, who has gone on to great fame since then. And the other one was a fellow by the name of Donald Petterson, who is the current ambassador to Dar es Salaam. That was a subordinate post since it was a consulate reporting through Dar es Salaam.

I arrived there in June and was out in January, and also out three weeks in the London Hospital for Tropical Diseases, so I didn't spend an awful lot of time there. I just barely got myself oriented where I started producing something when the ambassador was called in by the President who told him that Frank and I were declared *persona non grata* and we had 24 hours to get out of town. Never gave any reason or anything, which you don't have to do.

And one of my ambitions has always been to find out exactly what the reason was. We found out through a quirk that they had tapped the telephones and were listening to conversations I had with Carlucci. He would phone me or I would phone him back and forth just keeping in touch on things. And we had a long discussion a couple days before we were declared PNG. He had called me and said the

Independence Day Anniversary of Zanzibar was coming up. I said yes. He said, 'I'd like to do something. Some message of some kind.'

I said, 'Don't forget it's now Tanzania. It's no longer Tanganyika and Zanzibar. It's Tanzania.' I said, 'I want to move fairly slowly on this.' I said, 'Let's wait and see what Nigeria, Ghana, Great Britain, Members of the Commonwealth, let's see what the members of the Commonwealth countries do about this type of thing, whether they are going to send a message or not. And if they do, then that will give us the ammunition we need to go back to Washington and maybe get a message out of Soapy Williams or somebody.' Now at that time we weren't aware that our lines were being tapped. Now, a few days later we were declared PNG and no reason given.

Many theories of why. One was the fact that I had used the word 'ammunition' with Frank and, theoretically, it was interpreted that Frank and I had plotted against the Government of Zanzibar behind the ambassador's back through direct contacts with CIA. Joe Palmer at that time was Director General and he sent a big rocket around to every post in the Foreign Service saying to be very, very careful when using slang. This and that could be misinterpreted and so forth. Giving credence to the fact that that was the real reason.

Well, baloney. I never had believed that. I still don't know. I can remember when I was going out as ambassador to Mauritius. I went over to CIA for the usual briefings. Frank Carlucci, at that time, was Deputy Director of CIA. I went up and had a cup of coffee with him. I said, 'Frank, now that you've got this job, find out what the hell was the reason.' He said, 'I've never been completely satisfied, either. And I can tell you there's not much here because one of the first curiosity files I poked into was that one.'

About two years ago, three years ago, I got a letter from Frank telling me that he had met a very high Soviet official at a reception. And this Soviet official told him that they had set us up on this and that they had fiddled with the tape of what we said and didn't say. I remember Nyerere, the President of Tanzania, said to our ambassador, 'Well, they used a word which I think is a very insulting word and they think I wouldn't know that word.' And the word was -- whatever the word was. I couldn't repeat the word now and it had no meaning to us. So that made me feel that those guys had been fiddling with the tape, too. Anyway, this may be the answer, that the Russians set us up.

Q: A disinformation campaign.
Gordon: Yes. The early days of it.
Q: What was your impression of President Nyerere?
Gordon: Of course, when we were there he was the great intellect in both the African independence movement and the movement of 'we will correct all of our ills with a well-organized socialist-directed society.' And, of course, we see that that brought him to no good. It helped ruin what agricultural base they had in the first place. I didn't have too much of an impression except I knew he was very highly thought of.

He was a great pain in the neck already to the United States. But he was somebody we had to work with and he could be very helpful because he had an enormous amount of influence with other black African leaders. He was so revered as the great father and so on, and so forth.

And I understand that he at one time was trying to be very helpful as one of the front line states in the Namibia-Angola-South African negotiations that have just come to fruition in the last months or so."[20]

Frank Carlucci, who was based in Zanzibar when the revolution took place, an event that helped to facilitate the unification of Tanganyika and Zanzibar, also recalled in an interview years later what happened during those days:

"**Q: You went from the Congo, were you assigned directly to Zanzibar?**

Carlucci: No. I came back and I was in effect Congo desk officer during the Katanga secession. Then I had a brief tour in Personnel. When Zanzibar broke – that is to say, when they expelled our consul and closed our consulate – and a few months later, I was asked to go out there.

Q: So you went to Zanzibar. You were there from when to when?

Carlucci: I arrived 1964 and I was there just about a year. So it would have been probably – I think I would have gone out in early '64 and I think I was expelled in January 1965.

Q: What had been the situation in Zanzibar that led to the previous expulsion?

Carlucci: Zanzibar had become independent in 1963. We had a consul, Fritz Picard was his name, who has since died. The Africans rose up and slaughtered the Arabs because the Arabs had been running the place. They drove a number of them right into the sea. They took over but they had a decided communist tinge. A lot of the Africans had been trained at the Patrice Lumumba University.

Q: Which is in Moscow?

Carlucci: Moscow. Now there were a couple of Arabs involved with them. Babu and Ali Sultan Issa, who had been trained in Moscow and Beijing respectively. By the way, they have since both become capitalists.

At the time, I remember shortly after I got there, the hospital was named the V.I. Lenin hospital and the stadium became the Mao Tse-tung stadium. All land was nationalized. In effect, all the Westerners were kicked out. There was a good deal of hostility toward the Americans and our consulate was shut down. Fritz Picard was marched out of the country, I think, literally at gun point. A long, intensive effort began to reopen our consulate, then turned embassy.

A number of us in the State Department favored reopening the embassy as soon as possible. The upper levels of the State Department wanted us to play a secondary role to the British. The British were more cautious. They didn't want us to open and their embassy had been closed down, too. It was quite a long negotiation getting back in. Actually I went to Dar Es Salaam and worked on the issue with then Ambassador Leonhart. We struggled to try to get me over there. Eventually the Zanzibaris agreed and I went.

Q: Now what was the situation in between Zanzibar and Tanganyika at that time?

Carlucci: They were independent countries.

Q: Two independent countries.

Carlucci: Two independent countries. It was later, in fact it at least partly our design, I think it was Bill Leonhart's idea as a matter of fact, that Tanganyika swallow up Zanzibar as a way of getting rid of the communist influence in Zanzibar. And eventually that proved to work, but it took time.

Q: Well, why were we pressing to develop or resume relations with this rather small, little island nation?

Carlucci: There was a lot of the focus on it. It was being called the African Cuba. But we also had a NASA [National Aeronautics and Space Administration] tracking station in Zanzibar which NASA at least thought was quite important. When I got to Zanzibar, I concluded that it was hopeless and we would have to dismantle the tracking station.

Q: What was it that in your estimate... In the first place, how did these negotiations go with Zanzibar? What was your role, what were the contacts like?

Carlucci: Well, the contacts, there were multiple channels. Basically, sometimes using the British, sometimes working with other African countries, or sometimes using Tanganyika to get in touch with the Zanzibaris. Eventually, Amani Abeid Karume, who was president, agreed that we could come back in.

Q: What was the rationality from their point of view to bring us back in?

Carlucci: I can't really answer that. I assume they didn't want to be totally isolated from the western world. Karume himself was not a communist. The government under him was basically communist and Karume was not a very sophisticated man (He was later assassinated.). He had a certain amount of goodwill toward the west. I assume that eventually he prevailed, allowing us to come back in.

One of the reasons that I think I got kicked out was that I managed to develop a good relationship with Karume. Karume spoke very little English and at one point I asked him what I could do to develop better relations with Zanzibar. He said learn Swahili, so I set to work and learned it. I was the only senior
diplomat on the island who could converse with him in Swahili and he loved that. So we had a very good relationship.

Q: Well when you arrived there in early '64, what was the situation from your perspective on the island?

Carlucci: It was pretty chaotic. People would be thrown in jail left and right. Asians sometimes literally were whipped in the streets. Mosques had been invaded and people killed. All land had been nationalized. The British club became the people's club, which was advantageous to me because tennis balls then became free and I was the only westerner left who played tennis. I found [locals] who could play with me.

There was just a lot of hostility toward the West. The Soviets and the Chinese flooded the place. There were well over a 100 Soviets attached to their embassy and the East Germans had a very significant presence. All doctors had fled except one female Asian doctor. The only doctors on the island were East German.

We had a North Vietnamese embassy. We had a North

Korean embassy and a very substantial Chinese communist presence, hardly matched by a very small British and American presence. I think there were three of us, a vice consul, one other officer, and a secretary or two. A very small British presence and that was it as far as the West was concerned.

Q: To me, one of enigmas is the large Chinese, at that time called Communist Chinese, presence in Africa which seemed to often have quite large missions and they were doing things, and yet I haven't heard anybody say it had any particular influence as far as getting involved. What was your impression in Zanzibar?

Carlucci: My impression was that the lead country for the Communists was East Germany. They had the most influence. They had a young, attractive ambassador, although the Soviets sent one of their most senior ambassadors. He had been ambassador to Canada. I think clearly the Soviets and the East Germans exercised more influence than the Chinese.

Q: Were the East Germans heavily into the security side as far as secret police and that sort of thing, because that seemed to be their specialty?

Carlucci: Yes, they got into that and they got into the media and the education system. They were building houses. Some of their projects turned out to be disasters. I managed to get one small aid project going. I built a school which I'm told is still functioning in Zanzibar today.

Q: With the expulsion of the Arabs, I would have thought that this would have been a disaster for the economy in Africa. Had the Arabs been sort of the merchant class and that type of thing?

Carlucci: The economy essentially was closed-tourism and some small trade. The economy spiraled down, such as it was. It wasn't a very significant economy to start with. They just planned to live on aid from the then Soviet

Bloc.

Q: Did you have any problems getting the small aid project rolling?

Carlucci: Oh, yes. I had difficulty getting it accepted. Once again the President had agreed to it and he actually, as I recall, came out and dedicated the school which was fairly major event because we couldn't get anybody even to attend our Fourth of July party. One of my neighbors, a minister named Jumbe, who later became vice president, had a tendency to drink a bit and one night he came over to my house. No sooner did he come in than the police arrived and essentially told him to get out.

We were pretty much isolated. We were socially ostracized. Virtually every Sunday there would be a demonstration against me. I would get my tear gas [mask] and my beer and I'd go to the embassy and watch the demonstrators. They would go around the block about three or four times to exaggerate the numbers. Sometimes I'd go down and mix with them as they were getting ready to demonstrate.

Q: Was there any focus or was there just…?

Carlucci: Anti-American. It got serious when the Belgians sent paratroopers into Stanleyville.

Q: This is Dragon Rouge?

Carlucci: Yes. That's the one time the demonstration got quite serious. By then we had had some Tanganyika police on the island. They managed to keep the demonstrators from breaking into the embassy. I guess it was then a consulate general because technically we had merged with Tanganyika. That demonstration by the way was led by the chief of protocol.

Q: How did this…Let's talk first about the NASA station. It was a space monitoring station was it? Had it been running during the time that we had no relations with the country?

Carlucci: No, I think it had been shut down temporarily. There were some NASA people-I'm not even sure if the NASA people stayed, they may have been evacuated. It was essentially dormant when I got there. To get back to the aura of your question, the only reason Zanzibar was important was U.S. domestic politics. I can remember before I left, Averell Harriman, who was Under Secretary of State, called me in and gave me essentially two instructions; get the NASA tracking station back in operation and to make sure that Zanzibar was not a political embarrassment to President Johnson during the campaign. Those were two difficult tasks.

Q: Was Zanzibar at all on the political map? Did you have correspondence coming in?

Carlucci: Oh, yes. There was quite a bit of press about the 'African Cuba.' It had become, I don't want to say it was a major story, but it had become at least a significant story in the U.S. press.

Q: Were you able to do anything about that or...?

Carlucci: Well, there was eventually, as I said, we merged with Tanganyika and the situation moderated, but that was over a period of time. During the first year, it was pretty chaotic. We didn't manage to score any major victory, I guess I'd have to say although it was clear that our influence was increasing as time wore on. To the extent that our influence increased, the Soviets and Chinese influence decreased and I was warned that they were going to try and get me.

Q: Was there a Soviet fleet presence there? If I recall, about this time, this was not too long after the Cuban Missile Crisis which was '62 and the Soviets really didn't have a very major fleet.

Carlucci: No, there was no Soviet fleet there.

Q: I mean it was really in the '70s when the Blue Seas Navy was developed.

Carlucci: No, it was really a civilian presence but they would spread scare stories. I can remember one time being called off the tennis court by the President of the country who said to me, 'There's an American submarine surfacing in our waters. Get it out of here.' Of course there was no American submarine.

Q: How would you conduct...What would a day's work be there for you when you say you were pretty well quarantined against most contacts?

Carlucci: The ministers would receive me in their offices and I had pretty good access to the President. When I asked to call on the President, invariably they would agree and I used to have some fairly good and lengthy conversations with him. Essentially, my time was spent providing political analysis, observing what was going on, establishing as many contacts as I could, talking to my colleagues in the British embassy, talking to the Israeli consul general, seeing what they had found.

I also had some contact with the Soviets. The Soviet ambassador became quite friendly. I remember he brought my daughter one of those Soviet dolls. And I spent a fair amount of time, at least in the early portion of my stay, learning Swahili.

Q: When you were having these conversations with the President, what were the subjects?

Carlucci: Trying to reassure him of our desire for a mutually beneficial relationship and to convince him that a lot of the stories that he'd been reading about us were not accurate. I talked to him about ways in we could help Zanzibar, working with him on the school project. Essentially, trying to regain their confidence because there were a lot of misleading and inaccurate stories that had been spread about the United States.

Q: What about relations with Tanganyika? Did you go over there fairly frequently?

Carlucci: Yes, I did. I never looked forward to the trip because the only way of getting over was a 1930, I think it was a '30s DeHavilland aircraft, which could hold about four or five people. The pilot, I remember, would pull out his novel the minute the wheels got off the ground, which was always a bit disconcerting.

Q: We're talking today, the 30th of June and on the 26th of June, Ambassador (William) Leonhart died. Unfortunately, I never interviewed him.

What was your impression of his support and how he ran his embassy?

Carlucci: His support as far as I was concerned was absolutely outstanding. He and I had an extremely good relationship. Bill Leonhart was a brilliant man. I'd have to describe him an intense man, a workaholic who spent hours and hours and hours in the embassy. No cable left his embassy unless it was perfect. He worked it over. I think he ran a really tight embassy. But he was always receptive to ideas from me and would take them and make them better if they were good ideas. He'd come up with a lot of ideas himself. I had such high regard for him, that when I later became deputy director of the CIA, I brought him over to the CIA and put him on a review panel for our analytical shop.

Q: Did you play any part, or our embassy in Tanganyika play any part, in this merger of Zanzibar and Tanganyika into Tanzania?

Carlucci: The answer to that is yes. I'm not sure exactly how Bill Leonhart did it, but clearly he played a significant role in it. Whether he convinced Julius Nyerere on a one to one basis or whether there were other channels that were used, I can't say because I was not party to those conversations. But I knew that Bill broached the idea to me long before it happened so there's something that was germinating at least through our embassy in Tanganyika.

Q: What were you reporting from the Zanzibar side as far as you saw through receptivity of the people on Zanzibar to this greater merger?

Carlucci: I think it was a mixed bag. The Communists were not favorable to it. They saw it as loss of authority for them. Karume was very much in favor of it. I think it was seen as a threat by the Revolutionary Council. Those were the days where African unity was very important.

You could not argue with the idea of African unity. It was a hard concept for them to argue against.

Q: As far as being in Zanzibar itself, was this a subject you could raise at all or was this something that almost better if you didn't raise this?

Carlucci: I can't recall whether I actually raised it. If I did, the only one that I could have talked to about it would have been the President. Certainly none of the Communist ministers had any kind of dialogue with me on that subject.

Q: What about the Soviets and the Chinese? Were they involved in this trying to stop this thing or were they...?

Carlucci: Not overtly. What they did behind the scenes I can't say. Clearly they were involved in getting me and Bob Gordon expelled.

Q: Bob Gordon was your...?

Carlucci: He was the DCM in Dar Es Salaam.

Q: The DCM, okay. Did you find that the East Germans, for example, were following you or harassing you or anything like that?

Carlucci: No. To the best of my knowledge nobody followed me or harassed me. The East Germans and I never talked because we didn't have relations. We would frequently be standing near each other in ceremonies. Everybody would gush all over him and ignore me.

Q: It must have been a little awkward on a small island with the diplomatic corps. You had the East Germans that we didn't recognize, the Vietnamese who we didn't recognize and the North Koreans that we didn't recognize?

Carlucci: The only people at ceremonies I could talk to were the Brit, the Israeli, and the Soviet. I'd have to listen to all the diatribes. In one of the more humorous incidents, I decided to visit the neighboring island of Pemba, which was being run by a Commissar, named Ali Sultan Issa, a man who was trained in Beijing. He was so indoctrinated that he insisted we even share the same bed. 'This is the way we do it in the People's democracy.'

He took me around the island with people chanting and singing since it was in the 'workers paradise.' Then he had a rally and meeting and I could see during the rally, this was in the early stages of my stay, that he would point at me and the crowd would applaud and yell and scream. So I asked someone what he was saying and he told me he was saying, 'There's the enemy. Why don't you applaud or don't you think we ought to throw the Americans out?' Right then and there, I decided that learning Swahili was essential.

Q: I would have thought that you would have been up against all these groups and you being sort of the butt of their attacks and speeches and all that at any ceremony you went to, you could almost stand up with a target painted on you or something like this. You must have had to make the decision, do I just stand here and smile or keep a stern face or what do you do?

Carlucci: Just smile and roll with the punches. There was one other African that I could talk to. He was the Chairman of the Afro-Shirazi party, Thabit Kombo, who was probably in his 70s or 80s at the time, and was such a revered figure in Zanzibar that he could talk to me without fear of retaliation. He and the President were essentially the only two that I could talk to.

Q: Turning again to the NASA station, they opened it up, reopened it while you were there?

Carlucci: No. Well I can't recall, to be honest with you, whether it was open for a brief period or not. I doubt it. We had to negotiate its removal and of course we stalled for time. Time was an issue because the government was demanding that we remove it within a matter of weeks and NASA said that just couldn't be done. It was very valuable equipment, which they wanted to get out. So I spent a lot of time trying to negotiate a reasonable period for dismantling the station.

Q: Was there any feeling about NASA one way or the other?

Carlucci: Of course, the communists had thoroughly planted the idea that this was a spy station; it was all run by the CIA and so the situation was almost hopeless. Everybody believed that it was a spy station.

Q: What about the Soviets, because if I recall, although space flight was in its early stages in those days, yet we had made offers that if the Soviets had a space problem they could use our space facilities and vice versa. Did they play any part in it?

Carlucci: I'd have to assume that the Soviets were behind the campaign to force us to remove our tracking station. That the attacks came from the communists, there is no question.

Q: How about the press. Is there anything to report on the press?

Carlucci: It was entirely government controlled. Anything the government wanted they'd give to the press. There was no free press. The only way that I could know about the real world was through tuning in VOA [Voice of America] on my radio.

Q: Did you notice any difference when Zanzibar and Tanganyika became Tanzania? You were there during the initial stages of the amalgamation?

Carlucci: Yes. I went from being chargé to being consul general.

Q: Did you notice how the amalgamation was working at that point?

Carlucci: Well, very slowly. We virtually couldn't feel any effects in Zanzibar, other than as I mentioned earlier we finally negotiated getting some Tanganyika policemen into Zanzibar. This was the first tangible presence. The island was very unwilling to give up its de facto independence.

Q: Could you do a little compare and contrast between the way things were run in Zanzibar while you

were there and what you'd seen in the former Belgian Congo?

Carlucci: Well, there was a certain similarity obviously. There was initial hostility toward the west but in the case of the Congo, there had not been the kind of thorough Communist penetration that you'd had in Zanzibar. The Congolese didn't know what communism was, although some of our politicians, particularly Senator Dodd, called them Communists – Senator Tom Dodd, not Chris Dodd, the son.

The Zanzibaris, a lot of them, had been to school in Moscow or in Beijing. They were much more sophisticated in their approach. Both situations were chaotic of course. I suppose the Congo might have been slightly more dangerous. We regarded Zanzibar as not particularly dangerous, although some people were killed. Of course during the revolution, a great number were killed.

Q: The similarity is the extreme nationalism and the anti-western overtones.

Carlucci: They were more explicit in Zanzibar than they were in the Congo. Zanzibar at least had a resolution. The Congo has never found its resolution.

Q: You were seeing the products of the Soviet training of Communists. Did you find that the people coming out of then named Lumumba University in the Soviet Union were pretty fairly indoctrinated?

Carlucci: Oh, yes. The big thing was the young pioneers, which was East Germany. I can remember large numbers of Zanzibaris being taken to East Germany and coming back as young pioneers in uniforms. Indoctrination was pretty thorough. Lumumba University hadn't really been established when I was in the Congo. By the time I got to Zanzibar, it was in full swing and there were large numbers of Zanzibaris, way out of proportion to their population, going to places like East Germany and Moscow and Beijing to study.

Q: Did you find any, were there any, Tanganyikan officials starting to drift over that you could talk to?

Carlucci: No. Not outside of the police. Even then I didn't have much contact. There was a Zanzibari police chief that I could talk to. He was not totally hostile to the West, but he was subsequently removed. While I was there, you could not feel much Tanganyikan presence.

Q: How did you expulsion come about?

Carlucci: Bob Gordon and I were having a phone conversation. This is about January of '65. We were discussing a message of congratulations on the second anniversary of the revolution. We did something very foolish.

Q: Where were you calling from?

Carlucci: I was in Zanzibar. And Bob Gordon was the DCM in Dar Es Salaam, Bill Leonhart's deputy. We started to double talk, which you should never do; it's easily decipherable. We started talking about the anniversary of the revolution and shouldn't we send a message, meaning a message of congratulations. Bob said, "Well, they are very reluctant in Washington and you will need more ammunition" meaning a stronger argument to make our case. I said, "I want to come over and discuss this." I flew over and I was at the home of Jack Mower, one of our embassy officials. He had the radio on and the radio announced that Bob Gordon and I had been expelled.

Bill Leonhart went to Nyerere and said, 'What's this all about?'

Nyerere said, 'We have a tape of this conversation.' And when Nyerere described it, it was obvious the tape had been doctored in some way to make it appear that we were plotting to overthrow the government of Zanzibar.

I went to see Karume, who even under those circumstances received me. He said this was wrong and should not happen. It was the Tanzanian government now that had expelled me, not the Zanzibar government. He said he'd call Nyerere, but there was nothing much more he could do. There seemed to be no alternative, so I left. A number of years later, I was at a reception at the State Department. A big Russian came up and almost swept me off my feet and said, 'Don't you remember me?'

I said, 'I'm not sure.'

He said, 'Well, I'm so and so. I was the Tass correspondent in Zanzibar when you were there.'

I said, 'Then maybe you can satisfy my curiosity. Who was it that plotted my expulsion and doctored the tape. Was it you Soviets or the East Germans?'

He said, 'Oh, we were all in it together.'

Q: It's interesting though that Nyerere got into this because he certainly must have...

Carlucci: Well, apparently somebody took the tape to the cabinet and played it for the entire cabinet. Of course the more radical members of the cabinet, insisted that we be expelled. What position Nyerere took in that cabinet meeting I don't know to this day. Don Peterson, who was my vice consul, later became ambassador to Tanzania. He told me that he had a conversation with Nyerere, this is years later, and Nyerere said they had made a mistake and that I was welcome to come back. But I don't know what transpired in that Cabinet meeting. I thought my career was at an end that day."[21]

After the two American diplomats – Frank Carlucci and Robert Gordon – were expelled from Tanzania, relations between the two countries soured and Nyerere himself once publicly addressed the subject.

Although Nyerere had profound philosophical and ideological differences with the United States, American diplomats in Tanzania did not question his integrity and commitment to his people and to the causes he espoused and acknowledged he was a man of deep intellect.

Presented below is a sample of what some American ambassadors, Democratic and Republican, said about President Nyerere.

Deputy American ambassador Robert Hennemeyer who was in Tanganyika, later Tanzania, from 1961 – 1964 described President Nyerere as "a great political theorist,...a charismatic figure,...a great leader of his people. I don't believe for a moment that he meant anything but to do the best he could for the wellbeing of his people....He had an enormous amount of influence with other black African leaders. He was so revered as the great father.... Clearly he was a world leader, not just an African leader."[22]

Ambassador Claude G. Ross described Nyerere as a leader who was "full of good intentions and the epitome of integrity. I don't think any kind of financial scandal was ever attached to him....He was a very interesting man, very articulate, you know, and had a better education. He'd gone to Edinburgh and had advanced training, not a doctorate, but advanced training." – (Ambassador Claude G. Ross interviewed by Horace G. Torbert, February 1989, *The Association for Diplomatic Studies and Training Foreign Affairs Oral History Project*, Copyright 1998 (ADST), pp. 64 – 65).

In the words of Ambassador John W. Shirley:

"I enjoyed the fact that during my tenure in Dar es Salaam Julius Nyerere was still President of Tanzania. I found him an interesting and extremely intelligent man. And since South Africa was in turmoil at the time, and because Nyerere was, to say the least, not particularly sympathetic to the policy of constructive engagement, my meetings with him were frequent, animated, sometimes sharp, but never acrimonious. It was as intellectually stimulating to deal with him, as it was to deal with Prime Minister Salim Salim." – (Ambassador John William Shirley interviewed by G. Lewis Schmidt, November 1989, *The Association for Diplomatic Studies and*

Training Foreign Affairs Oral History Project, Copyright 1998 (ADST), p. 30).

Ambassador W. Beverly Carter described Nyerere in the following terms:

"Julius Nyerere was...one of the early heroes, political heroes, of mine and of many other Africanists....(He) was an extremely popular person....(Other African) countries tended to look to Tanzania for leadership, and Nyerere was never hesitant about offering it and giving it and doing it well..He is probably one of the most principled men I ever met in my life....

I talked earlier about my Government's ambivalence about Tanzania....Nyerere should have been treated more like the world leader that he is and that everyone recognized him to be....Just unheard of for a man of his... Nyerere's worldwide leadership being treated, I felt, as, not as well as other people who didn't come nearly up to his size. It's sort of symptomatic of the problem I had in dealing with my own Government....

You didn't think of (President) Tolbert (of Liberia) as being ... a Kenneth Kaunda or Julius Nyerere. He didn't have that capability, was not an intellectual giant. He did not even have quite the quality that Botswana's Seretse Khama had, who was not a giant intellectually the way I think Nkrumah was or Nyerere is.....With Nyerere it was the kind of relationship that you have in a dormitory at night when you're engaging in a good debate (laughs)." – (Ambassador W. Beverly Carter Ambassador interviewed by Celestine Tutt, April 1981, *The Association for Diplomatic Studies and Training Foreign Affairs Oral History Project*, Copyright 1998 (ADST), pp. 6, 7, 8, 9, 15, 16).

Nyerere's high intellectual calibre was also acknowledged by a British journalist, Trevor Grundy, who worked at the *Standard*, renamed *Daily News*, in Dar es Salaam in the late sixties and early seventies. He was a sub-editor when I worked there as a news reporter. I left in October 1972.

Grundy wrote the following about Nyerere (a graduate of the University of Edinburgh) in his review of *Nyerere: The Early Years*, a book written by Thomas Molony, a senior lecturer in African studies at the University of Edinburgh, in spite of the fact that he disagreed with Nyerere's socialist policies and one-party rule:

"I worked in Dar es Salaam (1968-1972) for one of the English papers he nationalized in 1970....

He got into Edinburgh and that city and the people he met there left an indelible mark on his future career. Julius fell in love with the British and their great writers, economists and philosophers.

He went on to use his Edinburgh years to great advantage, bewildering (some might say bamboozling) liberal-minded journalists in the 1960s and 1970s with his formidable intellect which was the result of his reading of Jacques Rousseau and John Stuart Mill, T.H. Green's *Principles of Political Organization*, Benard Bosanquet's *Philosophical Essay of the State* and Harold Laski, the famous London School of Economics theorist.

He had a blotting paper brain.

Hardly a soul at Edinburgh guessed he would turn into Africa's number one brain box in years to come. As the historian George Shepperson put it in a BBC interview: 'We at Edinburgh were very surprised in the mid-1950s when Dr Nyerere's name became widespread throughout the world press. We never felt when he was here that he was going to become a leading politician.'

Statesmen and journalists were amazed at his knowledge....

With his eager tongue, (and) a formidable intellect,...he is presented by Commonwealth groupies as the politician who did the most to mastermind the downfall of Portuguese and British/Afrikaner rule in Africa....The Rhodesian leader Ian Smith several times referred to Nyerere as Africa's 'evil genius.'" – (Trevor Grundy, in his review of Thomas Molony, *Nyerere: The Early Years*, London: James Currey. The book was first published in June 2014. Trevor Grundy reviewed it in April 2015; see Africa Unauthorised).

The American secretary of state, Dr. Henry Kissinger who went to Dar es Salaam, Tanzania, to see Nyerere three times in 1976 also acknowledged Nyerere's stature as a towering intellectual and as an independent-minded highly influential leader who also played a central role as the spearhead of the liberation struggle in southern Africa. As he stated in his book, *Henry Kissinger: Years of Renewal*, in a section entitled, "Julius Nyerere and Tanzania: The Ambivalent Intellectual":

"Tanzanian President Julius Nyerere proceeded to arrange an official reception that could not have been more cordial. The motive, however, was altogether different from Kenyatta's. Nyerere...was, at heart, deeply suspicious of American society and American intentions.
 In international forums, Tanzania's ministers frequently castigated us. Nyerere would not have described friendship with the United States as a national priority; instead, he tended to think of relations with us as a necessary evil....
 Brilliant and charming, Nyerere had an influence in Africa out of proportion to the resources of his country, proof that power cannot be measured in physical terms alone....Because Tanzania was involved in the armed struggle that was taking place in Rhodesia, and because of Nyerere's intellectual dominance, Nyerere would be a key to any solution....
 Many of Nyerere's American admirers thought he and

his colleagues were the embodiment of American values and liberal traditions. By contrast, his American critics viewed Nyerere as a spokesman for Communist ideology. Neither view was accurate. Nyerere was his own man. His idiosyncratic blend of Western liberal rhetoric, socialist practice, nonaligned righteousness, and African tribalism was driven, above all, by a passionate desire to free his continent from Western categories of thought, of which Marxism happens to be one. His ideas were emphatically his own....

For our first meeting, Nyerere, a slight, wiry man, invited me to his modest private residence. It was a signal honor, and he introduced me to his mother and several members of his family. He was graceful and elegant, his eyes sparkling, his gestures fluid.

With an awesome command of the English language (he had translated *Julius Caesar* into Swahili), Nyerere could be a seductive interlocutor. But he was also capable of steely hostility. I had the opportunity to see both these sides during my three visits to Dar es Salaam....

Nyerere was the key to the front-line states....

The two most impressive leaders I encountered on this trip, Nyerere and Senghor, were at opposite ends of the African spectrum. In a sense, they represented metaphors for varying approaches to African identity. Nyerere was a militant who used ideology as a weapon...and considered himself as a leader of an Africa that should evolve in a unique way, separate from the currents in the rest of the world which Africa would use without permitting them to contaminate its essence. Senghor...sought a reconciliation of cultures." – (Henry Kissinger, *Henry Kissinger: Years of Renewal*, New York: Touchstone, 1999, pp. 931 – 932, 936, 949 – 950).

After his meeting with Nyerere, Kissinger was asked at a press conference in Dar es Salaam:

"Mr. Secretary, we've just come from a press conference with President Nyerere which was, to say the least, not encouraging for your mission. On both the Namibian and the Rhodesian questions, he said he received nothing of encouragement. In fact, on the Namibian question he said he is now less hopeful than before. Does this reflect your views on the future?...Isn't the fact alone that nothing has changed since last week an unhopeful sign?"

He said, among other things, in his response:

The purpose of my visit here was to get clear about the views of Tanzania." - (Henry Kissinger, at a press conference in Dar es Salaam, Tanzania, in Hanes Walton Jr., Robert Louis Stevenson, and James Bernard Rosser Sr., eds., *The African Foreign Policy of Secretary of State Henry Kissinger: A Documentary Analysis*, Lanham, Maryland, USA: Lexington Books, 2007, p. 243).

Nyerere had earlier stated at a separate press conference:

"A mission of clarity is not a mission of failure."

American ambassador James W. Spain described Nyerere this way:

"Nyerere's rule was relatively benign. I am quite sure he never ordered anybody killed. There were a few people in jail but not many. Some were from Zanzibar, under sentence of death there but kept alive on the mainland....People didn't get killed. They might get relocated under the ujamaa system of farming, but Nyerere never even thought of 'liquidating the kulaks'....
Nyerere's great aim was to bring education and medical facilities to his people. That was pretty hard to do

when they were scattered like that. So he set up the idea of ujamaa, the family village....and Nyerere did bring educational and medical facilities to the villages, far better than those in rural Kenya.... He was a hopeless socialist. Still, he was clearly a very sincere and humane man.

If I did anything useful, it was to convince Washington that Nyerere was not a brutal African dictator and a Communist stooge....

I found Nyerere fascinating. He had an MA from Edinburgh University and loved word play. I never read a book that he hadn't read. He translated Shakespeare into Kiswahili....I am very fond of Julius Nyerere....

Most Western development aid to Tanzania came from Scandinavia, particularly the Swedes. They liked the intellectual socialist, the benign father of his people who didn't kill or imprison people, while trying to create a new way of life with better prospects. The fact that it all didn't work very well didn't bother them....

For one thing, unlike other parts of Africa, no one was starving or dying of uncontrolled disease in Tanzania. For another, despite Nyerere's close identification with radical socialist theory, I don't think he cared much about economics. He was basically a humanist with a keen sense of both tribal traditions and modern politics, a social science type....

The fact was that Nyerere certainly wasn't on our side, but he wasn't a tool of the Chinese or the Russians either....

(On Uganda)...Nyerere replaced Amin with Milton Obote, a previous Ugandan prime minister who had been in exile in Tanzania for some years. He ran the grocery store (in Dar es Salaam)where we bought our food supplies. He was another intellectual socialist but without Nyerere's charm, humanity, or intelligence....

I was personally very fond of Nyerere--not necessarily a good thing for a diplomat. He was a very remarkable man and, I think, a very constructive element in the peaceful solutions to the problems of Southern Africa that eventually emerged." – (Ambassador James W.S. Spain interviewed by Charles Stuart Kennedy, October 1995, *The Association for Diplomatic Studies and Training Foreign Affairs Oral History Project* , Copyright 1998 (ADST), pp, 32, 33, 34, 35, 37, 41).

Ambassador Richard N. Viets said the following about Nyerere:

"At that time in mid-1979, the so-called front-line states in Southern Africa, I think there were five of them...the organization was chaired by Julius Nyerere, the President of Tanzania, a very remarkable gentleman. Nyerere really towered over the other four heads of state and this organization in many respects was a one-man operation. Because of his long association with the independence movements in East Africa and throughout Southern Africa he was highly respected.

Nyerere is an intellectual of very considerable dimensions, an extraordinarily articulate person. So the leadership of this group was essentially his without any challenge. He was offering almost daily advise to the Zimbabwean leadership on tactics, strategy, etc. in their negotiations with the British and the Americans and the others involved....

I decided I needed to know more about Julius Nyerere than anybody else on the face of the earth.... He is a very shrewd man.

He was...a most remarkable figure in contemporary African political history. I always said, and others who knew him well I think shared this view, that if Nyerere had been born in Western Europe or the Far East or even in North America, he would have been an exceptional figure in public life. He was a superb politician.

He had an acute brain, the memory of an elephant, intellectual horsepower that was second to none.

He was cunning. He could be warm-hearted one

moment and cut you off at the legs at the next if it met his political or personal needs. He had, of course, been the principal political figure behind the Tanzanian independence movement in the 1950s....

Nyerere... remains as far as I know the principal translator of Shakespeare from English into Swahili and one of the most gifted orators I have ever heard in English, and a marvelous drafter of the English language....

I can remember listening to him rail hour after hour against the IMF and the prescriptions the IMF was demanding of Tanzania that he argued would send it further into poverty, etc....

Nyerere regime's record is...in the human rights arena when one is talking about imprisonment and torture, or loaded legal shenanigans against opposition, I think his record is remarkably good. If human rights includes the right to a job, an education, hospitalization, etc., then you have to give him pretty good marks." – (Ambassador Richard N. Viets interviewed by Charles Stuart Kennedy, April 1990, *The Association for Diplomatic Studies and Training Foreign Affairs Oral History Project* , Copyright 1998 (ADST), pp. 56, 58, 59, 61, 67 – 68).

Ambassador David C. Miller, a staunch Republican, said the following about Nyerere:

"He was on his way to the Cancun summit, the only head of government from Africa among the 13 presidents at Cancun. He was the leader of the frontline states in the negotiations over Resolution 435, which was the Namibian independence resolution passed by the UN. In terms of national power at home, he was at quite a peak. Physically, he was old enough to be wise and young enough to be vigorous. He was a great guy to work with....

Nyerere had been a world leader of the non-aligned movement for a long time. His economic policies were well-known and the impact of his economic policies had been apparent for some period of time. In a nutshell, on the domestic front, Tanzania had succeeded in integrating itself as a political entity. At independence, there was Zanzibar and there was Tanganyika.

But there was also Julius Nyerere's belief that it was important for every citizen of Tanzania to move forward roughly together economically and to integrate themselves socially and that over a period of time his approach to the economic management of Tanzania would produce a more coherent, unified country than, as he was fond of pointing out, Kenya, his nextdoor neighbor, which was our favorite country. So, domestically, he had succeeded with a single party approach to governing Tanzania and thought that that had worked well for him...

Wonderful, warm, friendly, smart, honest, brave, humble. He was as great a head of government as Africa has seen as evidenced not by his ability to do the little day-to-day things of running a country but on the big accounts, the most important being his lifestyle, which remained humble throughout his whole time as head of government. Most remarkable, was his retirement from the presidency at a time when he was perfectly capable of going on physically.

Then, of course, he returned to his village upcountry as one of the few heads of government in Africa who behaved the way George Washington behaved here and said, 'We do not need presidents for life in Africa and I don't intend to be one.'

Frankly, he was probably happiest when he was back home in Butiama with his wife and grandchildren in a very humble home. It was hard to get to by vehicle. So, for me, he stands out in stark relief to the failed public leadership in Africa that can be found in almost every country....

Julius Nyerere because of his global leadership – and this is the thing that you have to remember: nobody in their right mind today can tell you who was president of Burundi or Rwanda 20 years ago – Julius was an international author, an international statesman, and used that effectively as a head of government to gain support for Tanzania well beyond either its objective importance or its internal economic performance. To a great degree, that's what a head of government in a developing country ought to be trying to achieve. Julius achieved that....

So, did the economy ever work perfectly? No. Did it achieve what he wanted? Yes, it did. It produced a level economic base that is now producing a solid Tanzanian economy without the disasters that befell Kenya. If Julius were here today sitting with us, he would say, 'I told you, David. Kenya turned into a corrupt mud hole. Tanzania is now slowly taking off the ground with responsible leadership in a country that's socially unified.' I'm happy to make that argument for him....

It was an outstanding diplomatic world simply because of Nyerere's presence and who he was and the importance of having Julius' support when he was head of the Non-Aligned Movement, of having Julius' support when he was running the Frontline States. When Julius Nyerere spoke or traveled, people listened to him. So, countries that were playing in that environment wanted to have a good mission in Dar es Salaam....

He had a position on the world.... He was first and foremost an intellectual and an ideologue.... Julius Nyerere was an intellect. He wanted to talk to people about his ideas and what worked and didn't work." – (Ambassador David Charles Miller interviewed by Charles Stuart Kennedy, January 2003, *The Association for Diplomatic Studies and Training Foreign Affairs Oral History Project*, Copyright 2004 (ADST), pp. 47, 48, 49, 50 – 51, 52, 55).

John H. Burns who served as the American ambassador to Tanzania from January 1966 to June 1969, not long after the Zanzibar revolution and the unification of Tanganyika and Zanzibar, had this to say in interview about Tanzania and Nyerere:

"Tanzania...had a highly intelligent and cultivated president, Julius Nyerere...

Q: Why did you want to go to Tanzania?

Burns: It was a very interesting time in East Africa. Tanzania had been independent only a few years and had recently experienced the much publicized revolution in Zanzibar--from which emerged the name Tanzania following the union of Tanganyika and Zanzibar. The country had a President, the remarkable Julius Nyerere, unique—then and ever since--in Africa.

The time in the CAR (Central African Republic) had stimulated in me a real interest in Africa; and then, from a personal point of view, I loved that out of doors life and Tanzania offered the best, Mt. Kilimanjaro, the Serengeti, the Selous and all. It is not that I am a hunter but I am a dedicated camper, animal watcher and all that.

Q: When you went out to Tanzania did you have any sort of brief? What were American interests and what were you doing?

Burns: Here I will say something that I have never recorded before. But that does not matter as no one would be interested this many years later. It harks back, perhaps, to Bill Blocker's telling me that if I followed the Foreign Service Regulations to the letter I would be a poor officer. Maybe I harked back to that counsel more often than I should have during my Service years but if so I have no regrets.

Tanzania placed a limit on the number of its own nationals each Embassy could have accredited. It was 14 or 15, as I recall, and applied to every country except the United Kingdom, which had, of course, many British citizens seconded at various functions throughout the Tanzanian government. During the briefings in Washington, before leaving for Dar es Salaam, both the CIA and the Department of Defense made it very clear to me that increasing the number of their personnel there (CIA) and opening an attaché's office (Defense), were, in their own words, 'their top priorities in Africa.'

I assured them that I would do my best but my fingers were mentally crossed. The Department never gave me actual specific instructions to present formal arguments for the removal of the American personnel limitation but it was clear that that was favored by most everyone.

I look on my three and one half years as what I might term the most 'singing' assignment of my entire career. And that was directly attributable to there being such a small staff.

We had one officer for each function: one political officer, one economic, one administrative, one consular (who also worked for CIA, as did the code clerk).

No one had to look for anything to do and we had little time for things like staff meetings; we'd have one every two weeks or so.

I have always thought meetings, generally, a terrible waste of time. I have also always thought that the more time officers spend out of the office the better and the staff at Dar, especially the Swahili speakers, did a lot of traveling around the country, as I did myself.

We had an old 4-wheel drive Land Rover and it was on the road most of the time. Not only did this add to the substance—and I might say validity--of our reporting, it was a practice extremely well received by the Tanzanian government. Because of our mandatorily limited staff, the Department was careful to send out the best qualified individuals. For instance Tom Pickering was DCM, followed by Jack Matlock.

Q: Both Ambassadors to the Soviet Union later on.

Burns: Yes. George Roberts was a witty, brilliant political officer and Earl Belinger the quietest, most efficient administrative officer I ever had the pleasure to work with. Roberts spoke fluent Swahili as did Pickering and Matlock. President Nyerere once said to me, 'Your Mr.

Pickering speaks better Swahili than half the members of my parliament,' which was true.

The result of all that was an operation of which I was immensely proud and, as I have noted, the most satisfying assignment of my entire career.

Before leaving I had a long, sort of retrospective, conversation with President Nyerere, sitting on the terrace of Government House, just harking back, with many laughs (President Nyerere had a fine sense of humor) over events of the three and one half years.

Just before leaving I said to him, 'Mr. President, there is one thing I'd like to say. As long as I have been here I have been urged by my government to try to persuade you to raise, or remove, the limitation on the number of Americans who can be assigned to this Embassy. As you know, I have never mentioned the subject to you and if I can bespeak anything in behalf of my successor, whoever that might be, it is that you never raise it.'

Laughing, he said, 'Of course I won't. What country could have an interest in little Tanzania to justify the diplomatic presence here of more than fifteen persons?'

And, of course, he was exactly right.

I recall a book written by Ambassador Ellis O. Briggs, who held, I believe, seven different missions, in which he said that the most efficient, and effective, of all seven had been Prague because the Czech government limited the number of Americans who could be stationed there.

Were I asked what single action would most improve everything about the Foreign Service I would without hesitation say, 'Reduce all staffs by a minimum of 25%.' Of course the chance of anything like that happening, or even winning measurable support, is about the same as that of Death Valley experiencing a snowstorm.

Q: Well, could we talk about, during the '65 to '69 period that you were there what the situation was in Tanzania?

Burns: There were no real political problems. Nyerere

had essentially no political opposition. When, years later, he finally left the presidency he did so entirely voluntarily. His problems were economic.

Tanzania is a miserably poor country, with no basis for hope of much change in the situation. Nyerere, realizing that, consistently worked to lower public expectations--which naturally soared after independence--or even hope of rapid economic advancement and stressed, rather, the importance of work and efforts to improve agricultural production and housing, simple advancements in living standards.

Although he attracted an immense amount of foreign aid, there was something about the idea of aid that was alien to him and he was anything but a petitioner. He, himself, lived very simply and he insisted that members of his government do likewise. There were no Mercedes limousines assigned to his ministers--or to himself. He resided in his own house, not a Government House, the old British palace, and it was by no means as grand as the average embassy residence.

He not only established diplomatic relations with communist China but paid a visit there. This agitated Washington tremendously, much more so than it did the British, Tanzania's erstwhile 'principal.'

I was frequently instructed to protest this or that action of Tanzania, which Washington found insufficiently 'pro-West' and, of course, there was the constant run of pressure about Tanzanian votes in the UN. I found this difficult when dealing with a man as innately sophisticated as Nyerere.

Once he laughingly said to me, 'Mr. Ambassador, we can't let our friends choose our enemies for us.'

He never showed the slightest resentment when, to tell the truth, he often had reason to do so.

Q: What was your impression of Nyerere during this period?

Burns: I have rarely known anyone more dedicated to

what he saw as his purpose in life. I once said that the song 'The Impossible Dream' could have been written for him.

He was a remarkably educated and cultured man, a graduate of the University of Edinburgh. One of his hobbies was translating Shakespeare into Swahili and one or two of them --Julius Caesar was one--were performed at the University of Dar es Salaam, an institution in which Nyerere, not surprisingly, took great interest.

His problems were, as I have said, economic and they were beyond his solution. I wonder if they, and the economic problems of Africa as a whole, do not defy solution.

It was frustrating to try to bring Washington to understand Nyerere. The first African chief of state invited to Washington by the Johnson administration was Colonel Mobutu of Zaire, who cooperated--one might almost say slavishly--with the United States in return for which he received untold millions in military and economic 'aid.' He is today one of the world's wealthiest men.

Incidentally, the week before he arrived in Washington on a state visit, he publicly executed several of his political opponents.

We could never even arrange to have Nyerere received on a personal call at the White House, when he went to the United States to address, at their invitation, the Council on Foreign Relations. This was all because he had established diplomatic relations with communist China.

Q: Did you find that he was open to you when you came there?

Burns: Completely. Originally I had feared that he might be tempted to refuse agrément to one coming direct from the office of the Supreme Commander Allied Powers Europe, and that at least that might inhibit our relationship. Not at all. He is a much bigger man than that. And, as I have noted, he was blessed with a most engaging sense of humor.

Q: Was he going through the, I don't know what the term was, but it was the creation of all those small village communes. I heard some remarks to the effect that this really broke up what was a viable agricultural system and did not help.

Burns: I don't believe that would be a fair contention in that, in my opinion, there was not a viable agricultural system to begin with. The country had not altogether emerged—if that is the proper word--from tribalism and the program called 'Ujamaa,' a sort of communal village scheme, was something of an expansion of the tribal arrangement based on an organized plan. I don't know how it turned out but I never believed it would work, anymore than planned economies have ever worked in any country. I don't think our own governmental farm programs really "work," however much they may benefit certain segments of our agricultural economy.

Q: This brings up an interesting situation. Nyerere was being accused of being too much of a devotee of the British Fabian Socialists and...

Burns: I have never known how Fabian socialism differs from plain socialism. I do know that Nyerere believed in socialism for Tanzania, a country with no capital foundation, other than land and that not very productive.

I believe that he thought that the introduction of large amounts of foreign capital into Tanzania would be simply a reversion to another form of colonialism.

His idea was to discourage great economic expectation among his people while endeavoring to raise the simple standards of their day-to-day lives, through work and education. For instance, during the years that I was in Tanzania there was no television; none at all. It was Nyerere's view that 1) they could not afford television in the first place, 2) it would keep people from the work they should be doing and 3) it would promote discontent by acquainting the mass of Tanzanians with a way of life they could not hope to equal, at least not any time soon.

As I said, Nyerere had an 'impossible dream.' One interesting sidelight of the no television situation was that almost every officer of the Embassy requested an extension of duty at that so-called 'hardship post.' They all had several children of school age--one had seven--and they found a life with no television to have many advantages; not to say that that was the only consideration affecting their desire for longer duty. There were many agreeable features about life in Dar es Salaam.

Q: Were you able to contribute anything to the educational thing through exchanges or...

Burns: Not to any great degree, no. We couldn't attract much attention from Washington for Nyerere. He was regarded by certain influential circles of the Johnson administration as a dangerous thinker. Despite the best efforts of Bill Leonhart, my predecessor, myself and Tony Ross, my successor, we could never persuade any of that particular group otherwise.

Q: You were there during some of the major periods of the civil rights movement in the United States. How did that play or not play, or was it...

Burns: It was of course of a certain amount of interest, mostly limited to university circles, journalists, etc. Nyerere, who, as I have said, was a sophisticated thinker, was very--but quietly--interested. He was deeply disturbed by Robert Kennedy's assassination. Kennedy had visited Tanzania about a year earlier, a visit which even anti-American elements of the Tanzanian press called 'a triumph.' Nyerere was deeply pleased by Kennedy's coming to Tanzania (it was Kennedy's own proposal) after his trip to South Africa and grieved--and I might say embittered--by his murder.

Q: Kennedy was assassinated about June of 1968, I believe.

Burns: Around that time. A few months later Robert Kennedy, Jr. came out to East Africa with Lemoyne

Billings, who had been probably John Kennedy's closest friend, and stayed a few days with me at Dar es Salaam. Nyerere was very gracious to him, receiving him in his office, talking seriously with him about wildlife preservation etc. and posing for pictures with him. Of course Nyerere was a gracious man by nature.

Q: Did you deal with Robert Kennedy when he came? How did that go?

Burns: It went as perfectly as anything like that can go. He and Mrs. Kennedy, as well as others accompanying him, stayed with me and of all the official visits with which I was involved over thirty years--and there were many--none equaled this one for its positive effect so far as US interests were concerned. Senator and Mrs. Kennedy charmed everyone and displayed sincere interest in everyone they met and everything they saw.

Q: Well, was there any problems...was Zanzibar pretty well in Tanzania at that time?

Burns: Zanzibar was legally a part of Tanzania but day-to-day governmental operations and politics were handled exclusively by a group headed by Sheik Karume, on Zanzibar. Karume held the title of First Vice President of Tanzania but his role on the mainland (where I do not recall his appearing while I was there) was essentially non-existent, as was Nyerere's on the island.

Nyerere early made it clear, in so many words, that he did not want the Embassy bothering his administration about questions concerning Zanzibar. It might be interesting to note that three successive Consuls at Zanzibar were Frank Carlucci, who later became Secretary of Defense, Tom Pickering, who went on to six subsequent embassies including the UN and Russia, and Jack Matlock, who also held several embassies, including the Soviet Union.

So Zanzibar, a post which was later closed, helped spawn three highly successful careers.

Zanzibar was regarded by Washington as a fermenting

problem when Tom Pickering arrived. Carlucci had been 'PNGed' not long before. Within a short time Zanzibar disappeared from the 'pending problems' lists in Washington offices and from the agenda of 'meetings.'

I don't know how familiar you are with Tom Pickering's career but that has happened wherever he has gone. For instance when he was moved from Nigeria to El Salvador--with Secretary Shultz saying, 'We are sending our best,' the 'media' was reporting explosive stories on a daily basis from that country. Within a month El Salvador had disappeared from the US headlines, or even the front pages. For some reason or other this has happened wherever Pickering has gone. Some officers have a talent-- if not actually the intention--of calling attention to their activities. Tom Pickering is the exact opposite."[23]

After John Burns left Tanzania in 1969, he was replaced by Claude Ross who served as the American ambassador from December 1969 to June 1972. When Ross arrived there, the union of Tanganyika and Zanzibar was still in its infancy but stable. As he stated years later in an interview about his service in Tanzania and on a number of subjects including Nyerere and the country as a whole:

"**Ross:** I got a call from John Burns, who had just left Tanzania and was now Director General, asking me if I would go to Tanzania.
Q: That was the second time he'd called.
Ross: Yes. I must say in all fairness, I wasn't that keen about it. I had rather hoped at that stage to go to another Latin American assignment at a larger embassy. As it turned out, there was one in the works that I didn't know about until I got back to Washington.

I got there to sit on a selection board in August or September of 1969, and the ARA executive director, Findley Burns, said, 'You know, Secretary Meyer wants to send you to Venezuela. Would you have any objection? I said, 'No. I told John I would go to Tanzania, but sure, if Meyer wants me to go to Venezuela, of course.' It's a class-one embassy. Maurice Bernbaum had come out sometime earlier. He'd come out through Haiti, and I'd seen him. I didn't know anything about this until Findley Burns tried it out on me.

Anyway, they sent the Under Secretary, to the White House, to see if they could undo what had been done regarding Tanzania and put me in for Venezuela.

Q: I think it was probably Elliot Richardson.

Ross: It might very well have been. Maybe it was Elliot. Anyway, no go. Over there they said, 'No, we've already processed it for Tanzania, so that's where he's going to go.' So that's where I went.

Q: That was a hell of a big country, but also another difficult one.

Ross: As I found out later, Venezuela might have been offered to me earlier on, but they had tried originally to send Ambassador Hurd there, and then it was discovered, belatedly, that he had all of those oil company connections. So his nomination was withdrawn. When I didn't go, Rob McClintock eventually did. I went to Tanzania and President Nyerere. That was an interesting experience, I must say.

Q: He's always been a fascinating person.

Ross: He was fascinating. There again, I had a very good personal relationship with him, although there were some issues on which we were on opposite sides of the fence. Vietnam was at its height then, and we were on opposite sides of that. He didn't think we were moving fast enough or firmly enough in Southern Africa to work changes in South Africa or in the Portuguese territories. Then, of course, as you know, he was a Fabian Socialist and had his own ideas about how the Tanzanian economy should develop. That didn't keep him from accepting a substantial amount of aid from us, and that aid being used fairly well.

On the fiscal side, there was very good accountability, because they had a Tanzanian, an Indian who had been born in Tanzania, as their Minister of Finance (Amir H. Jamal). He was very good and had very good standing in the international financial community, which helped them out over a long period, when otherwise they might not have had as much.

Q: Did the Indians have the same trouble there that they had in other parts?

Ross: It came before I left. It started coming in 1971, I guess. Yes, they changed a lot of the local laws. You couldn't own rental property after a while. If you lived in it, okay. But you couldn't have apartment houses or apartments for rent, etc. Also they clamped down on foreign exchange available for Tanzanian children to go abroad for study. Lots of the Indians, the ones who could afford it, had sent theirs to Britain or elsewhere.

Q: Ambassador Ross, we were talking about the problem of the Indians, particularly in Tanzania.

Ross: As I say, there were a number of measures that were, on the face of them, not discriminatory, but in the practical effect, only affected the Indian element of the population. So these people began pulling up and going out, and in the process, the Tanzanians lost a very productive element of their population--doctors, for example, merchants of one kind or another--because most of the merchants were Indian.

Q: In fact, it was the middle class, almost.

Ross: That's right. There were some relatively well-to-do Tanzanians, particularly up in the north in the coffee areas.

Q: Probably more in Tanzania than Uganda?

Ross: I don't know. I really don't know. There were a few Africans, but not very many. Of course, the whole thrust of Nyerere's policies was to make a kind of classless society, and he used this device of Ujamaa villages, where he hoped he was going to be able to develop centers of productivity throughout the country, establishing villages where, in effect, everybody worked for the common cause, and at the end of the harvest season, you all shared and shared alike, that kind of thing.

Well, that didn't go very well, because, as you might suppose, there were those who worked very hard and those who sat around. Obviously, they weren't about to share equally when that kind of thing existed. He tried, too, to convert to Ujamaa some things like coffee-producing areas, which would have been a real disaster.

He decided he wanted to move the capital out of Dar es Salaam to a place called Dodoma, in the middle of the country. He wanted to have a more centrally located place, and I think to get the government away from whatever foreign influence that came from being on the coast. They still haven't achieved this, although I gather technically the move is still on the books. It was obvious that there were going to be all kinds of problems.

I went up to Dodoma and there wasn't any water there. I mean, it was a very dry part of the country, and one wondered how you were going to support any kind of a population or put the capital there with all that entailed. That was just one overriding problem. But he was full of good intentions and personally the epitome of integrity. I don't think any kind of financial scandal was ever attached to him.

Q: And a man you could talk to.

Ross: Oh, yes, yes.

Q: You might not reach any conclusion, but you could talk.

Ross: That's right. But he was a very interesting man, very articulate, you know, and had a better education. He'd gone to Edinburgh and had advanced training, not a doctorate, but advanced training, and I think it during his British sojourn that he came under the influence of Fabian socialists and took a turn in that direction.

Q: Was his advanced training in economics?

Ross: I can't remember whether it was that or in the education field. Because he was a teacher. The Tanzanians all called him, in Swahili, Mwalimu, which means 'teacher.' That's what he was early on.

Q: What did we have there basically in the way of programs? Did we have a Peace Corps there?

Ross: We did not have a Peace Corps there.

Q: At no time?

Ross: No. We had had a Peace Corps, and it had been pulled out at the request of the Tanzanian Government the year before I was posted there. I think it was late 1968 or early 1969. It was not reinstated in my day. There again, you know, the idea being, I guess, that there was too much American influence out in the countryside.

Q: Corruption?

Ross: That's right. I was there at the time when, back here in the States, Afro hairdos were in style and things like that. Nyerere wouldn't have any of it. No Afro hairdos in Tanzania. There were several other things which he just didn't want.

Q: He was a conservative?

Ross: Yes. He wanted to keep his people free from this. But it was a fascinating place, and the relationship between Tanganyika and Zanzibar was an interesting one, because we had two vice presidents one from Zanzibar and one from Tanganyika. The vice president from Zanzibar who was assassinated shortly before I left, a man named Karume, was, in effect, the dictator of Zanzibar. Zanzibar was a big foreign exchange earner for Tanzania, because it is an island that grows cloves.

Q: And other spices.

Ross: Other spices, too, but cloves are the big crop, both on Zanzibar proper and on Pemba, which is part of the Zanzibar geographical entity. However, under Karume those revenues were kept by the Zanzibaris for their own use. They didn't come over as part of the total Tanzanian revenue. I think eventually this may have changed, but in my day it didn't.

Q: In other words, they ran their own foreign exchange.

Ross: Yes, and they had, as a carryover from the time they were independent before the union with Tanzania, consular posts there that Nyerere might not have authorized. The East Germans were there, the Czechs were there, etc. They gave assistance directly to the Zanzibaris without going through the Tanzanian apparatus. I don't think that sat terribly well, but I guess there were limits on what Nyerere could do.

Q: You said that he might not otherwise have authorized these things. Was he that strong a leader?

Ross: I think he would want to keep control of this, you see. We had a consulate there, a holdover from the old days, too. The Brits no longer had a resident consul there but the British High Commissioner used to visit periodically. I don't recall that otherwise there was much in the way of a Western presence there on Zanzibar.

Q: I never got into Tanzania at all when I was there, because there was always friction between Kenya and Tanzania.

Ross: Yes. They broke up their common market.

Q: Common services.

Ross: Yes. East African common services.

Q: That happened while I was there, and it was a great loss, I think.

Ross: It was. That happened while I was there, too, the termination of one common service and then another.

Q: The Ugandans got out very early, I think.

Ross: Yes.

Q: That was a great loss, because that was a good operating thing.

Ross: It was. Yes, they had a lot of good things.

Q: Of course, it was something installed by the British.

Ross: It was. It did tend to work much more efficiently than three separate entities would and probably less costly.

Q: The currency was an important thing, too.

Ross: That's right, as we've had occasion to note in other places, the various vested interests in a country.

Q: I think it was each one with national pride.

Ross: That's it.

Q: And the fact that Kenya was going well economically.

Ross: Yes. It was always a point of great resentment and dissatisfaction among the Tanzanians that all of the safaris from Europe and America and elsewhere came into Nairobi and then fanned out from there.

Q: They collected much of the foreign exchange.

Ross: That's right. Even to the point, you see, that the people on safari didn't know when they were in Tanzania. As you say, most of it was collected by the tour groups that were either headquartered abroad or in Nairobi. So that was another reason for the dissatisfaction.

But I must say, when the Tanzanians were handling it themselves, they never succeeded in really accomplishing a great improvement in the situation, at least during the time I was there. They would get tour groups, but they were all pre-paid, pre-packaged tour groups, so that the individuals who came would go to one of the beach resorts near Dar es Salaam. They might come into town once or twice, but for the most part, they were out there. It was all pre-paid. They spent very little money in the country.

Q: The hotel bills and so on, which were group rates.

Ross: Exactly. So one wonders. They had a few souvenirs that they may have bought, but one wonders how much the Tanzanians did get out of it.

Q: What were their principal sources of revenue and foreign exchange besides the spices?

Ross: There were the spices, there was tourism, and there were some gemstones. Just before I went out there, as a matter of fact, a stone called Tanzanite came on the market, a blue stone, semi-precious, really, which Tiffany's had the lock on. As I remember, when I went out through New York, I went to Tiffany's to see this. But Tanzania didn't have alluvial diamond fields as they did in the Central African Republic. That was one of the American interests there.

In Tanzania, diamonds were found in 'pipes' as they are in South Africa. In Tanzania they weren't all that extensive or important. Sisal and cotton had been important, but the markets for these had slumped as I knew from Haiti. For a little while, it looked like sisal might come back. Remember paper dresses? We had a period for things like that. But that never really developed. Coffee and tea were other foreign-exchange earners. The tea was in British hands on southern highlands, British companies.

Q: Was there any great American commercial penetration?

Ross: No, not a great deal.

Q: My experience is that eastern Africa is just too darn far away.

Ross: That's right. Then you ran into all kinds of difficulties. For a time the Lykes Lines used to come in, you know, and then they stopped, because the port was so congested that you'd have to stand off maybe for two weeks. What American freighter could do that? I think they were figuring it might be something like $30,000 a day. They weren't about to stand for that. So we stopped having American bottoms turn up there.

I only got one American naval vessel there, and that was near the end of my tour. We got one of them from the force in the Persian gulf, a destroyer. That took a lot of doing. It went off all right, no harm done. The U.S. Navy were very keen on doing it. They were always looking for ports of call.

Q: I had a very dichotomous attitude on that where

we were, but I had them come in, and it worked all right.

Ross: I had an unfortunate experience in that regard in Guinea, which I neglected to touch upon, which perhaps I'll add later on. I wasn't all that keen to have them come in, in the face of what I could see was, at best, a lukewarm attitude.

Tanzania, as you know, has Mozambique on its southern border, and Dar es Salaam was the center from which Eduardo Mondlane, the head of Frelimo the Mozambican independence movement, operated. He was married to an American. He was assassinated shortly before I got there, but the Mozambicans were a presence there, as were, of course, groups from Rhodesia and South Africa.

Q: What was the relationship with Malawi? Was that significant?

Ross: Not really. I think the Tanzanians all thought that Banda was a bit of an Uncle Tom. Relationships were all right. They shared the lake together, you know.

Q: And the transportation came through, I suppose, to Dar es Salaam, didn't it?

Ross: Not really, no. A lot of things from Zambia came through, yes, but not from Malawi. That was one reason that the Tanzanians got the Chinese in there to build that railroad to Zambia. They were hoping to eliminate Zambia's having to use the railroad that ran through Rhodesia and Mozambique. The Chinese came and built the railroad.

There was great suspicion and fear in Washington that the Chinese would never leave, having come in. I was at considerable pains to try to get some sense of balance on that question in my reporting, because we could find no evidence of this, or that the Chinese were having much of an impact on the Tanzanians. I'm sure they were grateful for the assistance, yes, but the Chinese weren't imparting any particular political philosophy, and certainly not any work habits, on the Tanzanians.

The Tanzanians were quite prepared to sit there and watch the Chinese work, but they weren't about to work the way these coolies were working on the railroad.

Q: You couldn't say that we did anything except have the Chinese build our railroads across the country anyway.

Ross: Yes. We were engaged in road building. That is to say, we had an American Company called Nello Teer, building a road from Dar es Salaam to Morogoro.

Q: Was this an actual paved road?

Ross: It was to be.

Q: Our road building in Somalia was mostly what they called "stabilized earth," which you mixed a little cement in with the soil.

Ross: Yes. They weren't finished by the time I left, so I don't know how it all turned out. But the first stages were paved. Incidentally, it might interest you to know that one of the other road-building outfits in Tanzania, particularly in the north of Tanzania, was the Frederics Company, owned by in-laws of Henry Tasea. They were also involved in building the international airport that was put up between Arusha and Moshi in the north, presumably for travelers to come in and go directly into the game areas of Tanzania. Whether that ever worked out or not, I don't know. Shortly before I left Tanzania, I went to the inauguration of the airport. But up to the time I left, there was very little traffic in and out, and I don't know if there were any scheduled flights.

Q: Does that pretty well wind up Tanzania?

Ross: I think so. When I knew that I was coming out, there was that chiefs of mission conference in Addis shortly before, in April of 1972, and David Newsom asked me if I would come in to be the senior deputy of the bureau. In anticipation of that, after that conference, I went first to Morocco to visit my son. Andrea went with me.

Then I went up to Lisbon, took a plane, and flew from Lisbon to Luanda and did a tour of Southern Africa, in preparation for my Departmental job. I went to Angola first and flew to South Africa--Pretoria, Johannesburg, Durban, and Cape Town. In Cape Town I had an hour's conversation with Forster, one on one, in the course of which his comments and attitude showed me how intractable the South African stand on apartheid really was. I then went to three former High Commission territories--Botswana, Lesotho, and Swaziland, and to Mozambique. It was all extremely useful.

When I got to Washington, Rogers was still secretary. I think we probably got a little more attention in the African bureau from him than we subsequently did from Kissinger, except perhaps as South African questions came up. We got his attention for them, but not for run-of-the-mill African things. For a few things in North Africa, yes. We still had the office of North African Affairs in the African Bureau and we were negotiating liquid-gas contracts with Algeria, which the seventh floor was interested in. But in general, we didn't receive a great deal of interest in the day-to-day operations.

One big problem that we had was the Ugandan flap when Idi Amin was there causing all that trouble. We pulled our Ambassador out and Bob Keeley ended up being chargé. Then it became a question of whether we were going to leave anybody in or whether we were going to wind up the operation."[24]

The preceding interviews with senior American diplomats including ambassadors who were accredited to Tanzania provide an American perspective or perspectives on Tanzania and on Nyerere as a leader during one of the most critical periods in the history of post-colonial Africa when some of the most important events on the continent took place: the Zanzibar revolution and formation of a union of two independent countries unprecedented in the history of the continent since the advent of colonial rule.

Some of the diplomats were there during the revolution and when the union of Tanganyika and Zanzibar was formed. Others were there when the union was going through a transitional phase of consolidation, adjustments and readjustments to prevailing conditions, domestic and external, especially during the Cold War when Tanzania and many other Third World countries were pursuing a policy of non-alignment.

The union of Tanganyika and Zanzibar featured prominently in discussions and in many debates during that time as President Nyerere kept it non-aligned between the two contending ideological camps: East and West. It is a union that continues to generate debate even today more than 50 years after it was formed.

Although the interviews featured here do not exclusively focus on what led to the formation of the union of Tanganyika and Zanzibar, they have been included in this work where they focus on Tanzania because they cover other subjects vital to a better understanding of what is the largest country in East Africa and one of the largest on the continent with a potential to be a major player in continental affairs once its potential is fully harnessed. For example, years later, it was no coincidence that three American presidents – President Barack Obama and former presidents Bill Clinton and George W. Bush – as well as the American secretary of state, Hillary Clinton, visited Tanzania around the same time within a two-year period; Obama and Bush were in Tanzania during the same time. Hillary Clinton went to Tanzania at least twice; Bush also, at least twice, including once when he was president; Bill Clinton, also at least twice.

One of the main reasons Tanganyika, now mainland Tanzania, drew the attention of world powers during the Cold War was its strategic significance; nowadays because of its abundant natural resources including a dazzling array of minerals, vast reserves of natural gas, as well as helium, and great potential for oil discovery; it is also still strategically significant.

Almost centrally located on the East African coast, Tanzania is the gateway to the heart of Africa, now the Democratic Republic of Congo (DRC), a treasure trove and potentially the richest country on the continent, and to the countries of southern Africa which are also endowed with abundant natural resources including strategic minerals vital to the industrial economies of the world.

Tanzania also shares borders with more countries than any other country on the continent besides the Democratic Republic of Congo which is bordered by nine countries; Tanzania is bordered by eight. But it is also bordered by the Indian Ocean (another strategic asset), a total of nine boundaries like Congo's.

And that made mainland Tanzania an important potential client during the Cold War, probably even more than Zanzibar was, an outpost in the Indian Ocean, isolated, without being surrounded by other countries like Tanganyika was.

And while it is true that the United States and Britain wanted Tanganyika to unite with Zanzibar in order to prevent the island nation from falling into communist hands, it must also be conceded that uniting the two countries was a goal Nyerere always wanted to pursue. It is something that he had in his mind as far back as the mid-fifties. Because of the indissoluble ties which had existed for centuries between the people of the mainland and the isles, Nyerere – and other people as well – had always considered Zanzibar to be an integral part of the mainland divided only by colonial boundaries.

Therefore, uniting the two countries was simply reuniting the people who had always been one. Unification was inevitable, sooner or later. Nyerere would have pursued it even if the United States and Britain did not exist on the face of the earth; hence his contention: "It is an insult to Africa to read cold war politics into every move towards African unity."

No amount of external pressure would have been enough to make him pursue the goal of uniting the two countries if he was not interested in doing so; if it was not in his best interest to do so, and if conditions within Tanganyika and Zanzibar – not only during that time but even before then – were not conducive to unification. Common bonds between the two countries – cultural and historical – were a major factor in the quest for unification although they were not given due prominence in the context of Cold War rivalries between the East and the West during that period.

Decades later about one year before he died on 14 October 1999, Nyerere again expressed his disappointment on his failure to form a larger union, the East African federation, in an interview with Ikaweba Bunting of the *New Internationalist*:

"I respected Jomo (Kenyatta) immensely. It has probably never happened in history. Two heads of state, Milton Obote and I, went to Jomo and said to him: 'Let's unite our countries and you be our head of state.' He said no. I think he said no because it would have put him out of his element as a Kikuyu Elder....

Kwame Nkrumah and I were committed to the idea of unity. African leaders and heads of state did not take Kwame seriously. However, I did. I did not believe in these small little nations. Still today I do not believe in them. I tell our people to look at the European Union, at these people who ruled us who are now uniting.

Kwame and I met in 1963 and discussed African Unity. We differed on how to achieve a United States of Africa. But we both agreed on a United States of Africa as necessary. Kwame went to Lincoln University, a black college in the US. He perceived things from the perspective of US history, where the 13 colonies that revolted against the British formed a union. That is what he thought the OAU should do.

I tried to get East Africa to unite before independence. When we failed in this, I was wary about Kwame's continental approach. We corresponded profusely on this. Kwame said my idea of 'regionalization' was only balkanization on a larger scale. Later African historians will have to study our correspondence on this issue of uniting Africa."[25]

If the British, who were the colonial rulers, wanted to form an East African federation, they would have done so a long time ago. They had plenty of time, decades, to do that: at least since the end of World War I when Tanganyika, the last territory in the region to be colonised by Britain, came under the League of Nations mandate ruled by Britain after Germany lost the colony in the war; Tanganyika later became a UN Trusteeship.

The British did, in fact, attempt in the 1930s to establish a giant federation stretching from East Africa all the way down to South Africa composed of all the British colonies in the region: Kenya, Uganda, Tanganyika, Zanzibar, Nyasaland (now Malawi), Northern Rhodesia (renamed Zambia), Southern Rhodesia (now Zimbabwe), Bechuanaland (today Botswana), Swaziland, Basutoland (renamed Lesotho), and South Africa.

But they wanted to form such a federation for a different reason: to consolidate imperial domination of Africa. The plan was strongly opposed and resisted by African nationalists in those countries.

In pursuing unification, Nyerere's intention was not to perpetuate imperial domination of East Africa by the British colonial rulers when he strongly advocated formation of an East African federation before independence and even offered to delay Tanganyika's independence if such a move would help to achieve that goal. And the British as well as other Western powers definitely had more influence on Jomo Kenyatta than they did on Nyerere, if at all. Yet Kenyatta was the least enthusiastic of the three East African leaders about forming a federation. It was also reported in 1977 – 1978 that Kenyatta was on the CIA payroll together with Mobutu Sese Seko and a number of other African leaders. Nyerere was not one of them.

Had Kenyatta and Milton Obote been as enthusiastic as Nyerere was, about regional unity, the East African federation would have been formed before the end of 1963 as the three leaders had agreed to do in the declaration they signed in June in Nairobi, Kenya, the same year.

Although the failure of the three East African leaders to form a federation in 1963 was one of Nyerere's biggest disappointments, he remained undaunted in his quest for unity and went on to form the union of Tanganyika and Zanzibar the following year; not because the Americans and the British asked him to do so.

His track record in pursuit of African unity and independence contradicts that line of reasoning. And formation of the union was one of his greatest achievements in the Pan-African context and in the area of foreign policy. It was also clear vindication of his non-aligned position in the bipolar world of the Cold War.

The new nation of Tanzania went on to forge strong links with the Eastern bloc – the nemesis of the West, which supposedly inspired the union in its ideological war against the communist bloc – and continued to maintain equally strong ties with the West contrary to the wishes of the Russians and the Chinese. In fact, Tanzania got more financial and technical assistance from the West than she did from the East, mainly because of historical ties.

It is also worth remembering that if Nyerere was subservient to – or took orders from – the West as supposedly was the case when he formed the union of Tanganyika and Zanzibar, he would not have been able to expel American diplomats from Tanzania in 1964 when they were accused of trying to overthrow him; and they would not have tried to undermine his government since he was their "ally."

Also, he would not have broken diplomatic ties with Britain in December 1965 over the Rhodesian crisis, the first African country to do so; nor would he have curtailed ties with West Germany when the latter objected to diplomatic representation of East Germany in Tanzania. The West German ambassador was shown the door, and the Canadians came in to train Tanzania's fledgling air force after the Germans threatened to withdraw their aid for the training programme. Nyerere told them to withdraw all their aid in all fields.

All those cases clearly show that Nyerere was an independent-minded leader who also demonstrated a degree of independence in his policy pursuits and initiatives rarely seen among Third World leaders.

Yet, in spite of all this evidence, the litany continues that the union of Tanganyika and Zanzibar was a product of Cold War intrigue, and not of Nyerere's own initiative in pursuit of his Pan-African goals. If the communist threat prompted Nyerere to unite Tanganyika with Zanzibar at the behest of Britain and the United States in order to stop communists from establishing a base in Zanzibar, why did he go on to establish strong ties with communist countries after the union was formed – instead of avoiding them? It seems he didn't pay very much attention to the British and the Americans who "told" him to form the union and avoid communists.

The union never served as a bulwark against communism – it did as a socialist state against capitalism – because it was never intended to be one; nor did it serve as a launching pad for communist penetration of Africa from the east coast – it was never intended for that either. And communism never penetrated Tanzania in spite of the strong ties the country had with the Eastern bloc. It remained a non-aligned nation; hence Nyerere's contention that we are not going to allow our friends to choose enemies for us. As he stated in a speech, "Policy on Foreign Affairs," 16 October 1967:

"We shall not allow any of our friendships to be exclusive; we shall not allow anyone to choose any of our friends or enemies for us. It should also be clear that we shall not allow anyone – whether they be from East or West, or from places not linked to those blocs – to try and use our friendship for their own purposes."[26]

Also, if Nyerere formed the union to neutralise communists in Zanzibar, and in Tanganyika itself, he not only would not have established strong ties with the People's Republic of China and other communist countries; he would also have tightened his grip on Zanzibar, the potential base for communist subversion; and he would not have appointed to cabinet posts Zanzibaris who were known to have communist leanings. The president of Zanzibar who formed the union with Nyerere, Sheikh Abeid Karume, wanted a complete merger, hence a stronger union. But Nyerere refused to go that far. He preferred, instead, to have a weaker union in which Zanzibar would continue to have its own government and enjoy considerable autonomy virtually as a sovereign entity in a number of areas except foreign affairs, defence, immigration, and others specifically placed under the jurisdiction of the union government.

He was concerned that if a complete merger of the two countries and governments took place, the people of Zanzibar would feel that they had been swallowed up by Tanganyika, a much bigger country. It would not be a union of equals since, as a sovereign entity, Zanzibar was entering the union as an independent country, not as a junior partner.

Another Zanzibari leader who was strongly in favour of a much stronger union was Kassim Hanga who served as prime minister and vice president under President Karume and was one of the leaders on the isles known for his communist sympathies.

Another leader from Zanzibar with known communist leanings was Abdulrahman Mohammed Babu, leader of the Umma (The People's) Party, who became minister of defence and external affairs under President Karume. Yet, in spite of his communist ties and ideological orientation, he was later appointed to cabinet posts in the union government by President Nyerere and went on to become one of the most distinguished and influential leaders in Tanzania whose influence as a scholar and Marxist theoretician extended beyond Tanzania. He held key ministerial posts serving as minister of economic planning and minister of commerce and industries between 1964 and 1972. He was also one of the strongest supporters of the union and African unity in general, despite his earlier misgivings about the union which took place in his absence.

Nyerere's approach to unity between the two countries probably saved the union more than anything else. Had Zanzibar not been allowed to have its own government and its own president who also served as the first vice president of the united republic – the second vice president automatically came from the mainland – the union would probably have collapsed.

Even soon after it was formed, there was strong opposition to the merger by some elements in Zanzibar who argued that their smaller country had been swallowed up by Tanganyika in what amounted to "annexation," as Professor Ali Mazrui erroneously characterised the merger.

Had Zanzibar indeed been swallowed up, without allowing it to have its own government, secessionist sentiments in the former island nation – which have existed since the union was formed – would have increased, providing momentum to a separatist movement which could even have led to an insurgency on the islands plunging the country into chaos.

But the secessionists were robbed of this momentum by allowing Zanzibar to continue having its own government, under its own president, and under its own constitution, enabling it to enjoy extensive autonomy.

Although it was intended to maintain the union by being fair to Zanzibaris, even such extensive devolution of power, if not properly managed, could have had unintended consequences by encouraging people opposed to the union to demand even greater autonomy, progressively leading to a return to the status quo ante: restoration of Zanzibar's full sovereign status, hence dissolution of the union.

Yet it was skillfully managed by Nyerere under a unique arrangement, what was essentially a unitary state – with some federal features as a concession to Zanzibaris – which did not allow such extensive devolution of power to the regions on Tanzania mainland except to the former island nation of Zanzibar.

Nyerere's formation of the union was criticised even by some of his fellow socialists although of the Marxist bent; Nyerere was not a Marxist. As Ann Talbot, a Trotskyite, stated in "Nyerere's Legacy of Poverty and Repression in Zanzibar":

"The late President Julius Nyerere, the first president of independent Tanganyika,...formed a union with Zanzibar to create Tanzania in 1964.

Nyerere remains an icon of the Pan-Africanist movement and the limited welfare measures that he introduced in Tanzania are still held up by some as an example of the benefits of what was known as African socialism. To many he remains as saintly a figure as Nelson Mandela has become....

Nyerere formed the union with Zanzibar when a spontaneous popular uprising had just overthrown the government of large estate owners that Britain had given power to on independence. Neither of the two opposition parties, the Afro-Shirazi Party (ASP), or the Umma Party, were in control of the uprising. Power fell into their hands because the movement lacked a programme that represented the interests of the dispossessed estate workers or the workers on the docks....

Nyerere recognised that the uprising was a threat to his own position. In the weeks following it... encouraged by the events in Zanzibar, his army mutinied against its British officers.... The ease with which the mutiny had taken place revealed the weakness of his regime to popular opposition. Nyerere realised that if he could not control the political aspirations of the mass of his population, he would be of little use to Britain or any other imperialist power....

Nyerere had an object lesson close to hand in what happened to an African leader who could not control popular movements. Only four years before President (sic) Patrice Lumumba had been assassinated by Western agents because he could not maintain control of the volatile situation in the Congo.

Lumumba had appealed to the Soviet Union for military aid and in doing so had threatened to tip the balance of the Cold War in Africa. Now the new Zanzibar government had established relations with the Soviet bloc, allowed East Germany to open an embassy and accepting their help to train the army.

Nyerere was looking at Lumumba's fate when he initiated the union with Zanzibar. He knew that he would not survive if he allowed the movement in Zanzibar to continue and could not demonstrate his usefulness to imperialism by bringing Zanzibar into a union with Tanganyika.

For his part Zanzibar's President Abeid Karume, who led the Afro-Shirazi Party, saw the union with Tanganyika as a means of undermining his opponents in government. His particular target was Abdulrahman Mohammed Babu, leader of the Umma Party, who favoured close links with the Soviet bloc and Cuba. Babu, whose power base was on Pemba, as the CUF's (Tanzanian opposition Civic United Front's) is today, was forced to take refuge on the mainland as Karume arrested or killed his opponents. In 1972 Karume was assassinated, probably at Babu's instigation."[27]

Factual errors aside – the army mutinies in all the three East African countries of Kenya, Uganda and Tanganyika took place in January 1964, therefore within days, not after weeks as Talbot says, following the Zanzibar revolution which took place on January 12th; the first mutiny was in Tanganyika on January 20th and lasted for six days; Patrice Lumumba was prime minister, not president, of Congo and his ouster was externally engineered by the United States; and Babu's political base was on Zanzibar, not on Pemba Island – there is a distinct ideological line, Trotskyite, Ann Talbot is pursuing in her deeply flawed analysis of Nyerere instead of focusing on objective inquiry regardless of one's ideological oorientation. It is these ideological blinders which have thrown her off track in what should be a scholarly pursuit involving dispassionate analysis. And Babu, of course, differs with Talbot on the role of the Umma Party in the Zanzibar revolution. As he stated in "The 1964 Revolution: Lumpen or Vanguard?":

"Although the Umma Party did not fire the first shot of the uprising, it nevertheless rose to the occasion with revolutionary zeal and skill. It helped to transform a wholly lumpen – in many ways apolitical – uprising into a popular, anti-imperialist revolution, which, left to its own momentum, and without the external intervention that followed, would undoubtedly have opened up a new path – the road to socialism."[28]

The revolution itself was an indigenous expression of mass discontent, not a foreign-inspired uprising as some still maintain. And to contend, as Ann Talbot does, that Nyerere was an imperialist agent at the beck and call of the British and other imperialist powers – presumably the United States and other Western nations as well, since as a Trotsykite socialist, she would never conceive of a scenario in which she would see the Soviet Union, now dead, acting as an imperialist power – is, once again as I argued earlier, to deliberately ignore Nyerere's record of independent domestic and foreign policy initiatives which irritated and even infuriated both ideological camps at different times during his long political career; not only as a Tanzanian or as African leader but also as a Third World leader and one of the most influential world leaders in the twentieth century.

Yet, as a Trotskyite, Talbot is obsessed with "proving" in every conceivable way that Nyerere was "wrong" because he didn't toe the Trotskyist party line; he didn't the Maoist either. Any socialist – including Nyerere – who deviates from this or does not toe this party line is considered to be an apostate or a traitor. And I don't use the term Trotskyist – as opposed to Trotskyite – in a disparaging way in this context, as it is normally used in the description and analysis of Trotskyism by some of its critics.

Nyerere's independence from Marxism-Leninism – and unimpressed by Marxist-Leninist dogma – did not earn him endearment in the socialist camp anymore than it did in the West for his relentless criticism of Western imperialist policies towards Africa.

Trotskyites, like other Marxist-Leninists who include Maoists, see themselves as the standard-bearers of Marxism-Leninism even though it is a discredited ideology as has been validated by experience and by the collapse of communist regimes around the world since the end of the Cold War. Even some of the most hardline

Marxist-Leninist states have renounced the ideology.

There is no question that Nyerere was independent-minded. He demonstrated such independence even during the Congo crisis as the leader of Tanganyika before uniting with Zanzibar and after the two countries were united under his stewardship to form Tanzania, at a time when the East and the West were locked in the most bitter and intense rivalry on African soil right in the heart of the continent in the turbulent sixties.

In spite of Tanzania's weakness, Nyerere openly supported the Congolese nationalist forces – followers of Lumumba – against the Western puppet regime in Leopoldville installed and supported by the CIA and other Western interests including French and British. He also allowed Cuban troops led by Che Guevara to use Tanzania as a conduit to enter Congo and even allowed them to have a rear base in western Tanzania to support the Congolese nationalists fighting the CIA-backed Congolese government.

Kigoma, a town on the eastern shore of Lake Tanganyika, was used by Che Guevara as his rear base. Fidel Castro did not sneak Cuban troops and Che Guevara into Congo through Tanzania. He sent hundreds of Cuban troops, and Che Guevara, to Congo through Tanzania with the full knowledge and permission of President Nyerere and his government. And the CIA knew this; so did the British and other Western intelligence services, as did their governments, from Washington to London, Brussels, Paris and the rest. They also knew that Nyerere allowed the Russians and the Chinese to send weapons to the nationalist forces in the Congo through Tanzania.

This does not seem to be the kind of leader who was a servant of Western imperialism, as Ann Talbot contends, or as someone who took orders from the United States and Britain – the very powers he fought against – to form the union of Tanganyika and Zanzibar as others claim.

And it is worth remembering that even after the

Congolese nationalist forces failed to dislodge the CIA-backed regime in Leopoldville, Nyerere never changed his position. He continued to oppose Western domination and exploitation of Congo – and the rest of Africa – and supported the Congolese pro-Lumumbist nationalists and liberation movements in other parts of the continent. And when Che Guevara failed in his Congo mission, he retreated to Tanzania and stayed in Dar es Salaam, the nation's capital, for many months from October 1965 to early March 1966, during which he wrote his famous book, *The African Dream: The Diaries of the Revolutionary War in the Congo*, before returning to Cuba. As Jorge Castañeda states in his book, *Compañero: The Life and Death of Che Guevara*:

"His secretary during those crucial months in Tanzania...was...Colman Ferrer....During the time he spent with Pablo Ribalta, the Cuban ambassador to Tanzania and his old comrade-in-arms, in the Tanzanian capital, Che made two crucial decisions: he would not return to Cuba, and his next destination was Buenos Aires....His wife arrived in Dar es Salaam. They were staying at the Embassy....

Che spent his free time writing – his favourite activity, apart from combat and literature.

Working from notes taken in Congo, he began drafting...*Pasajes de la guerra revolucionaria (el Congo).* Colman Ferrer, a young secretary at the Cuban Embassy in Dar-es-Salaam, served as his assistant. Che dictated his text, Ferrer transcribed it, then Guevara revised and corrected the final manuscript. In the words of Ferrer, Che basically spent the days 'marking time, preparing the conditions for a change of scenery.' As Oscar Fernandez Mell recalls it, 'One of Che's great virtues was the way he enjoyed reading, though he also had more exacting tastes and ways of spending his time. He could read for hours; he had a good time even when he was alone.'

He was extremely meticulous in his work. In Ferrer's words, 'he was careful in the things he was going to write, avoiding any mistakes. He took great care, he analyzed and reread the transcription repeatedly.' The book left little time for other activities. 'He wrote day and night. His only distraction was an occasional game of chess with me. One day when I was about to checkmate him, he looked at me as if he had not realized what was happening; it was obvious that he wasn't really in the game.'

Finally, at the end of February or beginning of March 1966, Che agreed to leave....'Everybody returned to Cuba and he stayed on alone in Tanzania, and then I decided to get him out of Tanzania and take him to a safe place until he decided what he was going to do,' Ulises Estrada, (in) interview with the author (Castañeda), Havana, February 9, 1995."[29]

The CIA and other Western intelligence agencies knew Che Guevara was in Dar es Salaam, Tanzania, for months, after the failure of his Congo mission. He settled in Dar es Salaam in October 1965. And they knew when he left. Much as they hated him for spreading revolution to other parts of the Third World, they would have pressured Tanzania to expel him from the country if President Nyerere was their stooge as Ann Talbot claims. And if they tried, then they failed to speed up his exit.

Che Guevara left Tanzania when he was ready to do so. And he stayed in Tanzania for as long as he did because he was allowed to. One can't think of him staying, even for one day, in a country whose leader was subservient to the West. He would have been expelled the same day, let alone been allowed to have an operational base, as Che Guevara was, to support anti-Western nationalist insurgents in a neighbouring country.

That Nyerere allowed the Cubans to operate from Tanzania, and communist powers to funnel weapons through Tanzania to support nationalist forces in Congo,

168

demonstrated a degree of independence and his commitment to non-alignment one would hardly characterise – if at all – as a sign of weakness and subservience to the West.

And his opposition to American involvement in Vietnam during the Vietnam war, and to the invasion of Czechoslovakia in 1968 by the Warsaw Pact forces led by the Soviet Union, once again demonstrated his independence and commitment to positive neutralism without taking orders from either side of the Iron Curtain.

It is in this context that Nyerere's establishment of the union of Tanganyika and Zanzibar must be viewed as a realisation of his policy objectives, a triumph of Pan-Africanism, and a rejection of imperial domination by any of the world powers regardless of their ideologies. Yet, because of his modesty, even his adversaries underestimated him. As Gamal Nkrumah, son of the late president of Ghana, Dr. Kwame Nkrumah, stated in the obituary he wrote about Nyerere, "The Legacy of A Great African," in *Al-Ahram*:

"Nyerere's presence at political rallies, remote poverty-stricken villages, academic conferences and international forums where he pleaded the case of the South always lit up the occasion. He had a way with the words....He was the philosopher-king, intellectual, enlightened, the polar opposite of the despotic ruler so common in the Africa of his day. But he was also a man of the people....

Two years ago, at celebrations marking the 40th anniversary of Ghana's independence, I met and spoke to Nyerere for the last time. I would never have guessed that he was ill....

He was not only a man of integrity, but he also had the courage and modesty to admit to past mistakes.

I have heard him speak in London, at the Commonwealth Institute, in several forums in the United

States and at the United Nations, as well as in many an African setting.

To me personally, Nyerere was always the attentive father figure, never missing an opportunity to remind me that my own father's vision for a united Africa was the only way forward.

With his wit, humour, sharp intellect and disarming sincerity, Nyerere was always a winning personality. But, to say that he was an uncontroversial character would be a grave mistake. From the beginning of his political career, Nyerere was widely seen as a moderate, and that at a time when more militant African leaders prevailed. As early as the late 1950s and early 1960s, official US documents, now declassified, interestingly reveal that America's Central Intelligence (CIA) regarded him as the only 'responsible' African leader. Nyerere himself was clever enough to realise that such a revelation was no compliment....

His greatest achievement is undoubtedly the successful unification of mainland Tanganyika with the Indian Ocean island of Zanzibar (and Pemba). The United Republic of Tanzania was born in 1964 out of that union with an overwhelmingly Muslim island-nation whose closest historical, economic and political ties were with Oman in particular and the Arab Gulf countries in general. Zanzibar was for two centuries the Omani official seat of government and the official residence of the Sultan.

In contrast, Tanganyika...had a more mixed population, equally divided between Christians and Muslims.

It was to Nyerere's credit that he managed to unite this most ethnically, linguistically and religiously diverse of nation-states and make it one of Africa's most politically stable countries."[30]

Contrary to what Amrit Wilson says, the union of Tanganyika with Zanzibar was not a product of a Western initiative. A Marxist, she saw the union as an imperialist plot by the United States to secure American and Western geopolitical interests in the region to the exclusion of her ideological allies – communists – on the other side of the Iron Curtain. Also a strong admirer of Zanzibari leader Abdulrahman Mohamed Babu, a fellow Marxist, she saw Babu as a staunch anti-imperialist, unlike Nyerere whom she dismissed as an agent of Western imperialism – he was not a Marxist – in spite of Nyerere's record to the contrary.

Amrit Wilson makes that clear in her books, *US Foreign Policy and Revolution: The Creation of Tanzania*, and *The Threat of Liberation: Imperialism and Revolution in Zanzibar*.

Like Ann Talbot, another Marxist who equally denounced Nyerere as an imperialist ally, Amrit Wilson is blinded by her ideological bias and loyalty to Babu and dismisses anyone who is not Marxist as an agent of imperialism since, according to this logic, only Marxists are true anti-imperialists; the hostility of both – Talbot and Wilson as well as other Marxists – towards Nyerere fuelled by his success in depriving Babu of a power base in Zanzibar and preventing the island nation from becoming a communist state under the leadership of their ideological comrade as they would have like to.

There is no question that Babu had profound ideological differences with Nyerere. But both agreed Tanzania should pursue socialism. However, they differed on how Tanzania should be transformed into a socialist society, and what kind of socialism it should pursue.

An advocate of scientific socialism, Babu did not believe that Nyerere's brand of socialism, *ujamaa* – which means "familyhood" in Kiswahili and was a form of African socialism – was socialist enough, if at all. He believed it would keep Tanzania in neocolonial bondage because it was not radical enough to enable Tanzania to break away from imperialist control.

Tanzania could be transformed into a truly socialist society only if its economy was owned and controlled by the people – the masses: workers and peasants who constituted the vast majority of the population – and not by international capitalists and their local allies. This could be achieved by embracing scientific socialism, not African socialism known as *ujamaa* as advocated by Nyerere. Babu articulated this position in his collected writings, *African Socialism or Socialist Africa?*

He never got the chance to see his vision come true. And that disappointed many of his supporters, especially Marxists such as Amrit Wilson and Ann Talbot.

Probably their condescending attitude towards Nyerere – as an ally of imperialism because he was not a Marxist like them, according to their logic – was compounded by frustration on their part because Zanzibar was not transformed into a Marxist state, as they hoped it would be under the leadership of Babu, but was instead united with Tanganyika under the leadership of Nyerere allegedly with the help of American imperialists, Nyerere's allies.

Amrit Wilson also contends that it is naïve to believe that Pan-Africanism played a role in uniting the two countries, as Nyerere and others argued. As she states in her book, *The Threat of Liberation: Imperialism and Revolution in Zanzibar*:

"To describe the union between Tanganyika and Zanzibar as an aspect of Nyerere's Pan-Africanism, as some writers have done, is perhaps naïve. At this point the cold war, like the war on terror today, led to constant interventions by the United States to try to influence and manipulate leaders of African countries, and where they were unable to do so, organize 'regime change.'" – (Amrit Wilson, *The Threat of Liberation: Imperialism and Revolution in Zanzibar*, London: Pluto Press, 2013, p. 63).

Yet there is evidence to show that the union of Tanganyika with Zanzibar was not a product of American or British efforts.

In her quest to demonstrate that Zanzibar would not have united with Tanganyika had it not been for American pressure on Nyerere and his colleagues in Zanzibar, Wilson either deliberately overlooked – in pursuit of a political agenda – or missed records in the American intelligence archives including reports and communications between American diplomats in Tanganyika and their superiors in Washington which clearly show that the unification of Tanganyika and Zanzibar was an African initiative, especially by the leaders of Tanganyika who also had the support of the main leaders in Zanzibar, especially Karume and Hanga and even Babu himself who was perceived and even portrayed himself to be against the union. That was not his position during the first days after the revolution even if he supported the idea of uniting Zanzibar with Tanganyika purely for his own political survival in the isles because security for the new government would be provided by the union government dominated by Tanganyika.

There are records showing that the leaders of Tanganyika, together with their counterparts in Zanzibar, worked hard on their own to form the union without being forces or pressured by the United States and Britain to do so; although American officials showed great interest in the merger. They felt it could serve their interests as well because of Nyerere's neutrality as a strong proponent and advocate of the policy of non-alignment, refusing to align his country – and Africa as a whole – with either ideological camp: East or West.

He maintained that position throughout his political career, contrary to what Amrit Wlison says that he was pro-Western simply because he was not a Marxist like Babu, an anti-imperialist par excellence because of his Marxist credentials. As James Spain who once served as the American ambassador to Tanzania stated in an interview:

"Nyerere certainly wasn't on our side, but he wasn't a tool of the Chinese or the Russians either....If I did anything useful, it was to convince Washington that Nyerere was not a brutal African dictator and a Communist stooge." – (Ambassador James W. S. Spain, interviewed by Charles Stuart Kennedy, October 31, 1995, *The Association for Diplomatic Studies and Training, (ADST), Foreign Affairs Oral History Project*, copyright, 1998, pp. 36 and 34).

US Secretary of State Henry Kissinger who was in Dar es Salaam, Tanzania, during that time (in 1976) on his trip to the region to discuss with Nyerere the contentious issue of the liberation struggle in Rhodesia and southern Africa in general, expressed the same sentiment in his conversation with Ambassador James Spain. As Spain explained:

"He (Kissinger) said,'I want to warn you about one thing. This fellow Nyerere is not our side." (Ibid., p. 36).

And he was not their side when he united Tanganyika with Zanzibar. He did that in Africa's not America's interest.

Nyerere also proved to be an extremely brilliant and tough negotiator, as Kissinger found out, when the two leaders met to discuss the subject of white minority rule in Rhodesia and in other countries of southern Africa and how to end it. As David Martin, a prominent British journalist who worked in Tanzania for many years – he knew Nyerere very well – and who covered southern Africa, stated:

"Tanganyika became independent on 9 December 1961 and a year later when the country became a republic, Nyerere, elected by over 96 per cent of the voters, became its first president.

For the next 24 years Nyerere was to fill the African and international stage like a colossus. When he met the astute American Secretary of State Henry Kissinger for the first time in Dar es Salaam in 1976, the two men began a mental verbal fencing match of David and Goliath proportions.

One began a quote from Shakespeare (some of whose works Nyerere translated into Swahili setting them in an African context) or a Greek philosopher and the other would end the quotation. Then Nyerere quoted an American author. Kissinger laughed: Nyerere knew Kissinger had written the words.

Neither man trusted the other. Kissinger wanted the negotiations (over Rhodesia, now Zimbabwe, and southern Africa) kept secret. Nyerere, understanding the Americans' duplicity, took the opposite view and as Africa correspondent of the London Sunday newspaper, *The Observer*, I was to become the focal point of the Tanzanians' strategic leaks. That year the newspaper led the front page on an unprecedented 13 occasions on Africa. All the leaks, as Kissinger knew, came from Nyerere. One political fox had temporarily outwitted the other." – (David Martin, "Mwalimu Julius Kambarage Nyerere: Obituary," Southern African Research and Documentation Centre (SARDC). A former news editor and deputy managing editor of the *Standard*, renamed *Daily News*, Dar es Salaam, Tanzania, David Martin was a founder-director of the Southern African Research and Documentation Centre (SARDC) of which Julius Nyerere was patron. He lived in Tanzania for 10 years from 1964 to 1974 and frequently talked with Nyerere through the decades, a period of 35 years, until Nyerere's last days.)

Nyerere always put the interests of Africa first just as he did when he united Tanganyika with Zanzibar; not the interests of the imperial powers as some of his critics allege happened in the case of Tanganyika and Zanzibar when the two countries united under his leadership.

His involvement in Zanzibar was nothing new. Right from the beginning, he was involved in the island nation's struggle for independence and supported the Afro-Shirazi Party which represented the majority of the people in the isles. They were mostly black African. He also continued to be involved in the affairs of Zanzibar even after the end of colonial rule which led to the assumption of power by the sultan representing the Arab minority.

When the British handed over power to the sultan on independence day, 10 December 1963, it was clear justice had not been done. The black African majority were excluded from power. Their leaders sought to end this injustice by overthrowing the Arab minority regime and went to Nyerere to seek assistance.

There was also a group of militant Arabs who were against the new regime. They were members of the Umma Party led by Abdulrahman Mohamed Babu. They also plotted to overthrow the sultan. As Helen-Louise Hunter who was a member of the CIA/DDI Research Staff stated in her study of Zanzibar, 21 February 1966, two years after the revolution which removed the sultan from power:

"Intelligence reporting before the coup had concentrated on the Arab political minority from which the party in power was drawn, not on the African majority.

This reporting indicated that active plotting for the overthrow of the government was being done in the Umma Party by followers of the radical Arab leader Abdulrahman Mohamed Babu. There were no reports of such plotting centered on the Afro-Shirazi Party, the chief spokesman of the African majority.

Thus we did not know then what has since been established from good sources – that in the Afro-Shirazi Party a radical group of African trade union leaders led by Abdulla Kassim Hanga was also making plans, independent of those of the Arab Babu and his Umma

Party group, for a revolution. As early as the middle of 1963 a group of ASP leaders including Hanga had gone to Tanganyika to ask President Nyerere for money and arms in support of their projected uprising." – (Helen-Louise Hunter, "Zanzibar Revisited: A Case Study in Political Research: Reconstruction of the 1964 Revolution," pp. 1 – 2).

It was this revolution which helped pave the way for the unification of Tanganyika and Zanzibar at a faster pace than would otherwise have been the case – had it not taken place.

One of the leaders who played a critical role in facilitating formation of the union of the two countries was Tanganyika's minister of foreign affairs, Oscar Kambona. He facilitated consummation of the union, especially in its initial phase involving negotiations, more than any other leader besides Nyerere.

There have been attempts to ignore John Okello or minimise the role he played as a liberator of the black African majority in Zanzibar. Some people have even tried to write him out of history. But he deserves a lot of credit for helping create conditions which led to the unification of Tanganyika and Zanzibar. He was the one who overthrew the sultan, an ouster which helped pave the way for the two countries to unite even though that was not his intention. He did not even know that's what would happen as a result of the revolution he led.

The union itself was also seen as a step towards formation of an East African federation. Even Karume expressed that view. He also probably believed that Zanzibar would be treated as an equal partner in a larger federation, which would include Kenya and Uganda, than she would be in the union only with Tanganyika in which she would be a junior partner because of her small size.

The driving force behind the merger of the two countries was, of course, President Nyerere himself. The union would not have been formed and consummated without his participation, support and approval regardless of what Kambona and his colleagues did or may have tried to do on their own.

It was Nyerere who authorised Kambona and other Tanganyikan leaders to talk to Zanzibaris about the union. And there is no question that Kambona and his colleagues discussed the matter with Nyerere and told him what was going on.

Whatever Kambona did in pursuit of unification of the two countries had Nyerere's approval and support, for, in the end, it was Nyerere who would have to approve and sign the agreement to unite the two countries, together with his Zanzibari counterpart, Abeid Karume. And it was he who initiated the move towards unification of the two countries by sending his subordinates to Zanzibar to discuss the matter:

"Immediately after the revolution, Nyerere sent two successive delegations to Zanzibar to persuade Karume into the union. The first was led by Oscar Kambona, Foreign Minister, and Bibi Titi Mohamed, a cabinet minister; and the second one was led by Tewa Said Tewa and Job Lusinde, both cabinet ministers. Karume responded that he still needed time to put things in order (Jumbe, 1994: 15).

Later, on 21 April 1964, Karume went to Dar es Salaam following his telephone conversation with his counterpart, Julius Nyerere." – (Mohammed Bakari and Alexander A. Makulilo, "Between Confusion and Clarity: Rethinking the Union of Tanganyika and Zanzibar after 50 Years," *The African Review, Vol. 41, No. 1*, the University of Dar es Salaam, Dar es Salaam, Tanzania, 2014, p. 7).

The contention that Nyerere was the driving force behind the merger is also supported by the testimony of one of the main leaders of Zanzibar, Aboud Jumbe, who said it was Nyerere who wanted the union, and that he is the one who went to Zanzibar in pursuit of his goal of uniting the two countries:

"Ask Nyerere, because he is the one who went to Zanzibar. He is the one who wanted the union. He must have had goals. Has he achieved them? I can not speak for mainlanders on the achievement of the union." – (Aboud Jumbe, commenting on the union of Tanganyika and Zanzibar, at a press conference in Dar es Salaam, Tanzania, during the 34th anniversary of the Zanzibar revolution, 12 January 1998).

The leaders of Zanzibar themselves wanted close ties with Tanganyika for various reasons, including security for their new government.

Even Babu went to Dar es Salaam – together with Karume and Hanga – to talk to Kambona and Nyerere about the situation in Zanzibar after the revolution. The three Zanzibari leaders expressed interest in forming a federation with Tanganyika, even if it was for their own selfish motives and not out of Pan-African solidarity; thus refuting the claim that the idea to unite the two East African countries came from the Americans and not from the Africans themselves.

Was Babu, together with his colleagues, also pressured by the United States and Britain to do so, as was claimed – by Amrit Wilson, Ann Talbot and others – to be the case with regard to Nyerere?

One of the main reasons the three leaders – Karume, Hanga and Babu – expressed interest in uniting the two countries was probably security for their new government. That seems to be the case because they went to Dar es Salaam to talk to Kambona first, about uniting the two countries in a federation, soon after the sultan was overthrown. There were also reports, true or false, about 2,500 Arabs being trained in Arab countries in order to invade Zanzibar and reinstate the sultan.

The idea that a number of Arab countries were ready to support the invasion was enough to scare the new rulers of Zanzibar into seeking security from Tanganyika even if it meant forming a federation with their bigger neighbour to off the invasion.

It was obvious that the only country they expected to get help from, to provide security for the new government, was Tanganyika. Federation of the two countries would guarantee that security. As the head of government, Karume was concerned about that probably more than any other Zanzibari leader in the ruling revolutionary council.

His fear was compounded by the threat he faced from communists in the government, especially Babu, prompting him to seek union with Tanganyika even without external pressure or manipulation. He did not need to be coerced by the Americans and the British to ensure his own survival, although they did try a number of ways to influence him to exclude communists, especially Babu and Hanga, from the government. But they did not make the final decision on uniting the two countries. As Nyerere said:

"We ourselves voluntarily agreed on a union. Karume and I met. Only two of us met."

That was when the final decision was made by the two leaders to unite.

Why should Nyerere not be believed when he said he and Karume voluntarily agreed to unite, even if they had different motives – each had his own reason or reasons – in seeking unification of the two countries?

American diplomats in Tanganyika did not even know what was going on when the leaders of Tanganyika and Zanzibar met secretly to discuss formation of the union. Why did they not know if they were the ones who were behind it and initiated its establishment?

In fact, it was the leaders of Zanzibar who expressed interest in uniting their country with Tanganyika just a few days after the Zanzibar revolution took place. As Professor Paul Bjerk states in his book, *Building a Peaceful Nation: Julius Nyerere and the Establishment of Sovereignty in Tanzania, 1960 – 1964*:

"Within a week of the Zanzibar Revolution in January 1964, Oscar Kambona reported that the new Zanzibari leader Abeid Karume, together with Kassim Hanga and the influential Abdulrahman Babu, expressed interest in the idea of a 'union or federal relationship with Tanganyika in the near future.'[1]

After the mutiny on the mainland, which had ironically left Nyerere in a strong position both internally and externally, Tanganyika entered into a tense period of diplomatic jockeying over the fate of revolutionary Zanzibar.

In the union of Tanganyika and Zanzibar, the East African leadership found a solution that satisfied all sides enough to restrain an outside intervention, and so retain East African control over the islands. As Kambona explained, the key issue was to maintain local autonomy from foreign interference:

'Our first concern was the growing Communist presence, and second, the danger of the Cold War coming in. The Cold War was in the Congo already – it would have been a straight line across Africa....The problem was how to isolate Zanzibar from the East countries, yet not be used by the West for its own purposes.'[2]

The details of this account largely agree with those of Issa Shivji, Thomas Burgess, Ian Speller, Frederick Jjuuko, and Godfrey Muriuki, but my analysis suggests that both Nyerere and Karume were concerned about increasing superpower interference in Zanzibar and sought to minimize it, fearing that it would fuel further violence.

Western diplomats worked to retain a friendly government in Zanzibar as a strategic asset in the Indian Ocean, and Eastern countries made great efforts to cultivate the strong communist element in the Zanzibari leadership to create an ideological ally in East Africa.

The Tanganyikan leadership sought only to keep Zanzibar from becoming dependent on either side. To accomplish this, Nyerere and Karume agreed to end revolutionary Zanzibar's tenuous sovereignty and place it within the ad hoc framework of a new sovereign state that came to be known as Tanzania.

....The East African leaders kept superpower intrigue at bay through the careful manipulation of the discourse that governed the tense competition between East and West in the nonaligned world." – (Paul Bjerk, *Building a Peaceful Nation: Julius Nyerere and the Establishment of Sovereignty in Tanzania, 1960 – 1964*, Rochester, New York: University of Rochester Press, 2015, p. 206, and 207).

If Nyerere and Karume agreed to do so – "end revolutionary Zanzibar's tenuous sovereignty and place it within the ad hoc framework of a new sovereign state" – and went on to create a new nation by uniting their countries, as indeed was the case, it is clear the union was not something that was imposed on the two leaders and their colleagues by the United States and Britain or any other outside power.

American and British diplomats in Tanganyika and Zanzibar did not even know everything that was going until Kambona told the American ambassador, William Leonhart, that the leaders of Tanganyika and Zanzibar were discussing the possibility of uniting their countries. Other details were kept secret.

Even the East Germans, who were very close to Zanziba'r revolutionary government, including their intelligence chief, did not know the island nation was about to unite with Tanganyika until the last minute when the announcement of the merger was about to take place:

"Upon hearing that Agence France-Presse (AFP) got word of the union, Kambona called in the American ambassador (William Leonhart) late at night on April 22 to tell him that the union would be announced the following day." – (Ibid., p. 223).

There would have been no need for Kambona to call Ambassador Leonhart to tell him the union would be announced the next day if the union was conceived by the Americans together with their British counterparts. Ambassador Leonhart would have known that all along – when the union would be consummated and when it would be announced. In fact, after he heard about it, he said he did not believe – nor did the British believe – the union would solve the main problem the United States and Britain wanted to be solved: preventing the establishment of a communist regime in Zanzibar.

Leonhart said the only practical solution would be to get rid of Babu whom the Americans and the British considered to be the most dangerous communist in Zanzibar and in the entire East Africa.

Nyerere had the upper hand on Zanzibar – soon after the revolution – even before the union was formed. He was very much concerned about the future of the island nation in terms of security and its position in the East-West rivalry. As Bjerk states:

"Between pragmatic nationalists like Karume and idealists like (Ali Sultan) Issa and Babu, Nyerere hoped a progressive nationalist government could be established. He spent the first week after the revolution trying, in Leonhart's words, 'to use his leverage to reestablish order in Zanzibar and prevent a racial bloodbath.'

By the end of the week, before the mutiny threatened his own government, Nyerere had begun to consider long-term options. 'Left to himself [Karume] would merely replace Arabs with Africans in same feudal structure,' he told Leonhart. 'This is not enough. If real social reform did not [happen], Communists would take over. Babu had ideas necessary for thoroughgoing social reform.'[29]

But the Tanganyikan leader was also keen that Umma Party leftists did not lead Zanzibar into communist neocolonialism under the Soviet Union or China. Whether coincidentally or not, the revolution seems to have been timed when Issa and Babu were both off the island." – (Ibid., p. 210).

Babu was in Dar es Salaam; so was Karume, and Hanga as well as other Afro-Shirazi Party officials. They returned to Zanzibar on Monday, January 15th. They left Kunduchi, Dar es Salaam, in a boat around 12 midnight and arrived at Kizimkazi in Unguja (Zanzibar Island) around 6 A.M., three days after the revolution had taken place under the leadership of John Okello.

The revolution paved the way and facilitated the unification of Tanganyika and Zanzibar in a way that was not anticipated. Had the revolution not taken place, the union itself would not have been formed when it was; it is even possible it may not have been formed at all, mainly because of the refusal of Zanzibari leaders to unite their island nation with a much bigger country which would have "swallowed it up." But security considerations, especially by Karume, and Pan-African ideals on the part of Hanga, prevailed over any fear some Zanzibaris may have had about submerging their country in a larger political entity in which Zanzibar would no longer exist as a sovereign state.

Of all the factors which made Zanzibaris decide to unite with Tanganyika, security for Karume and his colleagues besides Hanga was of paramount concern.

Hanga was motivated by Pan-African solidarity probably more than anything else when he urged his colleagues in the Zanzibar Revolutionary Council – some of whom had doubts about the merger – to ratify the articles of union.

With formation of the union, Nyerere achieved the goals he wanted to achieve and even kept the Americans out of Zanzibar where they contemplated intervening to keep the Chinese and the Russians out:

"With the Union Treaty articles unanimously ratified by the Tanganyikan National Assembly and pushed through the Zanzibar Revolutionary Council by Karume and Hanga on April 25 and 26, respectively, Nyerere had successfully preempted both American intervention and communist domination in Zanzibar.

....The Tanganyika-Zanzibar Union had forestalled the Western rationale for intervention by containing the influx of communist influence, but it did not do so by becoming subservient to American demands. Tanzania moved steadily to the left after the Union.

Translating the hasty arrangement into a real country would take time, but it strengthened African control of Zanzibar's political trajectory. 'Can't you see,' explained another Tanganyikan minister, 'that what we have done is first build a roof....After that, the window, walls and doors will come.'[161]

....Nyerere estimated that 'the initial organizing period' would last six months, but that it would take five years to fully harmonize the institutions of the two governments.[162] Major issues like defense, finance, foreign affairs, and ministerial appointments would be in the hands of the Union government based in Dar es Salaam under Nyerere's presidency, but Zanzibar would retain autonomy in its internal affairs under Karume as the first vice president. Tanganyika's laws were to be supreme, however, allowing its Preventive Detention Act to be used to detain any obstructionists in Zanzibar or the mainland.

After successfully concluding the treaty, Nyerere was elated, aware that he had forestalled outside intervention in Zanzibar, in what he called 'the biggest gamble of my life.'[163] More important, he had taken a step toward his closely held vision of progressively building an East African federation." – (Ibid., pp. 224, 225, and 226).

The role played by Nyerere and his colleagues in forming the union is minimised because of the politics of the Cold War, and Cold War intrigues, which were prevalent during that period, obscuring what really happened behind the scenes between Tanganyikan and Zanzibari leaders in forging the merger.

Everything was viewed and distorted through the prism of the Cold War, tipping scales in favour of the super powers and competing ideological camps. Their perceptions were considered to be reality, totally ignoring how Africans themselves felt, what they wanted, and what they did.

More than 50 years after the union was formed, questions are still being asked concerning its formation: Who was behind it? Did African leaders really form the union? Or was it the Americans and the British who orchestrated the whole thing? As Professor Ethan Sanders states in his paper, "Conceiving the Tanganyika-Zanzibar Union in the Midst of the Cold War: Internal and International Factors":

"To what extent was international pressure placed on Nyerere and Karume to unify their two states in April 1964?

The argument made is that even though Americans were initially very pleased with the outcome of the Union —because they thought it would help stem the spread of communism in the region—this was not a Western-initiated plan forced upon East African leaders. Indeed, the evidence shows that Americans were largely in the dark and in fact very frustrated by their lack of influence on the situation. Instead, the Union merely served as a confluence of African and American interests....

On 20 April 1964 the Union between Tanganyika and Zanzibar was agreed upon in principle by Abeid Karume and Julius Nyerere in a closed-door meeting in Dar es Salaam attended by only a small handful of high-level ministers. Two days later across the Zanzibar Channel the two heads of state signed the Articles of Union, binding the states together in a political merger.

The question that historians and other commentators are still trying to straighten out fifty years later is why, exactly?

The standard reply for years has been that the Union was a shining example of the ideals of Pan-Africanism and served as the model which proved that there could be political unity between African nations.

However, in 1989 author and activist Amrit Wilson came out with the provocative thesis that the Union was not an African initiative, but was engineered and orchestrated by the Americans and British in order to stop the spread of communism in eastern Africa. In her view the United Republic of Tanzania was an American and British creation through the means of manipulation and subterfuge.[1]

This interpretation seemed feasible in light of the revelations about the CIA's involvement in the Congo just prior to the Zanzibar Revolution that demonstrated the obvious lengths Americans were willing to go in order to engender regime change in Africa.[2]

As tensions have risen between the mainland and the islands in the last few years, this debate over the role of foreigners in engineering the Union has been discussed by prominent academics Issa Shivji[3] and Haroub Othman, writer Godfrey Mwakikagile, as well as a host of commentators in the Tanzanian media and the East African blogosphere.

A close reading of recently released American National Security files, CIA documents and interviews with the Tanganyikan Attorney General who drafted the Articles of Union, reveals that while the Americans were initially very pleased with the outcome of the Union—because they thought it would help minimize the influence of the 'radical elements' in the Zanzibar Revolutionary Council and stem the spread of communism in the region— this was not an American or British initiated plan forced upon East African leaders. Indeed, the evidence shows that the Americans were largely in the dark and in fact very frustrated by their lack of influence on the situation with regional leaders.

The idea of federating Tanganyika and Zanzibar was clearly an African one, an idea which had its own long and complicated history stretching back to the 1940s well before Anglo-American concerns over the Zanzibar Revolution.

The actualization of the union agreement in April of 1964, however, was principally the responsibility of two individuals, Julius Nyerere and Abeid Karume, and was built out of both their longtime interests and desires as well as their complex concerns over the evolving situation in the early months of 1964.

Therefore the Union between Tanganyika and Zanzibar served as a confluence of interests. It helped meet the needs of the principal African leaders involved and was also an outcome that the Americans were temporarily pleased with as they thought it would be beneficial to their own geopolitical interests.

However, neither the Americans nor the British were the prime movers or significant shapers of this plan. Instead, the Union was conceived by Africans and largely fashioned by Nyerere and Karume's key advisers, Tanganyikan Minister of External Affairs, Oscar Kambona, and Zanzibari Vice President Abdulla Kassim Hanga. It was the agendas of the two heads of state and the initiative shown by a few of their top ministers that guided the unification process.

The merger was not a plan cooked up by British or American agents and diplomats and then forced upon the leaders of these two nascent postcolonial states." – (Ethan Sanders, "Conceiving the Tanganyika-Zanzibar Union in the Midst of the Cold War: Internal and International Factors," *The African Review, Vol. 41, No. 1,* the University of Dar es Salaam, Dar es Salaam, Tanzania, 2014, pp. 35 – 37).

Nyerere and Karume had their own interests in forming the union. The Americans and the British did not even know everything that was going on between the two leaders in their quest for unification of the two countries. As Professor Sanders goes on to state:

"The very first record in the American files of any discussion about federating or uniting Tanganyika and Zanzibar came just days after the Revolution when Oscar Kambona requested a meeting with William Leonhart to discuss the arrest of Americans in Zanzibar. Meeting at Kambona's house on January 16, Kambona mentioned that Karume, Hanga and Babu had come to see Nyerere to ask him for police advisers and help. During this initial meeting the Zanzibar delegation 'said they would like to discuss union or federal relationship with Tanganyika in [the] near future.'

This piece of information must not have initially struck Leonhart as too important because he made no comment on it in his report nor did he bring it up with Nyerere at his next meeting with the Tanganyikan president.[37] This exchange at Kambona's house was reported by the CIA a couple of days later.[38] (Most CIA reports at this time were commentaries based on gleanings from State Department telegrams as they did not have any agents on the ground in Zanzibar during the weeks following the Revolution.)[39]

This first mention of some sort of union or federation is illuminating because it indicates several things.

First, the very idea of some sort of federation or union was first brought up by Kambona, and not the Americans.

Moreover, American understanding (and misunderstanding) of such a plan was always based on the information they received from Africans.

Second, it shows that Babu was privy to the early discussions of federation.

Finally, it demonstrates that there may be some evidence that the idea was first suggested by Karume and not Nyerere, although there is quite a bit of disagreement on this point as various parties involved have told different versions.[40]

A little over a week later Kambona again mentioned to Leonhart that 'the new GOZ [Government of Zanzibar] leaders continued to press for early EA Federation including Zanzibar.' Kambona's response to the Zanzibaris was that it was still too controversial to be undertaken quickly because the Afro-Shirazi Party, the political party that made up the bulk of the Revolutionary Council, had long been accused of being mainland agents. He told the visitors that he felt Zanzibar should exist as an independent state for some months before discussions on federation resumed.[41]

Whether or not this is exactly how the discussion between Kambona and the Zanzibar leaders unfolded, or instead just how Kambona wanted Leonhart to think they unfolded, cannot be ascertained. However, it does speak to the fact that Tanganyikan-Zanzibar discussions on federation or union began almost immediately after the Revolution and that initially the discussions were focused on a larger East African Federation and not just a partnership between the two countries.

After Kambona's second mention of high-level discussions about federation, Leonhart and the State Department took more notice of this idea and wondered if it was worth further exploration to see if some sort of federal solution could possibly help alleviate the communist threat in the islands.

Coming just after the mainland mutinies when the US was contemplating a number of actions including a British military intervention and approaching East African leaders to do more to help, Secretary of State Rusk asked Leonhart to arrange a meeting to discuss the Zanzibar situation with Nyerere.

He gave Leonhart a list of twelve questions to ask Nyerere which were mostly focused on obtaining Nyerere's assessment on the situation and various Zanzibar actors, but also to see if Tanganyikan or Kenyan police could do more to support Karume and disarm the communist elements. The very last question was, 'What are Nyerere['s] views on possible federation Zanzibar with Tanganyika'?[42]

Nyerere's answer to Leonhart the next day was that even though he was much closer with the current government of Zanzibar than the previous one, that, 'there was not practical possibility of Federation (of) Zanzibar and Tanganyika alone and EA Federation 'very distant prospect.''[43]

Nothing was made of this at the time, but it did alter American perception that Nyerere was unwilling to have a federation between the two countries, and that if anything was to happen it needed to be a regional federation in which Kenyatta was again believed to be the key.

The next mention of a federation in the American correspondence was not until a month later when there were a flurry of meetings and discussions to devise a new action plan.

In Rusk's talking points memo sent out to the various American diplomats involved (mentioned above), he noted that one 'long-range solution might lie in some form of federation.' He observed the government of Zanzibar's possible interest in a federation from Leonhart's earlier reports and wondered if Nyerere might be asked again about this issue despite his 'previous objections [to the] idea.' However, because Nyerere was viewed as unwilling to go it alone, and because it was believed Kenyatta was more concerned over Babu than Nyerere was, Rusk thought it best to seek Kenyatta out first to see if the Kenyan prime minister would not raise the issue with Nyerere in a discussion about a larger East African federation.[44]

But the consensus that March at the meeting between (Colonial Secretary Duncan) Sandys, Leonhart, Carlucci and the others in Dar es Salaam was that the Americans 'nor the British believe Tanganyika-Zanzibar Federation practical possibility.' They suggested the only 'outside chance Nyerere might consider' some form of federation was if Kenyatta was willing to bring Kenya into a regional federation.[45]

Once again the idea was dropped and it would be another month before there was any revival of British or American interest in this outcome.

The next brief mention of a potential federal arrangement was only in a passing comment in early April when a distressed Nyerere approached Leonhart and shared his grave concerns over a rumor about a 2500-strong Arab force training to prepare to invade Zanzibar and retake it for the Sultan.

Nyerere asked both the American and German ambassadors if they had any intelligence about this counter-revolutionary force.

Leonhart obviously did not and in fact wondered if this frantic plea was not some sort of political cover by Nyerere to send more Tanganyikan troops to Pemba, or possibly some form of incorporation 'by Kenya or Tanganyika or both.'[46]

More substantially, American interests were again raised a couple of days later in light of the impending East African Federation talks between Kenyatta, Nyerere and

Obote to be held in Nairobi on 10 April.

The day before on their way to this conference a Zanzibar delegation stopped in Dar es Salaam to have a meeting with Tanganyikan officials. Hanga, Babu and Twala were at this meeting but Karume was not present due to the illness of his wife.

Mbwambo, the Tanganyika Chief of Protocol, informed Leonhart that the major topic was whether or not Zanzibar would seek membership in the East African Federation.

Mbwambo would not elaborate any further, but he revived American interests in such an arrangement.

Babu and Hanga attended the meeting in Nairobi as spectators as 'the big three' tried to hammer out a plan. According to Kenyan minister Murumbi this meeting went poorly. The climax came when Nyerere gave the emotional plea, 'We want federation now!' Kenyatta instantly agreed, but Obote went silent.

It is questionable whether Kenyatta was truly eager for federation, but the result of these talks made it clear that there would be no East African Federation, or at least not anytime soon.[47]

It was the following week that Hughes (Thomas Hughes, Director of the Bureau of Intelligence and Research at the US State Department) put out his major memorandum on US alternatives sombrely stating that any hopes of minimizing radicals through a regional federation were extremely doubtful.

It was the day after Hughes' memo was written that Leonhart first discovered that there were serious talks scheduled to take place to discuss some sort of political arrangement between Zanzibar and Tanganyika without Kenya or Uganda.

Reporting on a private meeting he had with Kambona on 16 April, Leonhart explained that Kambona had come to him in 'the strictest confidence' that secret talks had begun with certain Zanzibar leaders regarding a

Tanganyika-Zanzibar federation after the breakdown of the East African Federation talks in Nairobi. He mentioned specifically working with Abdulla Hanga, his long-time friend since their university days in London in the 1950s, as well as Saleh Saadalla, but specifically pointed out that cutting Babu down to size was an intended outcome of the federation—a sentiment obviously pleasing to American ears.

In his report to the State Department, William Leonhart questioned whether Nyerere would support such an initiative, but promised he would keep an eye on developments with the 'Kambona project.'[48]

Two days later Leonhart received a call from Kambona stating that if the plan was going to work then the best opportunity would be the upcoming weekend—a reference to Babu's absence from Zanzibar on a trip to Asia. He noted that he had brought other Zanzibar leaders in on the talks, Abdul Twala who was the acting Foreign Minister while Babu was abroad, and Yusuf Himidi.

Kambona had to travel to Tabora that weekend but he had recruited Harue Tambwe, a TANU stalwart who had strong connections to Zanzibar, to go talk to Hanga to see what he needed so that the deal could be sealed within the week.

Importantly, Kambona mentioned that Karume had already 'given tentative agreement' to an association and reconfirmed that the project had Nyerere's support as well.

Believing the plan may actually have the consent of the two critical players needed to pull off such a project certainly piqued Leonhart's attention, but his initial response was still somewhat cool.

Leonhart obviously wanted Babu out of the picture, but the prospect of a Zanzibar dominated instead by Hanga and Twala was also unpleasant. In fact, in classic Cold War paranoia style, Leonhart warned Washington that the Soviets might be behind this plan to unite Tanganyika and Zanzibar in order to counteract Chinese influence (via

Babu) in the islands, have their man Hanga installed instead and then expand their influence on the mainland.

Leonhart recommended that the US needed to proceed cautiously and gain more information before they considered giving full US support to what was still being referred to as Kambona's plan.[49]

When Leonhart informed Carlucci of the secret talks the next day, the Zanzibar chargé agreed that Hanga was preferable to Babu, but that he too would hopefully be removed at a later date.[50]

The response from the State Department was to wait and see what this 'Tanganyikan initiative' for some sort of federation or incorporation would entail. They thought since it was an 'African initiative'—something they were originally hoping would come through Kenyatta—that this was the best and maybe even 'the only possibility of reversing [the] present critical situation in Zanzibar.'

But they were also wary of stepping in and risking precipitating Soviet or Chinese involvement, and thus Leonhart was told to wait for Kambona to come to him before any offers of US assistance were made. But certainly the US was willing to give its 'blessing' if the plan would exclude Babu and his clique from power.[51]

The nature of these American cables indicates that the idea of a Tanganyika-Zanzibar union was clearly conceived by Tanganyikans and Zanzibaris and not American diplomats, who even initially suspected the Soviets of being behind it (italics added by Godfrey Mwakikagile).

When the Articles of Union were signed by Nyerere and Karume the only Western officials that had any clue of what was happening were Leonhart, Carlucci and the State Department higher-ups back in Washington like George Ball who had read Leonhart's incoming telegrams.

Subsequent cables indicate that the American Embassies in Nairobi and Kampala were still in the dark, as were all of the British officials who as of the 22nd of

April were still talking about putting pressure on Kenyatta to talk to Karume.[52]

Moreover, in the following days it became clear that the Americans and British were anxious over the feasibility of what was now being referred to as Nyerere's evolving strategy or the 'African solution.'[53]

The African formula brought with it the possibility of reactionary violence or, maybe worse, conniving counter-plans by Babu and his followers to use the larger mainland platform to spread their radical influence even wider.

Less than a week after the Union the British and Americans were complaining that little had been done to reduce communist influence in the islands and they once again began considering alternative courses of action to bring 'outside forces' to bear on the situation. Again, this hand-wringing and strategizing happened mostly at the level of internal discussions between Americans and their British allies and there was little direct action taken.

Different kinds of support for Nyerere and Karume were considered, both 'quiet support' as well as gifts of aid and other assistance. Previous strategies were dragged back out such as getting other African leaders to persuade Karume or Nyerere to cement the union and the non-aligned character of the new Union government.

There were also contingency plans for military intervention and sending in emergency forces.[54]

It was not until the very end of June that the Americans felt they could breathe a little easier and that they were 'at [the] end this overheated period.'

For the foreseeable future it looked as if the Union would last and that the African plan had gone a long way to reduce the threat of Zanzibar becoming a communist bastion in Africa.[55]

Internal Motivations behind the Union

The Union *was not* an Anglo-American idea and the

process of political unification was not pushed through due to direct pressure from the Americans, British or any other outside forces promoting such a plan.

But if Karume and Nyerere did not give in to 'irresistible pressure from Western powers,' it remains to be asked what factors compelled these two African leaders to take this extraordinary step?[56]

The answer to this question has usually been formulated in an either/or construct, it was either Pan-Africanism or a product of Cold War.

But in order to fully answer this question, one must understand the complicated local power dynamics, the inter-personal relationships that were at play, and importantly, understand that the aims of Pan-Africanism cannot be extracted from the problems of decolonization and the Cold War from which it was born.

The first thing to point out was that many of the players involved had a certain amount of idealism regarding African unity, what one might call the more romantic side of Pan-Africanism. Many of the Afro-Shirazi and TANU politicians had cut their political teeth in the African Association in the 1940s, a group declaring that all Africans were one and whose motto was '*Umoja ni Nguvu*' (Unity is Strength).

As early as 1947 the members of this trans-territorial organization explicitly declared at an Association-wide conference that they were willing to see the political federation of Tanganyika and Zanzibar. At this time both Karume and Nyerere were heavily involved in the Association and Karume was undoubtedly at the conference and among those that passed the resolution supporting federation while Nyerere, if not in attendance himself, would have certainly read about the resolution through the organization's highly-organized communication network.[57]

The desirability of such a federation was again confirmed in 1958 when leaders of the ASP and TANU agreed that they wanted to amalgamate the countries into one republic after independence had been achieved.[58]

The general atmosphere throughout the late 1950s and early 1960s was very pro-unity, to the point where declaring loyalty to the ideals of Pan-Africanism was widespread. This genuine, if not surface-level, desire for political unification is likely *part* of the reason why Babu had been interested in unifying some of the countries in East Africa as seen in his participation in a number of discussions on federation and his later assent to the 'idea of unity.'[59]

It can also be seen in Aboud Jumbe's response on the discovery that the union had taken place in his absence. When Karume asked his opinion, Jumbe's instinctual reaction was, 'unity is strength.'[60]

But as the case in the rest of Africa has seemed to prove over the years, the ideals of unity and the discussions of Pan-Africanism rarely translated into transfers of power or political unification or federation. Thus other factors must have helped precipitate the unification of these two states.

In the case of post-Revolutionary Zanzibar and Tanganyika it seems to have been a concern over outside intervention, a mutual reliance on the outcome of each state for purposes of domestic stability, and a desire by Karume and those loyal to him to consolidate his position and power.

From the standpoint of Karume and the Revolutionary Council, they very clearly relied on the help and support of the Tanganyikans after the unexpected Revolution. The new leaders had been thrust into the position of having to first calm the situation and then start providing for the people of the islands in this post-crisis period.

Zanzibaris immediately turned to long-time allies and friends in Dar es Salaam for assistance.

In the week following the Revolution there were multiple trips to the Tanganyikan capital by Hanga and

Babu and even a trip by Karume himself to request various support from the Tanganyikan government. They needed medical experts and supplies, technicians to restore essential services, help in organizing a police force and basic food items.

Nyerere sent a Tanganyikan police force to help restore order along with medical supplies, sugar and other food stuffs in aid.

Karume also turned to Nyerere for guidance in how to deal with political liabilities, ex-government ministers he wanted removed from the scene, and the problematic John Okello who had given Karume his position, but who could not be trusted in the new cabinet.[61]

From the record it appears that it was during these initial talks about Okello and assistance that the idea of unifying the two states was specifically discussed in light of Karume's political concerns. Karume not only saw the mainland as a place where he could get rid of his political adversaries, but it seems likely that he felt Tanganyika's assistance could help stave off foreign intervention from a number of directions.

From the beginning Karume was deeply concerned about a counter-revolution. He was highly suspicious of both the Americans and the British whom he felt had supported the outgoing regime, and at several points over the early months of 1964 he appeared concerned they would try to reinstate the old order. They had shored up the other post-independence East African regimes after the mutinies, why would they not help the ZNP government as well? He even arrested four American journalists he believed to be 'CIA Counter Revolutionaries.' This deep mistrust explains in part his coolness towards the Americans and British throughout the period.[62]

But Karume also apparently feared a number of Arab Gulf monarchies whom he believed wanted to reinstall the Sultan.[63]

In the months following the Revolution Karume's

growing concern centered on the rising power of Abdulrahman Babu and other non-Afro-Shirazi Party members of the Revolutionary Council like Ali Mafoudh who had become the de facto commander of Zanzibar's armed forces after the removal of Okello.[64]

Karume and Babu had been thrust into their positions by Okello who intentionally wanted members from both the ASP and the recently banned Umma Party of Babu to serve in the Revolutionary Council after he overthrew the ZNP-led government.[65]

Even though Karume worked with Babu out of necessity at first, inside sources indicate that there were always real fault lines between those RC (Revolutionary Council) members who were leaders of the ASP before the Revolution and those who were not. Indeed, there was deep mistrust and opposition towards Babu by some ASP leaders.[66]

Certainly, the progression of events and the way in which the Union was pushed through clearly indicate that sidelining Babu and consolidating Karume's power and influence in the islands was a central motivation on the Zanzibar side.

Babu had been involved in early talks regarding some form of federation in January and again in early April, but the timing of the final agreement was intentionally arranged to align with his trip to Asia.

There had been previous private meetings between Karume and Nyerere, but events sped up rapidly once it was clear that a larger East African federation was not going to happen and Babu was going to be away from Zanzibar.

In the week leading up to the signing and ratification of the Articles of Union, when messages were going back and forth between Kambona and Hanga, Kambona made it clear that if anything was going to happen it needed to be within the next week and the reason must have been to avoid any efforts by Babu to block the agreement.[67]

This is corroborated by the Tanganyikan Attorney General, Roland Brown, who had been secretly brought into knowledge about the potential union by Nyerere who wanted him to draft a legal document laying out how a union agreement would work. With Babu's temporary absence, tremendous pressure was put on Brown to finish the Articles of Union quickly so that Nyerere and Karume could sign them before Babu's return.[68]

After secretly meeting in Dar es Salaam on 18, 19 and 20 April, Karume and Nyerere finally came to an agreement.[69]

The last touches to the Articles were completed and brought to Zanzibar by Nyerere, Kambona, Job Lusinde, the Minister of Home Affairs, and three other Tanganyikans. The signing between Karume and Nyerere was also witnessed by some of Karume's top advisers including Abdulla Kassim Hanga and Abdul Twala who had both been in on the secret talks.[70]

The Articles were then whisked away by Kambona and Roland Brown to be shown to Kenyatta and Obote in Nairobi and Kampala, respectively, who had both been excluded from any knowledge about the talks. (There were concerns they would be upset for not previously being made aware of the secret talks.)

After giving Karume and Hanga a couple of days to politic for the Union, the Articles were then returned to Zanzibar with Kambona, Lusinde and Brown for their ratification by the Revolutionary Council on the evening of 25 April.

Brown was sent to the ratification to answer any legal questions which were raised, but was asked to sit outside the meeting.[71]

Salim Rashid had tried to stall the meeting until Babu's return (which ended up being later that night) by bringing in a lawyer from Uganda to raise legal objections with Karume.

Karume was undeterred by his meeting with the lawyer

earlier that afternoon,[72] and the ratification meeting went ahead even without the presence of several Revolutionary Council members, including Rashid who was possibly on his way to pick up Babu from the airport.[73]

A passionate plea was given by Hanga that the Union was necessary and that the Articles must be approved. Hanga was clearly Karume's closest ally who had stuck by the Sheikh during an earlier period of division within the ASP, he had a long-time personal relationship with Kambona, and being Karume's number two he also stood to gain the most by having Babu's power checked.[74]

The ratification by the Revolutionary Council took longer than expected, but Karume received the endorsement of enough members, with several others abstaining.[75]

With the approval of the RC, Kambona, Lusinde and Brown immediately headed back to Dar es Salaam where the Tanganyika National Assembly was waiting on their return to start the process for Tanganyikan approval. This was a much smoother process with nothing but positive speeches led by Nyerere himself.[76]

The manoeuvre was complete, but Kambona was still concerned about how Babu would react to the news, telling Leonhart that 'If Babu agrees, he will be a fool, but he may do so.'[77]

Babu finally met with Karume the next day and the president reportedly told him in front of other ministers that the Revolutionary Council had 'voted unanimously in favor of Union,' (only if one did not count the abstentions) and that 'he could either agree or resign.'

The extremely bright Babu must have recognized that something subversive was afoot and decided not to challenge Karume at that moment but carefully responded that 'he agreed with the *idea* of Union.'[78]

When the new Union cabinet was announced the following day Babu was given a high position, but one in Dar es Salaam directly under Nyerere and away from the

Zanzibar scene.[79]

Babu was the first casualty of Karume's use of the Union arrangement to clip the wings of political threats in the island.[80]

Nyerere, Kambona and Lusinde also wanted to see Babu's influence diminished, although not for reasons of securing personal power, but due to a desire to avoid external interference in African affairs. For them, Babu was just one part of a larger concern over foreign intervention. Similar to the Americans, the Tanganyikans too were concerned about too much communist influence in Zanzibar, but for slightly different reasons.

Nyerere and Lusinde both thought a prosperous communist-backed Zanzibar would serve to destabilize the domestic scene within Tanganyika. If the small islands were turned into a showcase of the financial fruits of aligning with the socialist powers, Nyerere was afraid it would undermine all his claims that remaining non-aligned held out the best solution for Tanganyikans.[81]

Lusinde too was worried about potential contrasts between Dar es Salaam and Zanzibar, noting that it was the urban poor who were involved in acts of mob violence during the mutiny and who were the most likely to cause problems for the government. They needed no new inspiration from Zanzibar social revolutions.[82]

Direct intervention from outsiders, be it the West, the Soviets or the Chinese, was something that needed to be avoided according to the minds of Nyerere and Kambona. Kambona was concerned that Karume was making the mistake of relying too heavily on the various communist groups that were promising aid and giving military assistance.

He was concerned that they were 'trying to smother Karume with advisers and aid, never giving him time or room to stand off and see what's happening,' and Kambona was also offended that the Soviets and Chinese were acting like Africans could not think for themselves.

Kambona noted that the union was a 'gamble' but that something had to be done before the 'Easterners' took over the island. He felt it was the mainland African states' responsibility to help keep Zanzibari Africans from such a fate.[83]

On the other hand, Nyerere was also concerned over a possible Western military intervention in Zanzibar.

Even though Nyerere never received any direct pressure from the West to unite Tanganyika and Zanzibar, (as demonstrated above and confirmed by Roland Brown)[84] he was aware of discussions over British military intervention which created a type of indirect burden to do something to find an African solution to the problem before there was another embarrassing show of force by the ex-colonial powers.[85]

Nyerere did not want either side in the Cold War meddling in the affairs of East Africa. This is seen in part through his constant rebuffs of US and British assistance when it was offered in the early months of 1964.[86]

This concern also played into his reasoning for why he was willing to take on the risk of merging with Zanzibar without the other East African states.

Even though some form of union between Tanganyika and the Zanzibar islands had long been discussed, it was still only second best to Nyerere's larger vision of an East African Federation. Nonetheless, the exigencies of the situation compelled Nyerere to act.

So was this Pan-African idealism?

The answer can only be yes if one recognizes the strong utilitarian strand in the Pan-African Movement of the 1950s and early 1960s.

The desire for African unity was born out of the desire to fight imperialism in all of its forms and was imbued by the Spirit of Bandung which sought a way out of the binary world of the Cold War.

The Pan-African Manifesto and the All-African People's Congress promoted a united and strong Africa which would not tolerate interference from any of the big powers and which hoped to solve its own problems and become a significant player on the world stage.[87]

Thus the Union was not founded solely on some abstract or romantic notion of unity, but it was forged through a process shaped by both Karume's concerns over losing power and Nyerere's utilitarian Pan-Africanism that desired to protect Zanzibaris, and ultimately Tanganyikans, from non-African intervention into East African affairs." – (Ibid., pp. 44 – 55).

Professor Sanders has cited extensively cables and telegrams – as well as other communications including CIA intelligence reports – between American diplomats in Dar es Salaam, Zanzibar, Nairobi, London and American officials in Washington, D.C., including those at the White House, to document his study, showing that formation of the union of Tanganyika and Zanzibar was not the work of American and British officials and diplomats.

There is also evidence showing that Nyerere's interest in uniting Tanganyika and Zanzibar to form one country goes back to the 1940s. Job Lusinde, who was minister of home affairs in Nyerere's cabinet soon after independence, said Nyerere made that point during a debate back in 1948, contending that a merger of the two countries was a goal that must be pursued. As Sanders states:

"Job Lusinde also tells a story about how the first time he met Nyerere was in 1948 when the future president was taking part in a debate in a secondary school in Tabora where he gave arguments in support of federating Tanganyika and Zanzibar. Interview with Job Lusinde." – (Ibid., p. 63).

The Americans and the British had nothing to do with that. They did not tell Nyerere back in 1948 he should consider forming a union of Tanganyika and Zanzibar, or support such a merger, if he became a national leader one day.

Tanganyika's attorney-general, Roland Brown, a British lawyer who was invited – from Britain – by Nyerere to serve in that capacity after Tanganyika won independence, played the leading role in drafting the articles of union:

"Brown recollects being told, 'get on with it please, can we have the final draft, Babu is one his way. . . .'

Brown was permitted to bring in his aide Paul Fifoot, the Chief Parliamentary Draftsman, to help him in drafting the document because of the short timeframe. Brown states that basing the structure of the Union on the relationship between Northern Ireland and Great Britain was actually Fifoot's idea. He did not share any information regarding the potential union with anyone other than Fifoot, and he denies the suggestion that Paul Bomani played a role as would later be suggested by Shivji (2008). Interview, Roland Brown; Roland Brown, 'Jammed Gatling.'" –– (Ibid., p. 65).

Meetings between Tanganyikan and Zanzibari leaders to discuss formation of the union of the two countries were held in secrecy:

"One controversial point surrounding these meetings was whether or not Karume was pressured into making a decision through Tanganyikan threats to pull their police forces from the islands if Karume did not act. Whether or not such an ultimatum was made or how it was worded is not clear, but certainly American observers mentioned that East African Airways had scheduled flights to remove the police from Zanzibar, but that this order was then withdrawn on April 19.

Later Kambona told Leonhart that it was indeed meant

to serve as a wakeup call for Karume to consider what the situation would be like without Tanganyikan support. LBJ NSF Country Files, Box 103, Zanzibar, Cables Vol. II – Incoming Telegram Department of State from Leonhart, 20 April 1964; LBJ NSF Country Files, Box 103, Zanzibar, Cables Vol. II – Incoming Telegram Department of State from Leonhart, 23 April 1964." – (Ibid.)

The secrecy of those meetings meant excluding even some of the people who would have been considered to be key players in the formation of any kind of union of the two East African countries:

"Roland Brown notes that his Attorney General counterpart in Zanzibar, Wolf Dourado, had no foreknowledge of the Union and had not seen the Articles until the ratification meeting, and thus he did not give Karume legal advice on the Union. The reason Dourado was kept out of the discussions was that he had previously served as Babu's personal secretary and it was feared he might leak information to Babu. Interview with Brown.
Ironically, Dourado seems to have been feeding information to Carlucci, informing the American chargé that Rashid had come to his office frantically looking for the resolutions of the Revolutionary Council to try and find a loophole or something to stall the ratification process.
Wolf Dourado's name is protected in the cable, but given the context and details it seems certain that he was the 'reliable GOZ source' who had been talking to Carlucci after the American heard about the Union project. LBJ NSF Country Files, Box, United Republic Tanganyika/Zanzibar, Cables Vol. I – Incoming Telegram State Department from Zanzibar [Carlucci], 25 April 1964; Shivji has a slightly different account of these events, (2008), 79-80." – (Ibid., p. 66).

An argument has persisted through the years that the articles of union were never ratified by Zanzibar's Revolutionary Council, the island nation's supreme ruling body. One of the leading figures in Zanzibar's revolutionary government who did not attend the ratification meeting was Salim Rashid who wanted it to be delayed until Babu returned from his trip abroad so that he could participate in the discussion of whether or not the union should be approved by the governing Revolutionary Council.

But there is evidence showing that the meeting did take place, and the articles of union were ratified although not by all the members, some of whom – such as Rashid and Babu – did not attend the meeting. And there were those who abstained.

One of the most memorable moments of the ratification process was when Kassim Hanga spoke, passionately pleading with his colleagues to ratify the articles of union and explaining why the union was vital to the wellbeing of the people of Zanzibar and Tanganyika and Africa as a whole. His plea helped to change the minds of some of the members of the Revolutionary Council who were not very enthusiastic about the merger:

"Rashid told Shivji he was not at the meeting and that it did not take place. However, there seems to be plenty of corroborating evidence that a meeting did take place, (see below) and Brown is quite certain that neither Rashid nor Babu were there.

We also know from a US report that Rashid was one of only two people to greet Babu at the airport that night at around the same time, and this could explain his absence from the meeting. Interview with Brown; LBJ NSF Country Files, Box 100, United Republic Tanganyika/Zanzibar, Cables Vol. I Incoming Telegram State Department from Carlucci, 25 April 1964; LBJ NSF Country Files, Box 100, United Republic

Tanganyika/Zanzibar, Cables Vol. I - Incoming Telegram State Department from Zanzibar [Carlucci], 25 April 1964." – (Ibid.)

It is true that Western powers, especially the United States and Britain, were concerned about communist penetration of East Africa if communist leaders came to power in Zanzibar. Some American leaders even described Zanzibar as "the Cuba of Africa" after the January 1964 revolution led by John Okello who toppled the Arab-dominated regime and transferred power to the predominantly black majority and their allies including a number of Arabs, some people of Iranian origin (originally from Shiraz in Iran), and others. But it is also true that the people who led the revolution were not interested in substituting one master for another – capitalist or communist – and their uprising was not communist-inspired. It was an expression of indigenous aspirations triggered by the racial injustices the black majority suffered at the hands of the Arab rulers for centuries.

Transfer of power to the Arab minority regime by the British colonial rulers at independence on December 10, 1963, at the expense of the black African majority, provided the spark that ignited the revolution a month later. It had nothing to do with communism.

The communist threat in Zanzibar was overly exaggerated. Even the leaders who could have established communism on the isles dismissed this threat. They were explicit in their intentions and would not have shied away from acknowledging that they were going to establish a communist state in Zanzibar. They included Abdulrahman Mohammed Babu, the most prominent Marxist leader in Zanzibar who was being closely watched by the CIA. According to one of the declassified documents in the US Archives written by Averell Harriman – the American roving ambassador who was in Nigeria during that time – to President Lyndon B. Johnson and Secretary of State

Dean Rusk on 25 March 1964:

"In long talks with Prime Minister Abubakar (Tafawa Balewa) and Foreign Minister (Jaja) Wachuku,...both minimized concern I expressed for Communist takeover in Zanzibar, assured me that Karume was sensible and Babu was primarily African nationalist and would not permit Communist takeover. When I pressed Wachuku, he firmly insisted he could guarantee Babu whom he had personally known a long time." – (Averell Harriman, Johnson Library, National Security File, International Meetings and Travel File, Africa, Box 31, Harriman's Trip, 3/64. Confidential; Priority; Exdis. Passed to the White House. See also, US Diplomatic Archives: Nigeria (1964 - 1968), *Foreign Relations of the United States 1964 - 1968, Vol. XXIV*).

The preceding telegram was followed by other reports on the potential for communist penetration of Africa during the early years of independence in the sixties. Ambassador Harriman himself in another report to President Johnson on 28 October 1964, about nine months after the Zanzibar revolution and just one day before the Union of Tanganyika and Zanzibar was renamed Tanzania (on October 29, 1964), conceded: "Not a single new African nation has succumbed to Communist domination."[32]

Officials in the Johnson Administration were convinced that communists had played an active role in the Zanzibar revolution on 12 January 1964, according to released documents contained in the 850-page volume of *Foreign Relations of the United States 1964 - 1968*. As one US State Department background paper, 7 February 1964, asserted: "There was obvious communist involvement in Zanzibar."[33]

Yet, the same officials admitted that disturbances in other parts of East Africa – the army mutinies in

Tanganyika, Kenya, and Uganda in January 1964 – around the same time did not appear to be communist-inspired. In fact, President Nyerere himself resolutely maintained that there was "no evidence whatsoever to suggest that the mutinies in Tanganyika were inspired by outside forces – either Communist or imperialist."[34]

But there was a common logic that linked the mutinies to the Zanzibar revolution. The revolution was an African uprising against Arab domination and had a distinct racial component (it was also a class conflict between dispossessed blacks and the merchants and landowners who were mostly Arab and Indian), as was clearly demonstrated during the revolution in which hundreds of Arabs and Indians, but mostly Arabs – probably no fewer than 2,000 – were massacred. Some estimates put the death toll at 13,000 – 25,000. But they mostly come from the supporters of the old Arab regime, especially Arabs, who are also strongly opposed to the union of Tanganyika and Zanzibar.

The army mutinies in Tanganyika and in the other two East African countries (Kenya and Uganda), partly inspired by the uprising in Zanzibar, also had a racial dimension. In addition to demanding an increase in salary, the mutineers also demanded the replacement of British army officers with African ones to Africanise the armed forces in a true spirit of independence by eradicating the last vestiges of colonialism. But the mutiny in Tanganyika almost ended up as a military coup, according to the evidence gathered from an analysis of records and documents contained in the archives of the East Africana Collection at the University of Dar es Salaam, Tanzania:

"(The) abortive military mutiny on January 20, 1964, (was) motivated by demands for higher pay and the replacement of British officers by Africans.

The six-day mutiny, which began at Colito Barracks (renamed Lugalo Barracks) in Dar es Salaam and spread to troops stationed at Tabora (and Nachingwea), appears to have been well-planned.

After arresting their British officers, soldiers built roadblocks at strategic points throughout the city, seized the State House (the president's official residence, although Nyerere did not live there but in a simple house on the outskirts of the city in Msasani, and used the State House, popularly known as Ikulu, only for official functions), police stations, airport, radio station, and railway station, and placed guards at critical postal, telegraph, and bank buildings. The Tanganyikan mutiny sparked similar uprisings in the Ugandan and Kenyan armies as well as the looting and pillaging of Asian shops in Dar es Salaam.

Hundreds of people were arrested during the looting in the commercial areas of the capital. Local forces of order were weakened by the government's earlier decision to send the Dar es Salaam Field Police (known by the acronym FFU - Field Force Units), a contingent of 300 men, to Zanzibar to help restore order on the troubled island.

The fear that racial violence might escalate was linked to the revolution in Zanzibar, which took place in the preceding week and was accompanied by race riots, the murder of hundreds of Arab and Asian shopkeepers, and the mass exodus of Asians to the mainland.

Field Marshal John Okello, who had seized power in Zanzibar, declared: 'We are friends of all Europeans and other foreigners. It is only the Ismailis and certain other Indian groups and people of Arab descent we do not like.' (*Tanganyika Standard*, January 17, 1964).

The racial antagonisms behind the army mutiny were evident in the behavior of the mutinous soldiers stationed in the town of Tabora, who beat up all Europeans and Asians who crossed their path. (Listowel, 1965: p. 433). During the looting of Asian shops in Dar es Salaam, 17 people were killed and 23 seriously injured. (*Tanganyika*

Standard, January 22, 1964).

Rumors spread throughout the capital that Nyerere had fled the country and a general strike was imminent. Nyerere, while still hiding, broadcast a radio message on the second day of the rebellion, to reassure the country that he was still in power.

Had they moved quickly, the mutineers could probably have seized control of the government, but the rebellious army units had no plans to launch a coup d'etat. Rebellious soldiers negotiated with Minister of Defence Oscar Kambona and agreed to release the 30 captured European (British) officers, who were quickly flown out of the country. Kambona had offered to replace all European officers with Africans and discuss wages, provided the troops release the officers and return to their barracks.

Nyerere's first public act, after he emerged from hiding on January 22, was to tour the city on foot, visiting the areas of looted Asian shops to express his condolences to Asian shopkeepers who had been targets of violence. (*Tanganyika Standard*, January 23, 1964).

Only after the mutineers began to negotiate with militant leaders of the trade union movement did the government reluctantly ask the British to intervene (the British were soon replaced by Nigerian troops at Nyerere's request at an urgent OAU summit he called in Dar es Salaam to deal with the crisis). Trade union leaders hoped to take advantage of the situation and turn the mutiny into a coup d'etat.

The two most prominent proponents of Africanization, trade union leaders Christopher (Kasanga) Tumbo, who had returned from Kenya, and Victor Mkello, met in Morogoro to plan a new government. (Listowel, 1965: pp. 437 - 38). On January 25, British troops quickly took control of the barracks and disarmed the rebels, killing five African soldiers in the confrontation.

The army mutiny proved to be a great embarrassment for the government, which was forced to call on troops of the former colonial power to restore public order. Yet the uprising also provided the occasion to move decisively against those who had continued to press for Africanization.

After the abortive mutiny, the government arrested 50 policemen implicated in the uprising, reorganized the military (while Nigerian troops sent to Tanganyika by the Nigerian Federal Government provided defence for the country), and replaced British officers to defuse the issue of Africanization. It used Preventive Detention Law, rarely invoked since its passage in 1962, to order the arrest of more than 200 trade union leaders, many of whom were released after questioning. Fifteen soldiers were sentenced to prison for their role in the mutiny.

The trade union movement was brought firmly under the control of the government by the dissolution of the Tanganyika Federation of Labour (TFL) and establishment in its place of the TANU-controlled National Union of Tanganyika Workers (NUTA).

Several days after the suppression of the mutiny, on January 28, 1964, Nyerere announced the appointment of a presidential commission to pursue the plans that had been announced earlier to create a single-party state, subsequently instituted in the constitution of 1965."[35]

Therefore, from all available evidence, it is clear that communism – or any form of external involvement or manipulation – was not a factor in the army mutiny in Tanganyika or those in Kenya and Uganda; three inter-related incidents in a chain reaction that almost plunged the three countries into chaos during those fateful days in January 1964.

Probably more than anything else, even more than salary demands, the mutinies were inspired by black nationalism and were a military expression of indigenous political aspirations; so was the Zanzibar revolution, although it transcended race and included some Arabs and

Persians in the vanguard in the quest for racial justice.

But since the oppressive regime which was overthrown was Arab, oppressing and exploiting black people more than anybody else, the revolution assumed a racial dimension as an indigenous expression of the political and economic aspirations of the black majority – who did not need communism to wake them up to reality and show them that they were being oppressed and exploited by the Arabs because they were weak and black. Experience is the best teacher.

Although it is true that American policy towards Africa during the Johnson Administration (as well as preceding and future ones) was one of communist containment, there was little evidence to show that communism was gaining ground anywhere on the continent; hence Ambassador Harriman's observation as early as 1964 that – "not a single new African nation has succumbed to Communist penetration"; and the conclusion, in the same year, by the US State Department that: "There is no hard evidence at this time that the trouble in East Africa (the army mutinies) was part of an inter-related communist plot to take over the area."[36]

A plausible explanation for American involvement in "facilitating" the establishment of the union of Tanganyika and Zanzibar may lie in the fact that the interests of the United States with regard to Zanzibar coincided with those of Julius Nyerere who had always wanted all the countries in the region (including Zanzibar) to unite, and therefore the American government – at best – did not interfere and try to block the union from being formed; but not in the fact, the erroneous fact, that the union was conceived and engineered by the United States and Britain.

Whereas the United States may have been concerned about the potential for the establishment of a communist regime in Zanzibar which could serve as a beachhead for communist incursions into the African continent and threaten her geopolitical and strategic interests on the continent and in the Indian Ocean as a world power – since the island nation would be turned into a communist satellite dominated by the Soviet Union or the People's Republic of China; Nyerere, on the other hand, saw the establishment of the union as a step towards African unity and a realisation of his Pan-African ambition to unite countries in the region; an ambition he had always cherished long before the "communist-inspired" revolution in Zanzibar took place, and even long before Tanganyika and other countries in the region won independence.

But even if the Americans thought that by uniting Zanzibar with Tanganyika, communists would be deprived of a base in the island nation under a radical regime, they were not very comfortable with Nyerere himself under whose leadership Zanzibar's radicalism was supposed to be contained or neutralised; thus raising a number of question including – why would they help such a leader to unite his country with Zanzibar in the first place.

Therefore, the legitimacy of the fundamental assumption – or argument – itself that Nyerere united Tanganyika with Zanzibar at the behest of the United States and Britain, and not on his own initiative, loses credibility.

In fact, recently declassified documents show that President Lyndon Johnson and members of his administration, as well as many – if not most – members of the United States Congress, were not comfortable with Nyerere's socialist beliefs and policies. According to a memo written by a National Security Council staff member, Ulric Haynes, on 8 June 1966:

"Under the mercurial and fiery independent leadership of Nyerere, Tanzania is the bastion of radicalism in East Africa.... Soviet and Chicom influence is considerable, especially in Zanzibar."[37]

According to the documents released, the Central

Intelligence Agency (CIA) was actively involved in covert operations in East Africa in the mid-sixties (and later, of course), although they don't specifically say what the activities were; no one expects them to, given the clandestine nature of their operations. But such explicit admission by the CIA of its activities in East Africa only corroborated some of the accusations made against the United States in her attempts to sow dissension in the region.

It also confirms the accusation by President Nyerere that the United States tried to undermine his government, leading to a deterioration of relations between the two countries and prompting the expulsion of American diplomats from Tanzania. As Nyerere himself stated in 1966:

"We have twice quarrelled with the US Government; once when we believed it to be involved in a plot against us, and again when two of its officials misbehaved and were asked to leave Tanzania....

The disagreements certainly induced an uncooperative coldness between us, thus suspending and then greatly slowing down further aid discussions. A comparison of American aid to Tanzania and other African countries supports the contention that at any rate our total policies (including support of the African liberation movements) have led to a lower level of assistance than might otherwise have been granted."[38]

It was later said the expulsion of the two American diplomats from Tanzania was based on false intelligence provided by the Russians – KGB agents based in Dar es Salaam – who worked with the Tanzanian authorities on the case which had been initiated by the Russians themselves.

But that does not change the fact that Nyerere did not flinch from making hard decisions – expelling American diplomats – and from taking a firm stand against the United States, or against any other power, if he had to; nor does it change the fact that the CIA did, at different times, try to undermine his government. The two diplomats, Frank Carlucci and Robert Gordon, were given 24 hours to leave Tanzania.

The United States itself, the most advanced country in the world and in the entire history of mankind, with highly sophisticated intelligence-gathering capabilities, has on a number of occasions taken decisive and even lethal action against its perceived enemies on the basis of false – even deliberately falsified – intelligence as happened in the case of Iraq when it invaded that country and became embroiled in a war which cost tens of thousands of lives to destroy "weapons of mass destruction" which did not even exist. It was later verified that Iraq never had those weapons which the United States used to justify its invasion. More than a decade later after the invasion, the Middle East is still in turmoil, with more lives – tens of thousands – lost, because of the decision by the Bush Administration to invade Iraq. The Islamic State (ISIS) is a product of that. There would have been no ISIS had the United States not invaded Iraq.

If the United States, a major world power, can make such a "mistake," what about a small and underdeveloped country like Tanzania making a mistake involving a case that required intelligence-gathering capabilities it did not even have? It is in that context that President Nyerere's decision should be looked at, as a rational decision any responsible leader would have made in the best interest of his country involving national security.

His decision was nothing to be ashamed of. It was based on the intelligence that was provided to him an his cabinet. He made an honest judgement based on the information he believed to be correct and which came from a credible source on a case that involved national security. Therefore, for anyone to suggest that his decision was hasty and irrational is to make an irrational judgement of what he did. And there was reason to be suspicious of the activities of the United States in Tanzania even with regard to the union of Tanganyika and Zanzibar.

Obviously because of his policies, the United States did not see Nyerere as an ally in the region and therefore had no reason to help him establish and consolidate a union – of Tanganyika and Zanzibar – except in strategic "partnership" to thwart communist advances, of which there were actually none, and about which Nyerere was not worried as he clearly demonstrated when he forged strong ties with Communist China and, to a lesser degree, with the Soviet Union and her satellites. If the United States had no strategic interests in the region, she would not have supported the union even if she knew formation of such a union would not militate against her interests.

In many fundamental respects, Nyerere's policies were the exact opposite of those of the United States. He was a socialist, opposed to capitalism. The United States was and still is capitalist, opposed to socialism. He was an implacable foe of apartheid South Africa and other white minority and colonial regimes on the continent – the Portuguese colonies of Angola, Mozambique, Guinea-Bissau and Cape Verde, and Principe and Sao Tome; Rhodesia (Zimbabwe); and South West Africa (Namibia) ruled by apartheid South Africa in defiance of United Nations resolutions which terminated its mandate to rule the former German colony. The United States, on the other hand, supported apartheid South Africa, Rhodesia, and Portugal as geopolitical and strategic allies during the Cold War and as a bulwark against communism in Africa – a red herring to perpetuate Western domination of the continent.

The United States also supported Portugal, a fellow NATO member, and refrained from criticising her policies in her African colonies because the Americans were allowed to maintain a military base on the Portuguese-controlled Azores islands in the Atlantic Ocean northwest of Africa. The United States and other Western countries also supported apartheid South Africa, Rhodesia, and Portugal for racist reasons, taking sides with their kith-and-kin regardless of the immorality of such a stance. As Nyerere bluntly stated in his article, "Rhodesia in the Context of Southern Africa," published in *Foreign Affairs*:

"The deep and intense anger of Africa on the subject of Rhodesia is by now widely realized. It is not, however, so clearly understood. In consequence the mutual suspicion, which already exists between free African states and nations of the West, is in danger of getting very much worse....

Successive Western governments have declared their hostility to apartheid, and their adherence to the principles of racial equality. They have frequently made verbal declarations of their sympathy with the forces in opposition to South African policies. But they have excused their failure to act in support of their words, on the grounds of South Africa's sovereignty. Africa has shown a great deal of scepticism about this argument, believing that it masked a reluctance to intervene on the side of justice when white privilege was involved. Now, in the case of Southern Rhodesia, legality is on the side of intervention. What is the West going to do? Will it justify or confound African suspicions?

So far the West has demonstrated its intentions by the gradual increase of voluntary economic sanctions; there has been a refusal even to challenge South African and Portuguese support for Smith by making sanctions mandatory upon all members of the United Nations. And there have been repeated statements by the responsible authority that force will not be used except in case of a break-down in law and order – which apparently does not cover the illegal seizure of power! What happens if the economic sanctions fail to bring down the Smith regime is left vague.

The suggestion therefore remains that, despite legality, the domination of a white minority over blacks is acceptable to the West....It is time...for Britain and the United States of America to make clear whether they really believe in the principles they claim to espouse, or whether their policies are governed by considerations of the privileges of their 'kith and kin.'"[39]

Therefore, whatever help Nyerere got from the United States and Britain to form the union of Tanganyika and Zanzibar – and there is no tangible evidence of that – it did not have any moderating influence on his Pan-African militancy. He continued to criticise the West, as he did the East, when he deemed it appropriate to do so. And his criticism was not confined to their policies towards Africa. For example, when the Warsaw Pact forces led by the Soviet Union invaded Czechoslovakia in August 1968, claiming they had been invited, Nyerere sharply responded: "Call an invasion, an invasion, not an invitation."[40]

The Tanzania government also issued a formal statement on 21 August 1968 condemning the invasion. According to Colin Legum and John Drsydale in *Africa Contemporary Record: Annual Survey and Documents 1968 – 1969*:

"The violation of Czechoslovakia's sovereignty by the Warsaw Pact countries evoked from Tanzania one of the strongest protests made by any African government. Expressing its 'profound shock,' the Tanzanian Government said that 'this act constitutes the betrayal of all the principles of self-determination and national sovereignty which the governments of these countries had claimed to support and uphold.'

The statement added that Tanzania opposed colonialism of all kinds, whether old or new, in Africa, in

Europe or elsewhere.

A week before the invasion of Czechoslovakia, the Tanzanian Government issued an unexpected warning to Communist countries not to interfere in Tanzania's internal affairs or external policies. *The Nationalist* (the daily newspaper of the ruling party TANU) said in an editorial that Tanzanians would not allow such interference just because their relations with some Western countries were strained. 'Let those Eastern countries who think they can do as they like in Tanzania take note of the fact that this is a free and independent nation, and it is determined to remain so'....

A protest note handed to the Soviet embassy in Dar es Salaam after a demonstration by TANU youths on August 21st demanded an immediate and unconditional withdrawal of the 'aggressive troops of the Soviet Union and her four satellite states from the territory of the Socialist Republic of Czechoslovakia'....

The demonstrators later went to the Czechoslovak embassy, where they expressed their sympathy at the suffering which the Czechoslovaks had been forced to endure under the oppressive hands of friends who have now turned against them."[41]

On American involvement in Vietnam, Nyerere had this to say:

"We are told that great principles are involved, and that the richest nation on earth is defending those principles against attack.

What are these principles? There is the principle of self-determination for the people of Vietnam. For twenty years, with unparalleled courage and determination, the people of Vietnam have been fighting for a chance to implement this principle – first against the French, and now against the Americans....(And) if this is a civil war, what are outside nations doing in that conflict?

Again, we are told that democracy is being defended, and only last month (September 1967) there were some 'elections' in South Vietnam. But these elections only covered the 'pacified areas,' and no candidate could stand on a clear platform of opposition to the war! And in any case these were the first elections since 1956, when South Vietnam came into existence, and no one could possibly call the governments of Mr. Diem, or his military successors, democratic.

Or we are told that the outside power responded to a request for assistance from a legitimate government, which was threatened by aggression. One can only look at the figures of soldiers operating in South Vietnam and ask whose aggression?...

The USA must recover from the delirium of power, and return to the principles upon which her nation was founded. Those millions of Americans who are now opposing their government's policies in this matter, and calling for peace, are working for the honour of their country."[42]

On Britain:

"We have quarrelled with the British Government on a number of issues, e.g. when we refused to associate ourselves with the Commonwealth communique on Rhodesia in June 1965; when we refused to support the proposed Commonwealth Peace Mission to Vietnam on the grounds that it was neither practical nor genuine; and when we received a Chinese offer to help with the building of the railway to Zambia while still discussing the possibility of British and American help on the same project."[43]

Tanzania was also the first African country to break diplomatic relations with Britain over Britain's unwillingness and refusal to take decisive action, including the use of military force, to end the rebellion by the white minority regime which illegally declared independence in Rhodesia on 11 November 1965.

On relations with West Germany, Nyerere stated:

"East Germany wanted Tanzania to give diplomatic recognition to her, and West Germany wanted us to ignore the existence of the German Democratic Republic and pretend there is no such administration over the Eastern part of Germany.

In fact we refused recognition to the East German authorities but accepted an unofficial Consulate General from them – a formula which had been accepted in one other African country.

As a result of our decision West Germany withdrew some types of aid – unilaterally breaking a five-year air training agreement – and announced that other aid was under threat if Tanzania did not change her policies. Tanzania refused to do this and told the West Germans to withdraw all their federal government aid."[44]

Nyerere continued to pursue an independent, non-aligned, foreign policy throughout his tenure as president of Tanzania just as he did when he was president of Tanganyika before the union with Zanzibar in April 1964. The union only widened the scope of his activities because of the merger itself as a subject of major interest in diplomatic circles and other international forums; also because it was the first union of independent states on the African continent, setting a precedent; and because of the controversy over Zanzibar as a potential communist outpost, and the revolution itself as a phenomenal event in the history of African decolonisation hailed across the continent for its Pan-African militancy.

And despite Nyerere's own commitment to African unity which inspired him to unite Tanganyika with Zanzibar, the political dynamics in the island nation itself also played an important role in facilitating the establishment of the union.

Therefore, even if Tanganyika did not have a leader of Nyerere's calibre and depth of Pan-African commitment, the unstable situation in Zanzibar only a few miles from the mainland – 24 miles or so – would perhaps have encouraged or compelled another leader to seek such a merger himself or herself, even if it was just for the security of the mainland without any concern for African unity.

And there is concern for security. Even today, in the minds of many Tanzanian leaders on the mainland, of paramount importance in the formation of the union was security for the mainland. Many of them, even Nyerere himself, may not have explicitly said so. But there is no question that in addition to Nyerere's quest for Pan-African solidarity in pursuit of regional and continental unity, security of the mainland and the entire region was also a major concern.

A radical or an unstable state just a few miles offshore which could destabilise the mainland and may be even spread chaos to other parts of East Africa, but especially to what was then Tanganyika, could not be tolerated by any leader on the mainland.

What if the island nation were to be torn by civil strife? What if it degenerated into chaos? Where would the people flee? Where would the islanders seek refuge?

What if an independent Zanzibar had a radical government and radical leaders across the spectrum – social and political – who wanted to spread their brand of radicalism and teachings to the mainland to upset the social order in order to have leaders who shared their social and political beliefs? What would the mainlanders have to do to ensure their own security, that they were safe from such upheavals, considering Zanzibar's close proximity to the mainland?

The best way to contain and even neutralise such

radicalism, any form of radicalism coming from Zanzibar, was to unite the two countries, and continue to maintain the union even today.

Had Zanzibar been 300 miles away in the Indian Ocean, it would have been an entirely different story. You could see the boats coming, after getting advance warning from the mainland's surveillance of her territorial waters that they were on the way, giving the mainland's authorities ample time to stop or intercept them. As Joseph Warioba who concurrently served as prime minister and vice president of Tanzania from 1985 to 1990 said in an interview in 1996, the mainland wanted to maintain the union for security reasons even decades after it was formed. According to Mohammed Ali Bakari in his book, *The Democratisation Process in Zanzibar: A Retarded Transition*:

"Joseph Warioba, former Prime Minister, for example, was asked as to why the Mainland is not willing to part with Zanzibar given the fact that the latter has on some occasions violated the agreements of the Union, and economically, it is a burden to the Union government for its failure to pay its share of costs in the running the Union government? And he categorically responded:

'Even if economically we do not gain anything from the Union, we are highly concerned with security implications. We cannot afford to dismantle the Union. Zanzibar is just a few miles from the mainland – the security of the mainland may be destabilized.'

A supplementary question was posed by another participant (in a discussion in Hamburg, Germany) as to how he could justify such fear when Zanzibar is a very small country with a population of only 800,000 and Tanganyika has a population of 27 million. Again, he responded: 'It might be that our fear cannot be justified, but certainly we have that perception.'"45

Perception is reality even if it does not correspond to reality. But in the case of the mainland and Zanzibar, concerning fear among some mainlanders for the mainland's security if Zanzibar were to become an outpost of instability and insecurity, that is the reality. One Tanzanian scholar, Mwesiga Baregu, went even further by being more explicit:

"It is quite clear to me that Tanganyika would not feel secure with an offshore Zanzibar controlled by Oman (where the former rulers of Zanzibar came from) or hosting a U.S. Naval or airforce base. Neither would Zanzibari indigenous nationalism – which precipitated the 1964 revolution – tolerate such a situation. The result would likely be chaos and internecine conflicts which would inevitably engulf at least both countries, if the ten-mile strip on the East coast of Kenya does not become an issue!!"46

What Professor Baregu calls "indigenous nationalism" is a euphemism for black African nationalism on the former island nation which is overwhelmingly black. The Zanzibar revolution can not be justified without them because of the social, political and economic injustices they suffered at the hands of the Arab rulers who were overthrown during the 1964 upheaval.

Although Tanganyika united with Zanzibar to form one country, the union was not a complete merger in all areas. Zanzibar retained its status as a separate entity, with its own identity, while Tanganyika lost hers and no longer exists as a political entity – not even as a geographical region. What was once known as Tanganyika is now simply known as mainland Tanzania or Tanzania mainland. But both countries lost their sovereignties when they united to form Tanzania. Their sovereignties were submerged in a larger entity, the macro-nation of Tanzania, although Zanzibar still exists as a political and geographical entity – but not as a sovereign state despite claims by some Zanzibari "nationalists" that Zanzibar is a separate country and an independent nation.

There is no such thing. Zanzibar is not a sovereign state anymore; it is not a country, and it is not an independent nation as it used to be. It is an integral part of the United Republic of Tanzania, although not as an administrative region or province. It is semi-autonomous.

But Zanzibar is semi-autonomous only because it does not enjoy international recognition as a legal sovereign entity. In reality, it is autonomous. It enjoys great autonomy, which is not equivalent to being semi-autonomous. It has its own government with complete jurisdiction in many areas. It has its own president who is not subordinate to the union president in many areas. It even has its own flag, and its own constitution which differs from the union constitution in many respects including its definition of Zanzibar as a separate country, not a part of another country, even though it is no longer an independent state.

Even Zanzibaris who support the union have, together with their brethren who are against it, always insisted on maintaining their separate identity as Zanzibaris. They also contend that Zanzibar is still a separate country even if it is an integral part of the United Republic of Tanzania. And there are those who want to break up the union. They want to return to the status quo ante when Zanzibar was an independent nation enjoying full international recognition because of its sovereign status.

Zanzibaris will *never* give up their identity as Zanzibaris. Many of them don't even want to call themselves Tanzanians, an identity they contend was imposed on them when they were forced into a union with Tanganyika.

But there are those who support the union. One of

them is Ali Karume, a son of Zanzibar's first president, Abeid Karume. He is a vocal supporter of the union and is resolutely opposed to the restructuring of the union which would lead to the establishment of three governments: a union government, a government for Zanzibar which already exists, and a government for Tanganyika, all separate with distinct jurisdictions. Like Nyerere who was also strongly opposed the three-tier government system for Tanzania which he said would signal the end of the union, Ali Karume contends that creation of three governments will lead to dissolution of the union which will not last even five years if the three-tier government structure is adopted.

He reiterated that position in July 2013 in an interview with the *Guardian*, Dar es Salaam, and in other forums. He articulated the same position together with many other Tanzanians on the union's 50th anniversary in April 2014.

During his presidency, Benjamin Mkapa issued probably the strongest warning ever given by a Tanzanian leader to those who want to disrupt the union. He emphatically stated that the government will do everything it can to protect the union even if it has to be ruthless. There will be no mercy for those who are trying to destroy it.

His strong warning was directed at the opposition, especially the Civic United Front (CUF) which is opposed to the union, and others who are against it.

The CUF also refused to recognise his victory after he won a second term in 2000.

He hailed the union as "a symbol of unity in the whole of Africa."[47]

There is no question that there is strong opposition to the union itself and to the two-government structure on both sides of the union. But the strongest opposition comes from Zanzibar. Therefore something must to done to resolve the matter.

In order for the union to continue to exist as a stable

entity, there is an imperative need to make major concessions to Zanzibaris.

Give them what they want, short of total independence, by granting them extensive autonomy in many areas – except vital ones such as security (intelligence services, police, and the military), immigration, foreign affairs, and monetary policy under which they can not have their own currency and their own central bank. There must be one currency, and one central bank, for the whole country: the United Republic of Tanzania.

That is probably one of the best ways to neutralise secessionist sentiments in the isles.

The union government, especially mainland leaders, must face this reality. Without extensive devolution, expect agitation and even unrest to continue in Zanzibar with some spillover on to the mainland.

The key is greater autonomy for Zanzibar. If that does not work, form a confederation as a last resort, but with a strong central government, and a constitutional provision which allows secession – only if wishes to secede have been determined in an internationally supervised plebiscite to be the expression of the majority of Zanzibaris. Mainlanders should be accorded the same right. That is the only way the union can be dissolved on amicable terms.

But for their own security, mainlanders should do everything they can – never to allow Zanzibar to secede. Zanzibar is not the Seychelles, Mauritius or the Comoros separated from the mainland by vast expanses of water of the mighty Indian Ocean. It's next door. It takes only simple canoes to get to the mainland.

Should the isles degenerate into anarchy or become an incubator and breeding ground for subversive elements bent on spreading chaos to the mainland in pursuit of their own agenda or whatever objectives they want to achieve, the mainland will be in danger.

Subversive elements can easily get to the mainland and

cause trouble, with Dar es Salaam, the largest city and commercial centre – and which for all practical purposes still is the capital of Tanzania – being the primary target in order to send shock waves and create panic throughout the mainland. They don't have to hit any other parts of the country. All they need is to hit the nerve centre, Dar, to paralyse the entire mainland. The country could be destabilised for years.

Denying Zanzibar greater autonomy through extensive devolution of power can only radicalise those elements even further and fuel secessionist sentiments in the isles. As a last resort, the only way they can be contained or neutralised is by military occupation of Zanzibar – a prospect too ghastly to contemplate – which in the end will mean the end of the union itself. Not only will it destroy the union; the mainland would have to be prepared to face even more enemies from the isles who have been radicalised by the injustices they have suffered as a result of the military occupation of their homeland by the union forces.

So, listen to Zanzibaris. They know what they want. Give them what they want – but within prescribed limits, taking into account security concerns of the mainland which were also major concerns on the part of Tanganyika when the union with Zanzibar was formed. But they were not the only reason Nyerere decided to unite the two countries.

However, there is no question that the revolution in Zanzibar was a major catalyst towards unification. But the revolution itself must be looked at in its proper context from an African perspective and without being blinded by ideological biases.

The Zanzibar revolution took place in the midst of the Cold War. Therefore, the communist threat could not have been ignored anymore than a threat from the West could have been: penetration and domination of the island nation by the United States and other Western powers after the revolution to secure their geopolitical and strategic interests in the region and keep the Russians and the Chinese out.

A threat to independence from the West is no more benign than a threat from the East; a "subtle" distinction that still seems to elude many Westerners, including political pundits, who think the West is a paragon of virtue and had the right to intervene and control Zanzibar to make sure the island nation was not dominated by the Russians or the Chinese and their local communist stooges.

Western domination of Africa was not a blessing. Otherwise African countries would have been happy to remain under colonial rule and would never have fought for independence.

It is also important to look at Zanzibar from another African perspective on why the union was important for black Zanzibaris who constituted the vast majority of the population in the island nation.

There was a racial element in the quest for unity between Tanganyika and Zanzibar. Black people in Zanzibar had been oppressed by the Arabs for centuries. The oppression included outright enslavement of blacks not only on the islands but also on the mainland which was the source of slaves who were taken to Zanzibar and beyond. Indigenous blacks themselves, in Zanzibar, trace their origin to the mainland from where they migrated many centuries ago.

The January 1964 revolution won them freedom. But with freedom was the residual fear that their former masters could reclaim the islands one day and re-institute tyranny with the help of the Arab states, especially the Gulf States, Oman in particular where the majority of the Arabs in Zanzibar including the sultanate came from.

Their only hope for security was a union with Tanganyika, a country much bigger and stronger than Zanzibar, and with more than 20 times the population, also mostly black just like the vast majority of the Zanzibaris themselves.

Security was undoubtedly a factor when the black leaders of Zanzibar promptly agreed to the merger, with Zanzibari President Abeid Karume calling for total unification; a formula rejected by Nyerere who felt that total renunciation of sovereignty by Zanzibar, without retaining extensive autonomy, would destabilise the union and even lead to its dissolution.

Therefore, the union was a product of a combination of factors, internal and external, but mostly internal. As Samir Amin said in the First Babu Memorial Lecture in honour of the late Abdulrahman Mohammed Babu (22 September 1924 – 5 August 1996), one of the "architects" of the Zanzibar revolution, in London on 22 September 1997:

"For me, speaking about Babu is speaking, not only of a comrade and an elder but of a personal friend whom I knew right from the post-war period – the whole of our generation in Africa. Babu was someone with whom I shared most political views for something like 40 years....

It was in London, in 1952, that we first met. Babu was then, like me, a young student, he was elder to me by a few years which at that point of time seemed a considerable difference – later of course the difference lost most of its meaning.

We were both very active among African students in Britain and France trying to start a unified movement.... Babu was connected to the East African anti-colonialist committee....

Babu did better than I (did in Egypt) because he was able... to participate in the creation of objective forces in his country – Zanzibar – which led to a revolution in January 1964, which potentially at least could go beyond nationalist populism.

I knew of course what Babu thought of all this. We had

been on the board of a magazine, *Revolution*, which was published in 62/63 i.e. just before the Zanzibar revolution.... We worked, both of us, with others on that magazine, to look at precisely this question. Is it possible and if so under what conditions for nationalist populism to move to the left?... provided the popular classes organised independently go into conflict with the system and go ahead. Babu tried to do this in Zanzibar with some success.... (The) merger...(of) Zanzibar with Tanganyika to form Tanzania...partly...was for reasons internal to Tanzania (Tanganyika) and Zanzibar."[48]

Even without external forces, internal factors alone – "reasons internal to Tanzania (Tanganyika) and Zanzibar," as Samir Amin put it, which also led to the merger of the two countries – constituted sufficient ground for the establishment of the union. But without the Zanzibar revolution, which was an expression of the collective sentiments of frustrated and downtrodden blacks, especially the young, the union of the two countries would probably not have taken place when it did.

The revolution provided a powerful impetus to the merger of the two predominantly black nations, and the leader of the revolution, self-styled Field Marshal John Okello originally from Uganda, provided an equally powerful rallying point for the frustrated black masses groaning under Arab oppression.

The ouster of the oppressive Arab regime was carried out by only a few hundred men – figures range from 300 to 600, but it probably was 300 – led by John Okello.

But after they seized the radio station and other vital installations including the police station where they seized more weapons, and Okello went on the air to announce the takeover, the majority of the African population welcomed the change and rallied behind the freedom fighters giving overwhelming support to the revolution.

Although the Afro-Shirazi Party (ASP) which

represented African interests did not participate in the initial phase of the revolution, including its actual planning and launching, it immediately gave full support to the uprising and acted as the official organ articulating the sentiments of the downtrodden black masses. It was joined by the Umma (People's) Party of Abdulrahman Mohammed Babu with which it went on to form a coalition government.

Thousands of supporters of the revolution and the Afro-Shirazi Party (ASP) struck back at their former oppressors, attacking landowners and merchants – who were mostly Arab and Indian – and their property including private homes. The killings spread further to include ordinary Arabs and Asians by virtue of their position as members of the oppressive races. In addition to the hundreds killed, thousands fled the islands and sought refuge elsewhere in Arab countries, Europe, Asia, and even in Africa itself. Many fled to Tanganyika as well, as they did to Kenya. In fact, the sultan of Zanzibar himself and his family and others fled to Dar es Salaam, Tanganyika, after they were denied entry into Kenya, at Mombasa, where they first sought refuge. Many other people also fled to the Comoro Islands.

Many of those targeted in the uprising were also originally from the Comoros, an island nation which has had historical ties with Zanzibar – and even with mainland Tanzania, formerly Tanganyika – for centuries. The Comorians are mostly of mixed Arab-Malay-African ancestry. And in the racially stratified society of Zanzibar, they were also, together with the Arabs and the Asians – mostly Indian – above blacks.

Also, in addition to the historical ties between the Comoros and Zanzibar, there are also racial ties, especially Arab, and linguistic ties. The main languages spoken in the Comoros are Shikomori and Arabic. Shikomori is heavily influenced by Arabic. It is also influenced by Kiswahili which is itself heavily influenced by Arabic, just like in Zanzibar. French is also spoken in the Comoros and is one of the official languages since the islands were once a French colony.

But in spite of the fact that many Comorians have African ancestry, they did not in general sympathise with the plight of black people in Zanzibar since they were members of a different "racial stock," or ethnic group, a confluence of three tributaries: Arab, Malay, and African. And because of their higher status in Zanzibar, as well as contempt for blacks they shared with the Arabs and the Indians, they were some of the primary targets during the revolution.

Estimates of the number killed vary. Some put it even as high as 20,000. But after some extrapolation, it was obviously in the hundreds; may be no fewer than 2,000.

It was virtually a one-sided conflict, with black Africans having the upper hand after Okello and his men seized weapons from the police station they had overtaken. Most of those killed were Arab. Although Indians, Comorians and other minorities were some of the victims, they did not perish in large numbers as the Arabs did.

It was one of the bloodiest conflicts in the history of post-colonial Africa and one of the most well-known. But out of this bloodshed emerged a new nation, born out of a merger of two countries, Tanganyika and Zanzibar, a union that would probably not have been formed when it was, had the revolution not taken place, prompting the Zanzibari Africans to seek immediate protection from Tanganyikans for their newly won freedom by uniting with them; lest their former oppressors launch a counter-attack some time in the future and re-impose tyranny on the islands.

Concern for security by blacks in Zanzibar; a deteriorating economic situation in the island nation; willingness – after some heated debate – of their leaders to unite with Tanganyika; the unstable political situation on the isles; Nyerere's desire to eliminate any threat to

Tanganyika that may come from an unstable, economically non-viable and weak neighbour whose weakness would have provided an opportunity for external forces to intervene and dominate the island nation – and that included possible intervention by the West, not just by the East; and his desire to unite all the countries in the region, probably more than anything else; all these factors combined to facilitate the unification of Tanganyika and Zanzibar on 26 April 1964, only three-and-half months after the revolution on January 12th, leading to the establishment of the first union of independent states in Africa, a feat that has not been duplicated anywhere else on the continent.

After the union, Tanzania also became one of the most stable and peaceful countries in Africa under the leadership of Julius Nyerere. Before the union, he had also presided over the establishment and growth of Tanganyika, one of the most ethnically diverse countries on the continent, yet which became one of the most cohesive states in the history of post-colonial Africa.

But in spite of all these achievements, most of Nyerere's critics give him little credit for them, focusing, instead, on his failed economic policies he pursued along socialist lines.

There is no question that his socialist policies were a failure in many cases, good intentions notwithstanding; something even his admirers should admit, as many of them indeed do. There is evidence of that. There is also evidence of his achievements in many areas including economic, not just social.

He did his best – which he himself once said would be a fitting epitaph for him after he died – and definitely meant well, as clearly demonstrated by his deep concern for the wellbeing of the masses which even had a saintly dimension in spite of all his flaws as a mere mortal like the rest of us, including hallowed saints, and one of the most humble, unlike most.

But his achievements must also be acknowledged and not overlooked or deliberately ignored because of what his critics consider to be his failed socialist policies. As Professor Ali Mazrui stated in his tribute to Nyerere at Cornell University in October 1999:

"Julius Kambarage Nyerere's radical thought was multifaceted. He began as an anticolonial African nationalist on his return home, seeking the independence of Tanganyika....

Linked to Nyerere's nationalism from quite early was his Pan-Africanism, a commitment to the pursuit of African unity and the adoption of the principle of African solidarity whenever possible. Sometimes he put his Pan-Africanism ahead of his Tanganyika nationalism, as when in 1960 he offered to delay Tanganyika's independence if this would help achieve the creation of an East African federation of Tanganyika, Kenya and Uganda. In the end, there was not enough political will in the other two countries – Kenya and Uganda – to achieve such a union. African researchers need to investigate why it has been so difficult to achieve regional integration.

Nevertheless, Tanganyika played host to other major Pan-African activities. It became a frontline state for the liberation of southern Africa from Portuguese rule and from white minority governments. Politically the colony for a while hosted the Pan-African Freedom Movement for Eastern, Central and Southern Africa (PAFMECSA). Tanganyika subsequently established major training camps for southern African liberation fighters.

Much later, Nyerere's Tanzania hosted the sixth Pan-African Congress (in 1974 at the University of Dar es Salaam, in Nkrumah Hall, named after another ardent Pan-Africanist leader), an attempt to re-establish the solidarity of Africa and its diaspora worldwide. This was the first of the Pan-African Congresses actually to be held in Africa. The fifth was in Manchester in 1945, with participants who included Kwame Nkrumah, Jomo Kenyatta, W.E.B. DuBois, and George Padmore. The Dar es Salaam Congress of 1974 was in a great Pan-African tradition....

Domestically in Tanzania he inaugurated three reforms – a political system based on the principle of the one-party state, an economic system based on an African approach to socialism – what he called ujamaa, or familyhood – and a cultural system based on the Swahili language.

The cultural policy based on Kiswahili was the earliest and most durable. Tanganyika – and later Tanzania – became one of the few African countries to use an indigenous language in parliament and as the primary language of national business.

Kiswahili was increasingly promoted in politics, administration, education, and the media. It became a major instrument of nation-building, and nation-building became the most lasting of Nyerere's legacies. Yet, Africana researchers have done little work on Nyerere's best contribution....

Why did ujamaa fail? Was it domestic factors? Was it external pressures? Was Nyerere building socialism without socialists? We need a postmortem on ujamaa....

(Also) Nyerere's Tanganyika did form a union with Zanzibar. This remains the only case in Africa of previoulsy sovereign states uniting into a new country – and surviving as one entity more than three decades. What used to be sovereign Tanganyika and Zanzibar became the United Republic of Tanzania in 1964.

Nyerere strengthened the union when he united the ruling Afro-Shirazi Party of Zanzibar with the ruling party of Tanganyika (TANU – Tanganyika African National Union – in 1977) to form the new Chama Cha Mapinduzi, the Party of the Revolution.

Will this union of Zanzibar and Tanganyika survive Nyerere's death? Once again have Africana scholars done enough to find out why Africans find it so hard to unite?

Has Nyerere's political behaviour sometimes reflected

his upbringing as a Roman Catholic?

One school of thought explains his recognition of the secessionist Biafra in 1969 as a form of solidarity with fellow Catholics against a Federal Nigeria, which would have been dominated by Muslims. This was in the middle of the Nigerian civil war. The Igbo of Biafra were overwhelmingly Roman Catholic. It seems much more likely that Nyerere recognized Biafra for humanitarian reasons.

What about the assertion that Nyerere's military intervention in Uganda in 1979 was motivated by a sectarian calculation to defend a mainly Christian Uganda from the Muslim dictator, Idi Amin? In reality, Nyerere might once again have been more motivated by a wider sense of humanitarianism and universal ethics. He was also defending Tanzania from Idi Amin's territorial appetites.

Most Western judges of Julius Nyerere have concentrated on his economic policies and their failures. Ujamaa and villagisation have been seen as forces of economic retardation that kept Tanzania backward for at least another decade.

Not enough commentators have paid attention to Nyerere's achievements in nation-building. He gave Tanzanians a sense of national consciousness and a spirit of national purpose. One of the poorest countries in the world found itself to be one of the major actors on the world scene.

Nyerere's policies of making Kiswahili the national language of Tanzania deepened this sense of Tanzania's national consciousness and cultural pride. Parliament in Dar es Salaam debated exclusively in Kiswahili. Government business was increasingly conducted in Kiswahili. The mass media turned away from English in favour of Kiswahili. Newspapers had not only letters to the editor but also poems to the editor in Kiswahili. And the educational system was experiencing the stresses and strains of the competing claims of English and Kiswahili.

Nyerere's translation of two of Shakespeare's plays into Kiswahili was done not because he 'loved Shakespeare less, but because he loved Kiswahili more.' He translated Shakespeare into Kiswahili partly to demonstrate that the Swahili language was capable of carrying the complexities of a genius of another civilization.

Above all, Nyerere as president was a combination of deep intellect and high integrity...(and) was in a class by himself in the combination of ethical standards and intellectual power. In the combination of high thinking and high ethics, no other East African politician was in the same league."[49]

That is probably an understatement. Hardly any other politician on the entire continent was in the same league with Nyerere in terms of high ethical standards and intellectual prowess; a rare combination. As Professor Mazrui himself stated – almost ten years after Nyerere died – in an interview with *The Gambia Echo* in July 2008:

"Intellectually, I admired Julius K. Nyerere of Tanzania higher than most politicians anywhere in the world. Nyerere and I also met more often over the years from 1967 to 1997 approximately.

I am also a great fan of Nelson Mandela. By ethical standards Mandela is greater than Nyerere; but by intellectual standards Nyerere is greater than Mandela."[50]

Nyerere's most enduring legacy is the nation he left behind as a united, stable entity; a phenomenon rare on the continent.

It all started with Tanganyika. He built Tanganyika into a cohesive state out of more than 126 different tribes and racial minority groups including Arabs, Asians, and

Europeans. And he went on to create a larger nation, Tanzania, by uniting Tanganyika with Zanzibar during some of the most tempestuous times in Africa's post-colonial era.

By the time he died, the union had survived 35 years. And it will always be remembered as one of his biggest achievements. Yet, as Nyerere himself conceded:

"My greatest success is also my greatest disappointment. We have established a nation – Tanzania – that is some achievement. Stable, united, proud with immense clarity of what it wants to do, committed to the liberation of our continent. It has played an immense role, poor as it is, in the liberation of our continent and it will continue playing it.

So that is what I think is our greatest achievement. But it is also our failure. I never wanted a Tanzania. I really do not believe that these African countries should establish different sovereignties. They are artificial creations, all of them."[51]

Africa is a natural entity. Achieving African unity is a goal to which he dedicated his life. As he said in Accra where he was invited by President Jerry Rawlings in 1997 to celebrate the 40th anniversary of Ghana's independence: "We are all Africans trying very hard to be Ghanaians or Tanzanians."[52]

He made that remark in a country whose founding father, Dr. Kwame Nkrumah, was one of the most uncompromising advocates of African unity and independence – twin Pan-African goals – and an ideological compatriot of Nyerere. As the first black African country to win independence since the partition of Africa at the Berlin Conference in 1885, Ghana set a precedent and became a source of inspiration to other African countries in their struggle to end colonial rule.

Liberia was, of course, the first black African country

to attain republican status, but in name only, and remained a virtual American colony throughout its history, as it still is even today: a client state, or America's "51st state" like Puerto Rico.

While Nkrumah blazed the trail for the African independence movement by being the first leader of the first black African country to attain sovereign status, Nyerere also set a precedent by being the first leader on the continent to unite two independent countries to create one nation, Tanzania; and the first East African leader to lead his country to independence. And while Nkrumah preceded Nyerere in political activism and in the struggle for independence – born on 22 September 1909, and Nyerere on 13 April 1922, he was his senior by almost 13 years – the two became peers in the post-colonial era and two of the most influential African leaders in the twentieth century besides Nelson Mandela; with Nyerere also earning the title, "The Conscience of Africa."

Yet, characteristic of his humility, he paid great tribute to Nkrumah when he visited Ghana after he stepped down as president of Tanzania. According to a Ugandan newspaper, *The Monitor*:

"Mwalimu Julius Nyerere paid a visit to Ghana shortly after his retirement in 1985 and reportedly berated the leadership of that country for the shabby way in which the republic's founder, Kwame Nkrumah, had been treated: 'This man is one of the greatest Africans that has ever lived. If you in Ghana don't respect him, the rest of us in Africa do. Independent Africa owes its liberty to this man. The least you can do is...give him a decent burial.'"[53]

Nyerere also acknowledged the inspiration he drew from Nkrumah when he was still a student at Edinburgh University in Scotland earning his master's degree in economics and history, while Nkrumah was leading the independence struggle in Ghana. And in one of his last interviews in December 1998, about a year before he died, Nyerere remembered Nkrumah and talked about the relationship they had in the quest for African unity and independence. He also talked about his attempts to form an East African Federation with Mzee Jomo Kenyatta and Dr. Milton Obote. The interview was published in *The New Internationalist*:

"It was events in Ghana in 1949 that fundamentally changed my attitude. When Kwame Nkrumah was released from prison, this produced a transformation. I was in Britain and, oh, you could see it in the Ghanaians! They became different human beings, different from all the rest of us! This thing of freedom began growing inside all of us. First India in 1947, then Ghana in 1949. Ghana became independent eight years later.

Under the influence of these events, while I was at university in Britain, I made up my mind to be a full-time political activist when I went back home. I intended to work for three years and then launch into politics. But it happened sooner than I planned....

For me liberation and unity were the most important things. I have always said that I was African first and socialist second. I would rather see a free and united Africa before a fragmented socialist Africa. I did not preach socialism. I made this distinction deliberately so as not to divide the country. The majority in the anti-colonial struggle were nationalist. There was a minority who argued that class was the central issue, that white workers were exploited as black workers by capitalism. They wanted to approach liberation in purely Marxist terms. However, in South Africa white workers oppressed black workers. It was more than class and I saw that....

Even now for me freedom and unity are paramount.... I respected Jomo (Kenyatta) immensely. It has probably never happened in history. Two heads of state, Milton Obote and I, went to Jomo and said to him: 'Let's unite our countries and you be our head of state.' He said no. I think he said no because it would have put him out of his element as a Kikuyu Elder....

It seems that independence of the former colonies has suited the interests if the industrial world for bigger profits at less cost. Independence made it cheaper for them to exploit us. We became neo-colonies. Some African leaders did not realize it. In fact many argued against Kwame (Nkrumah's) idea of neo-colonialism....

Let us create a new liberation movement to free us from immoral debt and neo-colonialism. This is one way forward. The other is through Pan-African unity....

Kwame Nkrumah and I were committed to the idea of unity. African leaders and heads of state did not take Kwame seriously. However, I did. I did not believe in these small little nations. Still today I do not believe in them. I tell our people to look at the European Union, at these people who ruled us who are now uniting.

Kwame and I met in 1963 and discussed African Unity. We differed on how to achieve a United States of Africa. But we both agreed on a United States of Africa as necessary. Kwame went to Lincoln University, a black college in the US. He perceived things from the perspective of US history, where 13 colonies that revolted against the British formed a union. That is what he thought the OAU (Organization of African Unity) should do.

I tried to get East Africa to unite before independence. When we failed in this way, I was wary about Kwame's continental approach. We corresponded profusely on this. Kwame said my idea of 'regionalization' was only balkanization on a larger scale. Later, African historians will have to study our correspondence on this issue of uniting Africa.

Africans who studied in the US like Nkrumah and Azikiwe were more aware of the Diaspora and the global African community than those of us who studied in Britain. They were therefore aware of a wider Pan-

Africanism. Theirs was the aggressive Pan-Africanism of W.E.B. DuBois and Marcus Garvey. The colonialists were against this and frightened of it.

After independence, the wider African community became clear to me. I was concerned about education; the work of Booker T. Washington resonated with me. There were skills we needed and black people outside Africa had them. I gave our US Ambassador the specific job of recruiting skilled Africans from the US Diaspora. A few came, like you (the interviewer, Ikaweba Bunting, who had lived in Tanzania for 25 years when he interviewed Nyerere in his home village of Butiama where he returned in 1985 after stepping down from the presidency and buried in 1999). Some stayed; others left.

We should try to revive it (Pan-Africanism). We should look to our brothers and sisters in the West. We should build the broader Pan-Africanism. There is still the room – and the need."[54]

The Pan-Africanism Nyerere talked about embraced people of African descent in the diaspora, as did Nkrumah's. It also assumed another dimension when the Organisation of African Unity (OAU) was replaced by the African Union (AU) in 2001, which was formally launched in 2002; the diaspora was represented in the OAU as it is in the AU.

The transformation was intended to facilitate continental unification, and strengthen institutions of regional cooperation and Pan-African integration, leading to the establishment of a common market, a common currency, a continental parliament, a Pan-African court and an executive body as an enforcement mechanism responsible for implementing decisions binding on all countries across the continent which the OAU never had.

And although the Ghana-Guinea union and later the Ghana-Guinea-Mali union – formed by Kwame Nkrumah, Sekou Toure, and Modibo Keita – were more symbolic than functional, they served to inspire other Africans across the continent to pursue regional integration and keep the dream of African unity alive.

The most successful of these efforts was, of course, the union of Tanganyika and Zanzibar formed by Julius Nyerere after he failed to convince the leaders of Kenya and Uganda – especially Kenya – to unite with Tanganyika and establish an East African Federation.

And even if the union were to collapse, if secessionist elements (especially with ties to Oman and other Gulf States) in the former island nation of Zanzibar are not neutralised through extensive devolution of power and formation of coalition government or some other institutional arrangements but without unconditional accommodation for separatists, it will still be remembered as one of Nyerere's biggest achievements; and one of the most ambitious experiments in regional integration on the African continent and in post-colonial history anywhere in the world. As he said in an interview with the *Black World*, an African-American journal, in the early seventies when he was asked how he would like to be remembered after he died, he hoped that people would say: "He did his best."

The Zanzibar Revolution and the Union of Tanganyika and Zanzibar: Reappraisal

THE Zanzibar revolution was one of the most significant events in the history of post-colonial Africa.

It was a victory in the struggle for African liberation; it brought fundamental change in Zanzibar; and it helped pave the way for the political union between Tanganyika and Zanzibar which was a major political transformation in the history of the continent.

On 12 January 1964, the Arab rulers of Zanzibar were overthrown in a revolution which went down in history as one of the bloodiest conflicts up to that time in Africa since the end of colonial rule, involving change of government by unconstitutional means.

The armed uprising was led by John Okello, a self-styled field marshal originally from Uganda who had lived in the island nation, on Pemba island, since 1959. He was born in Uganda in 1937 and also lived in Kenya for a few years.

After he moved to Pemba, he became a policeman and joined the Afro-Shirazi Party (ASP) led by Sheikh Abeid Amani Karume. He moved from Pemba to Zanzibar in 1963 where he started preparing secretly for a revolution to end Arab rule.

During the revolution, Okello led a group of about 300 men to seize power from the Arab rulers and overthrew Sultan Sayyid Jamshid bin Abdullah. Jamshid Abdullah, 35, ascended the throne after his father died. Okello was 26.

The people he recruited for the revolution were young men who were also members or supporters of the Afro-Shirazi Party which resented Arab domination. He had been meeting with some of them secretly for some time to prepare for the revolution. And they made history the following year.

When I was writing one of my books, *Nyerere and Africa: End of an Era* in 2002, I got in touch with one of the people who used to live in Zanzibar and who witnessed what happened on the island when the revolution took place. I asked him some questions and he sent me some information. He did not tell me back then exactly who or what he was when he was in Zanzibar. He said he was not a Zanzibari or a Tanzanian but an American – that is all he said to me in terms of his identity. I found out later he was the American consul in Zanzibar during the revolution and later served as the American ambassador to Tanzania. He explained the following in "The Zanzibar Revolution" which he also made publicly available:

"On the night of January 12, 1964 a band of some 300 people violently seized the Island of Unguja. They were led by a little known man named John Okello, who had lived on Pemba, having come to the islands some years earlier from Uganda.

In Zanzibar he developed a popular following among a core of young, tough men, many of whom were the Stevedores and Porters who worked the ships coming in and out of Zanzibar Harbor.

His group met in secret. He promised changes to these men, fellows long used to working together, in sometimes dangerous settings, and ready to follow orders of any 'captain' who could pay their fee. Theirs became a rebellion looking for a home.

Political unrest had been increasing on Zanzibar and Pemba since the death of Sultan Khalifa in 1960. He had reigned in Zanzibar for almost 50 years, since 1911.

After much jockeying for constituencies and coalitions the main political parties had narrowly split the two general elections of 1961 to the satisfaction of none. The British were leaving, their troops, including a contingent of Irish Guards, stationed near the golf course at the edge of Stone Town, pulled out in early 1963.

When the new Sultan, Jamshid, hoisted the flag of the independent nation of Zanzibar, on December 10, 1963, he marked the departure of the last British Resident, (Governor) of Zanzibar and the end of the colonial period.

Another election in late 1963 had given a slim majority to a coalition of two political parties, the ZNP (the Zanzibar Nationalist Party) and the ZPPP (the Zanzibar and Pemba Peoples Party). The ASP (the Afro-Shirazi Party) was to be in the minority in a British style parliamentary system with the sultan serving as the reigning but not ruling 'monarch.'

This nation, a full member of the British Commonwealth and a newly enrolled sovereign member of the United Nations was destined to last only 33 days.

Political debates raged and street demonstrations were not uncommon in those days.

I remember bicycling to school through crowds chanting the names of political leaders and traveling in the country past road-blocks manned by British soldiers.

The various factions debated everything; rights versus privileges, new-comers versus old-established families, capitalism vs socialism, merchants vs landowners, Zanzibaris vs Pembans, Asians vs Arabs, Swahilis vs Mainlanders, and all this against the backdrop of the Cold War and the other nationalistic and de-colonial movements abounding in Africa at that time.

John Okello didn't have answers to these thorny issues, but he did have the insight to realize that all of these competing interests presented an opportunity for a man of action like himself. After all, a few hundred determined men might be able to seize the few local centers of communication and the three police barracks.

Once he had those under his control and possessed the weapons stored there, who on the islands could throw him out?

Would the politicians join together to denounce and oppose his illegal actions? Or as he hoped, would they continue to distrust each other, to suspect that one or another of themselves must have put him up to it?

Would not they want to make a deal with him, quick, before someone else did? On that January night he rolled the dice.

The ASP leaders, though surprised by Okellos' actions, (many were not even on the island at the time) moved quickly to embrace the rebels.

Hundreds of party followers were whipped into a frenzy by those eager to seize this opportunity to cut the Gordian knot of democratic debate and go straight to the prize of ruling. They sought to gain the chance to remake society in accordance with their own ideals. Ideals were a dime a dozen in those days. Humanity was to become a much more costly item.

Having seen just how vulnerable a government could be, and not trusting their own mixed record in open elections, it was clear to some ASP leaders that drastic measures were warranted to secure the survival of what was now being called 'The Revolution.'

The mobs were unleashed. Law and order disappeared from the streets of Zanzibar. Landowners and merchants were dragged from their houses and shops, looting and killing spread throughout Stone Town. The city literally sacked itself.

Arabs and Asians, who had supported the other parties in large numbers, were killed indiscriminately. In a single night uncounted lives were lost and over the next few days thousands more fled the islands with only what they could carry.

John Okello established for himself the rank of 'Field Marshal' and, with his mob-battalions, established a reign of terror on the islands. He broadcast bizarre threats and promises of death to all who might oppose him....

When the dust settled the multi-cultural diversity of the islands was radically altered. A one-party state was decreed. Still nervous regarding the possibility of resurgent opposition from their now exiled opponents, the 'revolutionaries' further secured their positions by signing an agreement of confederation with mainland Tanganyika. This would allow thousands of mainland political allies to intervene in any future struggle.

The police forces on the isles were virtually replaced by mainland police loyal to the party and an isolationist curtain fell over the isles which was destined to persist for more than 20 years."[55]

Although the revolution was carried out by only a few hundred people, it had popular support among the majority of black Africans. Thousands of Arabs were killed and thousands more fled the island nation. Sultan Jamshid Abdullah first sought refuge in Mombasa, Kenya, but was denied entry.

He sailed back and went to Dar es Salaam, Tanganyika, where he and his family and others on the vessel were allowed into the country. He later left Tanganyika and went to live in Britain.

The exact number of the people killed in the Zanzibar revolution has never been officially acknowledged but estimates put the figure at least in the thousands. Some say about 17,000 – 20,000 people, mostly Arab, were killed. Other sources, including an American diplomat, Donald

Petterson who was in Zanzibar during that time, say 5,000 Arabs were killed. As he stated:

"The population (of Zanzibar) included about 250,000 Africans....In addition to the Africans, Zanzibar had 50,000 Arabs, and about 20,000 Asians of Pakistani and Indian origin. During the revolution, some 5,000 people were killed. Almost all of these were Arabs. That's one tenth of the Arab population. By the time I left the island near the end of 1965, the number of Arabs was less than 25,000....The Asian population was also down by half or more by that time. As the government of Zanzibar became more and more repressive, Asians wanted out, and those who could, left.

Karume, despite a lot of good qualities, became increasingly dictatorial. I didn't see the worst of it during my time and I got along very well with him, as did Frank (Carlucci)....My own relationship with him, and again, this was before he really got bad, was quite good because of the friendship we had established when I was a vice consul, and because I continued to deal with him in his own language, and, of course, treated him with a proper measure of respect."[56]

Probably the most controversial figure in the Zanzibar revolution was John Okello. He played the most important role in the upheaval in spite of attempts by the main leaders of Zanzibar to write him out of history. He was the one who launched and led the revolution. He was the one who was directly responsible for the downfall of the Arab regime in the island nation. And he was the one who announced to the world that the Arab rulers had been overthrown and that the black African majority would be the new rulers. The revolution was not led by Karume, Babu or Hanga. They were not even in Zanzibar when the revolution took place. They were in Dar es Salaam, Tanganyika.

When I was growing up in Tanzania, it was John Okello who was the most well-known leader of the Zanzibar revolution. He was acknowledged as the leader of the uprising. The revolution took place when I was 14 years old. And as Petterson explained:

"As the afternoon wore on, a phone call from the rebels finally came. It was from Aboud Jumbe, one of the ministers in the new government, who said that he wanted to come over and take Picard to the revolutionary headquarters. In due course he arrived in an open Land Rover with armed people in it. Jumbe himself was heavily armed.

Fritz and I, along with Jim Ruchti and the executive officer, got into the Land Rover and were driven to Raha Leo (about a mile away), the site of the radio station and the African community center. Raha Leo was now the command headquarters of the revolution. There was electricity in the air when we neared Raha Leo. Hundreds of Africans who were in a very fierce mood ringed the place, many or most armed with everything from sticks to old swords; an occasional rifle was seen.

As we approached the headquarters, better-armed revolutionaries came into sight. They carried police rifles, and a few had automatic weapons. We saw Arab prisoners, some of them bloodied, some lying near the entrance to the revolutionary headquarters, all looking despondent. The crowd was so excited because they knew that at that moment, or soon thereafter, Ali Muhsin, whom they hated, would be brought in....

It was so tense as they began to swarm toward the Land Rover, that Aboud Jumbe yelled at them in Swahili (he had a bullhorn) to get back or he would open fire. They obliged, and a way was cleared for us. We got out of the Land Rover and waited for somebody to come out of revolutionary headquarters.

After a while, a figure emerged, a man dressed in a

semi-military uniform. He had on dark shorts and a dark blue shirt, a peaked cap, knee socks in the British style. He approached us, went up to the executive officer, pulled a revolver out of his holster, stuck it right at the exec, either in his ribs as I remember it, or in his face as Jim Ruchti remembered it, and said, 'How do you do? I'm John Okello.'

With that, he put his revolver back in the holster and said there was going to be some target practice behind revolutionary headquarters. Would we like to join in? Well, figuring that the targets might well be some of the captured Arabs, we declined.

He escorted us into Raha Leo. We went up the stairs into a meeting room, where after another wait we were ushered into the room.

Sitting there behind a table with Okello were Abeid Karume, leader of the Afro-Shirazi Party and now the president of the new government, Babu, Hanga, and several others.

Back from Dar es Salaam. Karume had come back to Zanzibar by boat early that morning with Babu and Hanga. The British high commissioner had met with them just before we did, and as he left we entered.

The discussion began. Fritz, first of all, told Okello (who had put his revolver on the table with the barrel pointing at Fritz) that we would not negotiate at gunpoint. Okello made no reply, but picked up and reholstered his weapon. He didn't say much during the ensuing discussion, in which Fritz made the request for an evacuation.

Babu replied angrily, so did Hanga; Karume was uncomfortable. They were angry that the Americans had brought in this warship. And it seemed to us, as we thought about it a bit later, that they didn't know whether the Manley might open fire. In any case, they really didn't care for the evacuation. They didn't want to see it happen, but they agreed to it, fearing there might be consequences otherwise.

Finally, Karume indicated that he would not oppose the request. Then he turned to Okello and said, 'It's your decision.'

Okello sort of shrugged and said, 'All right.'

This made it clear to us there that Okello was indeed of great importance. I say this because later on there were those who belittled Okello's role in the revolution. In fact, the official history of the revolution barely mentions him. But he was the force that pulled it off. Weeks later, others with more political sagacity took control...."[57]

Petterson went on to state:

"I formed a friendship with Karume as a result, because I was the only American who spoke Swahili and my Swahili was getting better and better all of the time. We carried out our conversations in Swahili. I was very deferential to him; Fritz was not. Fritz, unfortunately, was a bit patronizing with Karume....

Now Babu was a factor to be reckoned with. He was not an African. He didn't belong to the Afro-Shirazi Party, but his followers, many of whom had been trained in Cuba or other Communist countries, had automatic weapons. They had more firepower than Okello's people, and therefore were a factor to be reckoned with. Babu was the Zanzibar government's foreign minister. I chatted with him, and we agreed we would talk later on. I was told to go back to my own house, which I did.

That began a period of five weeks, during which I was the only American in Zanzibar, pretty heady stuff, a junior Foreign Service officer in charge of the embassy!....

I formed a relationship...also with Babu, who was a very charming guy, a militant left-winger, to say the least, and very shrewd, very intelligent.

Karume was a stolid man, not nearly as bright as Babu, but a man of very real native intelligence. I don't mean to use that term in a derogatory sense at all. He was a very able man in many ways, but impressionable and unsophisticated. As time would go by the results of that would be harmful to Zanzibar...."[58]

Petterson further stated:

"In the early part of '64,...by this time, Okello had been eased out of power. He was simply not up to the skills of people like Babu and Karume. He had embarrassed them during the revolution. He had been on the radio giving very inflammatory announcements about who would be killed and who would be boiled in oil and all sorts of grisly comments, which embarrassed some Zanzibaris and terrified others.

But as much as Karume and others in the Afro-Shirazi Party leadership and Babu and his followers feared Okello for a time, they must had known that they would be able to get rid of him at some point. He had no political base. All he had was some mainly very unsophisticated people with weapons. Okello was not clever enough to see that disarming these people, which Karume had inveigled him into doing, and putting them into new military units would remove his base of power.

Sometime in March, he went over to the mainland, and when he came back to Zanzibar, Karume met him at the airport and said, 'You can't get off the plane.' Karume flew with him back to Dar es Salaam, where he stayed for a while before being ejected from Tanganyika.

He was a Ugandan who had gone to Kenya when he was a young man, worked as a laborer, then as a mason, and learned construction skills that he took with him to Pemba in 1959....

He ended up in Uganda. From Dar es Salaam, he went to Kenya, where he was expelled. Nobody wanted this man around. He had a fearsome reputation. People were afraid that wherever he went, he might foment a revolution. He had trouble with immigration authorities and was either expelled from places or put in jail.

Finally he returned to Uganda, where he was imprisoned. In 1971, he was seen with Idi Amin shortly after Amin came to power. Then John Okello disappeared from the face of the earth, no doubt killed by Amin."[59]

Petterson went on to say:

"In the meantime, Karume was concerned about Babu and his people, who had close relations with the Chinese and who were very well armed. Karume feared that they wanted to take over the revolution. So did Julius Nyerere on the mainland.

Nyerere and Karume decided that they would unify their two countries to undercut Babu. This they did, telling only a very few trusted advisors. Their decision, when announced, came as a complete surprise.

Babu was out of town. As Zanzibar's foreign minister, he was in Pakistan on an official visit. When he heard about the union, he was furious. He later denied that he was upset and said, untruthfully, that he knew in advance about the plan for union. When he came back, he found a new political dispensation. The government of Tanzania, the name chosen for the country later, was in the process of being formed.

Babu was given a post in the Tanzanian government, which was located in Dar es Salaam, since it was the new country's capital. In time, other Zanzibaris who were deemed as possible security threats were transferred to mainland jobs or sent off as diplomats. Babu was effectively stripped of his political power. From then on, he was bitter toward Karume and, especially, Nyerere. With Babu's departure from Zanzibar, Karume's power increased.

The marriage between Tanganyika and Zanzibar was a marriage of convenience. It had strains from the very beginning. As time went on the relationship became more strained as Zanzibar wanted to run its own foreign affairs, have its own military, and control its own foreign exchange. But the union continued. Nyerere wanted it and Karume wanted it, if on his own terms."[60]

There are those who, more than 50 years later, sill contend that the union was a product of the Cold War, formed at the behest of the United States and Great Britain, especially the United States, to contain or neutralise communist elements in Zanzibar who supported the Zanzibar revolution.

What is deliberately ignored or overlooked by the proponents of this view is Nyerere's commitment to African unity; a position he maintained until his last days. As he stated in an interview in December 1998 about a year before he died:

"I did not believe in these small little nations. Still today I do not believe in them. I tell our people to look at the European Union, at these people who ruled us who are now uniting." – (Nyerere in an interview with Ikaweba Bunting, *New Internationalist*, December 1998).

More than any other East African leader, Nyerere relentlessly sought to unite the countries in the region and even offered to delay the independence of Tanganyika so that the three countries of Kenya, Uganda and Tanganyika would emerge from colonial rule on the same day and form a federation under one government.

Just months before the Zanzibar revolution, the leaders of Kenya, Uganda and Tanganyika – Jomo Kenyatta, Milton Obote and Julius Nyerere – met in Nairobi, Kenya, and signed a declaration on 5 June 1963 which explicitly stated that the three countries would form a federation before the end of the year and invited Zanzibar to join the union after the island nation won independence. They issued the following statement, "Declaration of Federation by the Governments of East Africa":

"We, the leaders of the people and governments of East Africa assembled in Nairobi on 5 June 1963, pledge ourselves to the political Federation of East Africa.
Our meeting today is motivated by the spirit of Pan-Africanism and not by mere selfish regional interests....
Within this spirit of Pan-Africanism and following the declaration of African unity at the recent Addis Ababa conference (from May 22 – 25, which led to the establishment of the Organization of African Unity – OAU), practical steps should be taken wherever possible to accelerate the achievement of our common goal.
We believe that the East African Federation can be a practical step towards the goal of Pan-African unity...and wish to make it clear that any of our other neighbours may in future join this Federation."[61]

The federation was never formed. Nationalism won over Pan-Africanism. An even bigger federation including Ethiopia, Somalia, Zanzibar, and Nyasaland, was also discussed. But it also got nowhere.
But that did not discourage Nyerere from pursuing unity on a smaller scale with Zanzibar.
Some observers have questioned why Nyerere did not inform his colleagues – the leaders of Kenya and Uganda – about the impending union or invite them to join the merger since he was so determined to unite the countries in the region.
Informing them or inviting them to join the union would not have served any purpose in terms of regional unification. The three East African countries of Kenya, Uganda and Tanganyika had failed to unite just the month before, December 1963, which they had set as the deadline to form a federation that year when the leaders of those countries met in Nairobi in June and signed a declaration of intent, stating that they would unite their countries

before the end of the year.

Therefore, inviting his colleagues to join the smaller union would not have convinced them of the merits of unification anymore than the earlier attempt to do so – which failed – did. They were simply not interested; not as much Nyerere was in forming an East African federation.

So, Nyerere made the next move, which was to pursue a merger of Tanganyika and Zanzibar.

It is also worth remembering that even as far back as the mid-fifties, Nyerere worked closely with the leaders of Zanzibar in the quest for independence and in order to bring the two countries even closer than they already were. Prominent leaders of the political party in Tanganyika – the Tanganyika African National Union (TANU) which was campaigning for independence on the mainland – also went to Zanzibar to help the Afro-Shirazi Party (which came into power after the revolution) to mobilise the masses for the independence struggle in the island nation. One of those prominent figures was Bibi Titi Mohammed, a fiery campaigner and an effective mobiliser of the masses even in Tanganyika itself.

The two – TANU and the Afro-Shirazi Party – were already sisters parties even before the revolution. Therefore it was only natural that their leaders went a step further and decided to unite their countries which were already bound by historical, cultural and linguistic ties; in fact, Africans in Zanzibar were inextricably linked to the mainland. That is where they originated.

All those ties, which facilitated unification of the two countries, had nothing to do with the Cold War or pressure exerted on Nyerere by the United States and Great Britain to force him to form the union.

Even without pressure from the United States and Britain on Nyerere to form the union in order to eliminate a communist threat from the island, Nyerere would have pursued the goal, anyway, to unite the two countries because of the indissoluble ties between them and his Pan-African commitment in pursuit of African unity. As early as the mid-1905s, he already had an ambition to unite Tanganyika with Zanzibar.

The United States and Great Britain may indeed have wanted the two countries to unite in order to prevent communist leaders in Zanzibar from turning the island nation into a communist state or into "another Cuba" in collusion with Eastern-bloc countries. But Nyerere also wanted to form the union for his own reasons in pursuit of African unity.

Therefore, a more compelling argument is that the interests of the United States and Great Britain – to prevent a communist regime from assuming power in the island nation by placing Zanzibar under the control of Tanganyika – coincided with the interests of Nyerere who wanted to unite the two countries in fulfillment of his Pan-African commitment even if there was no such threat; a goal he had been pursuing long before the Zanzibar revolution.

Pan-Africanism was not a product of the Cold War. It preceded the Cold War. As a philosophy and ideology of decolonisation and unification, it started way back in the 1900s. It did not start after World War II, although it found concrete expression during that period, especially in the fifties and sixties, which became the era of decolonisation on the African continent.

The Cold War argument, competition between the East and the West as the driving force behind the merger of Tanganyika and Zanzibar to protect Western interests in the region and in Africa as a whole, is refuted even by the CIA itself which was active in Zanzibar – and in Tanganyika – according to some of its declassified documents.

While it is true that the United States and Britain wanted to contain Zanzibar to make sure it did not fall into communist hands, hence the imperative need for unity with Tanganyika which would enable Nyerere and his colleagues on the mainland to control radical elements in the island nation, there is no question that Nyerere pursued unification of the two countries on his own initiative.

He already had a track record of trying to unite African countries, first by forming an East African federation of Kenya, Uganda and Tanganyika, which would have become a reality had his colleagues in Kenya and Uganda shared his passion for unity. According to a CIA declassified report on the Zanzibar revolution, "Zanzibar: The Hundred Days' Revolution," 21 February 1966:

"Toward the end of 1956, Julius Nyerere, Tanganyika's foremost African nationalist and the founder of the Tanganyika African National Union (TANU), is reported to have come to Zanzibar t o urge Africans and Shirazis to stand against the Arabs and to form a political party based on pan-Africanism. On hisi initative, the Afro-Shirazi Party (ASP) was formed in 1957....

In late 1963 Mohammed Shamte, the leader the ZPPP (Zanzibar and Pemba People's Party) and the Chief Minister of Zanzibar's coalition government, stated privatelty that Nyerere and Kambona were basically unfriendly to the present government of Zanzibar 'including Zanzibar Africans like myself.' He expressed bafflement, saying he could not figure out what 'I or any Zanzibar Shirazi had ever done to the Tanganyikans.'

TANU leaders themselves usually advanced two basic reasons for their support of the ASP; first, their close feeling of kinship with the African element in Zanzibar and, second, their fear of Communisin or proto-Communism in the ZNP (Zanzibar Nationalist Party), especially people like Babu. Although there was no talk of alliance or annexation, it no doubt was even then the view of the Tanganyikan leaders that Zanzibar ought to be associated closely with Tanganyika.

Three other non-bloc countries, besides Tanganyika,

are known to have supported the ASP (Afro-Shirazi Party) before the revolution in 1964.

Ghana was, perhaps, rather slower than Tanganyika in coming out openly in favor of the ASP, but by at least 1961 the die was cast. In that year, the Ghana Bureau of African Affairs sent over $15,000 to assist the ASP in the election; later that year, Ghanaian legal assistance was afforded the ASP in defense of individual Africans accused of offenses committed during the election riots; at the end of 1962 the ASP opened an office in Accra; and in early 1963 the High Commissioner of Ghana in Uganda held private discussions with ASP leaders on the subject of financial assistance for the ASP.

Prior to the independence of Zanzibar, the Ethiopian Government also provided financial assistance to the ASP, on the grounds that it represented the majority and was the only predominately (sic) African political party. Haile Selassie, who was under considerable pressure from Egypt, was particularly sympathetic to the ASP's concern about Arab influence in Zanzibar. He was reportedly delighted when the coup ousted the Arab-dominated government in January 1964, and the Ethiopian Government was among the first to recognize the new regime.

While the ASP maintained liaison with these several ruling African parties and with Israel, the ZNP (Zanzibar Nationalist Party) found its major international ally in Egypt....

Sometime in mid-1963, probably soon after the June elections, a group of ASP leaders, including Hanga, went to Tanganyika to ask for money and arms in support of their revolutionary plan. Tanganyikan complicity with the ASP has been well established. Although President Nyerere may not have been aware of the extent to which Tanganyikan Defense Minister Kambona was involved in supplying arms and money to the Zanzibar revolutionaries, he obviously knew and approved of the general plan for the revolution.

Apparently, the coup was planned for March or April 1964. The most important figure in the plot was Hanga; Karume personally was never involved; it is doubtful that Othman Shariff knew of the plan....

Although Zanzibar's union with Tanganyika was in his interests – inasmuch as it got Babu off the island – Karume apparently was not initially enthusiastic about the idea; certainly, he was not as strongly in favor of the union as Hanga, who claims that he and Kambona agreed when they were students together in London that Tanganyika and Zanzibar should be united one day.

The idea of a union was not a new one. Nyerere probably had it in the back of his mind when he first became involved in Zanzibar politics, beginning around 1956. For years, he had looked forward to the time when an African government would come to power in Zanzibar, at which time he planned to merge the two countries. His feeling of urgency about the union in March and April 1964 was probably a reflection of his concern that Babu was well on his way to consolidating his position in Zanzibar and his belief that only decisive action taken in time could save Zanzibar's African revolution from Arab control.

There is evidence that Nyerere was concerned about the excessive degree of Communist influence in Zanzibar, but press and other comment in the West was probably wrong in emphasizing this as Nyerere's chief concern. It seems that the Tanganyikan President deliberately exeaggerated his fears that Zanzibar was falling under Communist control; it was an argument that he could use most convincingly in the West to win support for his move to absorb Zanzibar into Tanganyika.

Whereas in private conversations with Westerners, Nyerere has always emphasized the anti-Communist line as the main rationale for the union, in public he has taken the position that the the union was simply a natural step toward African unity.

The important point is that the union of Tanganyika and Zanzibar *was a Tanganyikan initative*. Although the idea had occurred to Western officials as the obvious solution to the Zanzibar problem, the subject was never officially discussed with the Tanganyikans. Thus, it appears that the move to form the union was strictly African in origin, without British or American inspiration; the news of the event caught all of the major world powers by surprise.

For more than a month, Nyerere and his representatives had been conducting secret negotiations with Karume and other Zanzibari leaders. Although they had suceeded in convincing several of them – including Hanga and Twala – that it was in their best interests to follow the Tanganyikan guidance, Karume was not immediately persuaded.

Finally, Nyerere's threat to recall the Tanganyikan police contingent had the force of an ultimatum. Faced.with the prospect of being deprived of the support he needed against Babu, Karume agreed to the union.

As an independent nation, Zanzibar had lasted just one hundred days. In its brief and turbulent career as a sovereign state, it had faced a bitter internal struggle for power, near economic collapse, and an intensive Communist offensive. It is not surprising that its new African leaders should have found it impossible to preserve their independence against these odds. Zanzibar was not really equipped for independence. To preserve the integrity of the African revolution they had just won, its leaders had to sacrifice the independence they had just been given. Zanzibar's future had always seemed in the long run to lie with Tanganyika. It was only surprising that this should have been realized so quickly....

During March and April Nyerere frequently invited Karume to Dar es Salaam for private talks, where he would be away from the influence of Babu and Hanga. Reportedly, the Tanganyikan President was very worried about what was happening in Zanzibar and was anxious to bolster Karume. In their talks, Nyerere first broached the subject of a Tanganyika-Zanzibar merger to Karume. Although it was not his sole reason for the union, he definitely believed that a merger would strengthen Karume's power position in Zanzibar. His feeling of urgency about the matter was probably due to his concern to ensure Karume's dominance as soon as possible.

Before the union, the main thing that kept Karume in power was the Tanganyikan police force contigent, which Nyerere sent to the island as a measure of protection for Karume against Okello and his armed followers. After Okello's departure, Karume kept the police as protection against Babu and the pro-Communist elements that were attempting to secure position of power in the government. Although they were nominally under the control of Karume, they took their orders from Nyerere. Without such concrete support from Nyerere, Karume would probably not have been able to stay in power in Zanzibar....

Even before the revolution, the affiliation of Zanzibar with Tanganyika had been under discussion in the context of a larger East African Federation. Nyerere, Karume and Hanga were on the record as favoring the Federation; Babu was opposed. It had never been a question of a union between Tanganyika and Zanzibar alone, however; that possibility arose as a direct result of the revolution.

As noted earlier, it was Nyerere who initiated the negotiations leading to the union. Much has been written about his reasons for wanting a Tanganyika-Zanzibar union. Press comment in the U.S. and other Western countries has tended to emphasize the cold war aspects of the situation....He has said on a number of occasions that he was personally furious with the way the American and British press treated the union....

On the question of the 'African revolution' Nyerere is deeply emotional. The possibility that Babu and his Arab followers might come to dominate the Government of Zanzibar was anathema; to Nyerere, it would have been a repudiation of the Zanzibar revolution.

By late March or early April, Babu had consolidated his position to the point where a take-over by the Arabs appeared imminent. Nyerere could have been expected to do anything and everything in his power to prevent such an eventuality. His solution was the union. As the best way to guarantee the integrity of the Zanzibar revolution, he decided on a union of the two countries in which the Zanzibar Arabs would be absorbed by an overwhelming African majority.

In the case of Zanzibar, Nyerere's natural concern to safeguard the 'African revolution' everywhere in Africa was closely bound up with Tanganyikan national interests. For years, Tanganyikans, including Nyerere, had had the idea that Zanzibar was really a part of T anganyika. They had looked forward to the time when an African government would come to power in Zanzibar, at which time they planned to merge the two countries. It may well have been his interest in a Tanganyika-Zanzibar union that prompted Nyerere to become involved in Zanzibar politics in the first place, beginning in 1956....

Besides Nyerere, Defence Minister Kambona is reported to have long believed that Tanganyika should absorb Zanzibar. Although the union was reportedly a Nyerere initiative and Nyerere remained in full control of the negotiations, this is one instance in which Kambona worked in complete harmony with the President....

Hanga was probably the most receptive to the Tanganyikan initiative. He has stated privately that he and Kambona agreed that Tanganyika and Zanzibar should unite when they were students together in London. Nyerere has also commented that Hanga favored the union even more than Karume. In July URTZ (United Republic of Tanzania) Foreign Affairs parliamentary secretary Tambwe said that Nyerere was 'paticularly pleased with

Hanga because he is, above all, an African nationalist who really supports the union'....

The U.S. Government did not have any earlier indication that a union between Tanganyika and Zanzibar was being negotiated....

By all reports, Karume and Nyerere are determined to see the union through.

Nyerere and Kambona and other Tanganyikan officials have said that they will never, under any circumstances, accept its dissolution, that they are prepared to maintain it at all costs – even to the point of armed intervention. So far, they have avoided anything resembling a showdown with the Zanzibaris, but apparently they are prepared to do everything, including intervene (sic) with force, before they see the union crumble. All indications are that the union is here to stay."[62]

In forming the union, Nyerere emphasised the imperative need for unity among African countries, even on a small scale as happened in the case of Tanganyika and Zanzibar. Even a communist like Kassim Hanga, prime minister and vice president of Zanzibar under Abei Karume, who strongly supported the union from the beginning, did so for the same reason.

Had he wanted to establish and consolidate a communist base for himself and his fellow Marxist-Leninists in Zanzibar, he would not have made an impassioned plea to unite Zanzibar with Tanganyika. And had the union been a product of Western powers to neutralise communists in Zanzibar, he would not have supported a merger which was deliberately intended to destroy him politically.

Hanga was widely known as an uncompromising African nationalist and gave an emotional speech in the Zanzibar Revolutionary Council urging his compatriots to approve the merger of the two countries. He supported the union, not to serve Western interests but to advance the cause of Pan-Africanism and the wellbeing of Africa. If he committed political suicide by supporting the union, he did so for the sake of Africa, not the West. Western powers did not exert pressure on him to support a union that would undermine him.

If the West wanted a union to undermine him and other Marxist-Leninists in Zanzibar, Hanga would not have supported it. His support for the union demonstrates the merger was an African initiative. If the West wanted the union for their own reasons, then their interests coincided with the objectives of the leaders of Tanganyika and Zanzibar who wanted the merger for their own reasons as well, mainly in pursuit of Pan-African goals to unite African countries and establish strong governments on regional basis and eventually unite the continent under one government.

Hanga was not a Russian stooge; nor was he manipulated by the West to serve the interests of the United States and her allies. He made it clear he was an African nationalist more than anything else and made that known to the Russians who were considered to be his allies and supporters but who expressed displeasure with the union; so did his friend Oscar Kambona who was Tanganyika's minister of foreign affairs at a meeting with the Soviet chargé d'affaires in Dar es Salaam:

"Tanganyikan Foreign Minister Kambona summoned Soviet chargé Ustinov in Dar es Salaam in the early morning hours of 23 April to tell him of the union agreement, a few hours ahead of the public announcement. Ustinov is reported to have received the news glumly, for the most part, in silence; he was obviously displeased. His only comments of substance were an oblique reference to Tanganyika's interference in the internal affairs of Zanzibar and a reminder that the Bloc countries were giving considerable material assistance to Zanzibar. He did not press either point, but the implication was clear that

Tanganyika should think twice before jeopardizing the continuance of Bloc aid.

Kambona answered that since Tanganyika was a non-aligned nation, the union would be also, and that assistance would be received gratefully from any quarter as long as that nonalignment was not disturbed.

The Soviet ambassador in Zanzibar is also known to have tried to convince Karume that the union was not in Zanzibar's interests. Hanga was present at the meeting and he reportedly answered the ambassador: 'Better to be exploited by our own brothers than by the West or East.'

The incident is interesting in that it was the pro-Soviet Hanga, and not Karume, who was the more forceful in resisting Soviet pressure. It is good evidence that Hanga is, first and foremost, an African nationalist – a communist and a Soviet sympathizer, to be sure, but not a mere instrument of the Soviets in Zanzibar."[63]

The Cold War context was clearly emphasised by the Western media, although in some of the analyses, African nationalism was also highlighted as a driving force behind the merger, not just cold-war politics. As Robert Conley stated in hi article, "Tanganyika Vote Completes Union," in *The New York Times*, 26 April 1964:

"DAR ES SALAAM, Tanganyika., April 25—The decision of Tanganyika and Zanzibar to unite as a single state was ratified by the two East African countries tonight with a visible sense of urgency.

Tanganyika's Parliament met in an emergency session to approve the merger in an attempt to protect African nationalism from Communist subversion.

Zanzibar's Revolutionary Council gave its assent at almost the same time. The way thus was open for the two countries to be joined tomorrow as the United Republic of Tanganyika and Zanzibar.

Tonight's ratifications meant that Tanganyika had

succeeded in carrying out what amounted to a 'counter-revolution' to prevent tiny Zanzibar from becoming Africa's Cuba.

Island Saved for Nationalism

Tanganyika pressed the merger to break the island, lying 24 miles off her Indian Ocean coast, away from increasing penetration by the Soviet Union, Communist China and their allies and to bring it back into the mainstream of African nationalism.

She also pressed it as a means of rescuing Zanzibar's President, Abeid Amani Karume, who is regarded as an uncommitted African nationalist, from domination by the Marxist faction around him. This faction is led by the Foreign Minister, Abdul Rahman Mohammed, called Babu, an advocate of Peking's theory of violent revolution.

The merger will make Zanzibar and her northern island of Pemba, with a combined population of about 310,000 and an area of less than 1,100 square miles, part of Tanganyika, which has a population of 9.2 million and is the largest country in East Africa.

Action Follows Sultan's Fall

The action comes three and a half months after Cuban-trained guerrillas led Zanzibar's African majority in overthrowing the Sultan, its traditional monarch, and his Arab minority Government.

Tanganyika's President, Julius K. Nyerere, has been openly apprehensive about the way Babu's Marxist faction seized almost every seat of real power in the revolutionary government, so that Mr. Karume was reduced to little more than a figurehead, giving an African image to the revolution while the Marxists solidified their gains.

Dr. Nyerere was known to be fearful that the Marxists would use Zanzibar as a starting point for penetration into the heart of Africa, a staging area for subverting African nationalism on the mainland.

Karume a Vice President

Dr. Nyerere will be the President of the combined republic and Mr. Karume a Vice President of the new state and executive head of Zanzibar.

Zanzibar will have a Parliament whose authority will be about equivalent to that of a provincial administration.

Tanganyika will take charge of Zanzibar's foreign affairs, defense, police, emergency powers, citizenship and immigration. She also will take charge of the island's foreign trade, communications, aviation, harbors, taxes and customs.

Dr. Nyerere sought to minimize the anti-Communist intention of the merger when he made a personal appeal to Parliament to ratify the articles of union. He said the merger had been agreed upon solely in the interest of African unity:

'Unity in our continent does not have to come via Moscow or Washington,' he said to cheers and applause. 'It is an insult to Africa to read cold-war politics into every move towards African unity. Africa has its own maturity and its own will.'

Babu and his faction, in the opinion of a number of influential sources, were left with almost no choice but to accept the merger and a reduced role on Zanzibar.

'If they try to oppose the merger or even fight it,' said one source, 'they will isolate themselves from the African nationalists.'

The decision of Dr. Nyerere and Mr. Karume to join forces appeared to have been timed to coincide with Babu's absence from Zanzibar.

Babu returned tonight from a visit to Pakistan and

Indonesia. No Zanzibar officials met him at the airport.

In Nairobi, Babu said at a news conference that he thought the merger would help toward creation of an East African Federation of Kenya, Uganda, Tanganyika and Zanzibar and said that he had been 'in on the planning of such a merger.'

Asked what his position might be in the unified Government, he said: 'I do not know. It is not important.'"[64]

Besides Nyerere and Kassim Hanga, as well as Karume for his own reasons of survival, other leaders who strongly supported the union included Oscar Kambona who was Tanganyika's minister of foreign affairs and defence and a close friend of Hanga since their student days in Britain.

Babu may have accepted the union as a *fait accompli*. But he also understood its significance in a Pan-African context in the quest for regional federation and continental unity and supported it, even if grudgingly, after the merger was announced in his absence when he was in Indonesia.

He initially had misgivings about the union because it deprived him of his power base in Zanzibar. He felt he would not be as influential in the new country – of the United Republic of Tanganyika and Zanzibar, renamed Tanzania on October 29th the same year – as he was in his homeland, Zanzibar.

He was also uncomfortable with the merger because he felt that by uniting with Tanganyika, Zanzibar had been robbed of its revolutionary momentum in its quest for a radical transformation of the the island nation into a socialist state which he eventually hoped or intended to lead. He was already the leader of the radical elements in Zanzibar who wanted to establish a socialist state. But in spite of all that, he supported the merger of the two countries soon after it was announced. Support for the union by Marxist-Leninists such as Hanga and Babu clearly shows the merger was not just a product of Western pressure to unite the two countries. As Professor Ronald Aminzade states in his book, *Race, Nation, and Citizenship in Post-Colonial Africa: The Case of Tanzania*:

"On April 24, 1964, Tanganyika joined with the islands of Zanzibar to create the new nation of Tanzania. The creation of this nation must be understood within the broader global context of the Cold War among Russia, the United States, and their allies....

There is considerable disagreement among scholars about why Tanganyika chose to unite with the residents of a relatively small island off its coast. One compelling account highlights the role of foreign powers, especially the United States, which was worried about communists in Zanzibar's government and feared a 'Cuba off the coast of Africa' that would spread revolution throughout the African continent.

The Union did take place at the height of the Cold War, amid rumors of a Cuban presence on Zanzibar....There is considerable evidence of U.S. State Department efforts to persuade Great Britain to intervene in Zanzibar to prevent a communist takeover and of subsequent U.S. pressures on Nyerere to create a union with Zanzibar to reduce the influence of communist leaders on the island....

For President Abeid Karume, a union with the mainland nation-state was not the fulfillment of any ideological commitment to African unity, but a response to his own worries that the Marxist-Leninist elements within Zanzibar, especially Babu and his supporters, threatened his rule....

An alternative account of the creation of the Union was that it was a victory for African unity and pan-African solidarity....This view is forcefully argued by Godfrey Mwakikagile, who contends that the Union was an African initiative and an expression of Nyerere's pan-African commitment rather than a product of Cold War pressures....

When Nyerere urged the Tanganyikan Parliament to approve the Union, he emphasized it was a first step toward a united Africa. It demonstrated that 'a single Government in Africa is not an impossible dream, but something which can be realized....If two countries can unite, then three can; if three can, then thirty can.'

In justifying the Union as part of an effort to promote Pan-Africanism, Nyerere emphasized commonalities between the mainland and the islands, including a common language and historical and cultural ties....Nyerere further portrayed the union as a product of 'the overall desire for African unity,' arguing that 'those who welcome unity on our continent must welcome this small move towards it'....

Support for the merger with the mainland from Abdulrahman Babu and Kassim Hanga, the two Marxist-Leninists who generated the most concern on the part of Western governments, suggests that the Union was also not simply the product of a Western anticommunist conspiracy engineered by the United States and Great Britain. Although these leaders may have accepted the Union as a fait accompli, there is evidence to suggest they saw it as an opportunity to gain a larger forum in which to pursue their goal, a United Republic that would be more immune from Cold War interventions."[65]

Nyerere himself, the driving force behind the union, stated in his speech to a special session of the Tanganyika National Assembly on 25 April 1964 concerning the merger:

"The union between Tanganyika and Zanzibar has been determined by our two Governments for the interests of Africa and African Unity. There is no other reason.

Unity in our continent does not have to come via Moscow or Washington. It is an insult to Africa to read cold war politics into every move towards African Unity. Africa has its own maturity and its own will.

Our unity is inspired by a very simple ideology – unity. We do not propose this Union in order to support any of the 'isms' of this world. We propose it in order to support and strengthen Africa, and our particular part of Africa....

We shall work for African Unity and African Freedom, and we shall remain non-aligned in world power struggles which do not concern us. Each international issue will be determined on its own merit and our friendship towards all nations will be affected only by their actions towards us. We shall not allow our friends to choose our enemies for us."[66]

There is no question that the Zanzibar revolution provided an impetus for unification of the two countries: Tanganyika and Zanzibar. But is was not the sole or even the prime determinant, as demonstrated above. It only facilitated the merger, and at a faster pace than would otherwise have been the case involving gradual formation of the union of the two countries.

The successful revolution led to the establishment of Zanzibar as a republic under the leadership of the Afro-Shirazi Party (ASP). Sheikh Abeid Amani Karume, leader of ASP, became president; Kassim Hanga became prime minister and vice president, and Abdulrahman Mohamed Babu, minister of defence and external affairs.

Babu was the leader of Umma, meaning the Party of the Masses, whose members defected from the Arab-dominated Zanzibar Nationalist Party (ZNP) to whom the British transferred power on attainment of independence on 10 December 1963.

The People's Republic of Zanzibar and Pemba, as the new nation was officially known, was ruled by a Revolutionary Council composed of 30 members. It was the new government. Zanzibar became a one-party state. Land and other assets including major means of production were nationalised in pursuit of socialist transformation of the country.

The Zanzibar revolution was hailed as a victory for the oppressed masses who had endured oppression including slavery under Arab domination for centuries and was supported by many people across Africa and in other parts of the world, especially in the Third World and in socialist countries.

Among African leaders who were the strongest supporters of the revolution were Nyerere and Nkrumah. Other African leaders who supported and defended the revolution included Emperor Haile Selassie, Nigerian Prime Minister Abubakar Tafawa Balewa, and Nigerian Foreign Affairs Minister Jaja Wachuku.

Castro also supported the Zanzibar revolution, as did East Germany, the People's Republic of China and the Soviet Union.

One of the leading figures in the Zanzibar Revolutionary Council, Sheikh Thabit Kombo, stated years later in one of his speeches to the members of Tanzania's ruling party – Chama Cha Mapinduzi (CCM) which means the Party of the Revolution or the Revolutionary Party – that besides Nyerere, Nkrumah also helped to finance the Zanzibar revolution. As Andrew Nyerere, President Nyerere's eldest son, stated in his letter in 2004 in response to a number of questions I asked him when I was working on the second edition of my book, *Nyerere and Africa: End of an Era*:

"As you look at the history of Mwalimu Nyerere and his contemporaries, you see that they were like a team who were born at the same time for the purpose of liberating the country from British imperialism.

So we do well to find out the truth about what these men did. We see, for example, that there is evidence that Kwame Nkrumah financed the Zanzibar Revolution.

In a speech to the Party, Sheikh Thabit Kombo gives an

account of it. He explains how during the election in Zanzibar, there had been great carnage and many Arabs were killed. And Nkrumah had financed this. He says it was not the fault of the Arabs that the disturbances started. They had masterminded it, and started the trouble.

But it is just modesty to say that the Arabs made no mistakes because this was a government which was based on slave trading.

So, during this election, there was a lot of trouble and many Arabs were killed, and Thabit Kombo and Mr. Karume fled to Dar es Salaam. They decided that they should go to Nyerere to discuss this with him, to find out what was his opinion.

And when they met Nyerere, they discussed this and he told them to go back, and said, 'I will send you money, I will send you guns.'

They went back and there was a trial. A white judge came from London. And Karume was asked by the prosecutor, 'Do you know, Mr. Karume, when you started that fracas, 75 Arabs died?' And Mr. Karume made a very memorable statement. He spoke out in exasperation. He asked, 'Who did you want to die?'

This is a statement which all the oppressed people of the world should remember. It is all on tape. I made copies of it and sent it to quite a few people."[67]

Tanganyika under Nyerere provided both financial and material support including security forces to restore order soon after the revolution. About three months later, Zanzibar united with Tanganyika to form Tanzania, the first union of independent states ever formed on the continent and which still exists today more than 50 years later.

One of the most dramatic pictures from that period shows Abdulrahman Mohamed Babu rowing a canoe reportedly from Zanzibar to Dar e Salaam, Tanganyika – although that was never confirmed. The new government under the Zanzibar Nationalist Party (ZNP) to whom power had been transferred by the British was getting ready to arrest him before he fled to Dar es Salaam, reportedly in a canoe. He later became one of the most prominent members in the union cabinet and one of the most influential leaders in Africa and in the entire Third World.

He died in London on 5 August 1996. He was 72. The government of Tanzania under President Benjamin Mkapa paid for Babu's funeral and brought his body back home from London. He was given an official burial – not a state funeral – in spite of the fact that he had not been a cabinet member since 1972.

He was buried in Zanzibar at a funeral attended by many Tanzanian leaders and others. And he will always be remembered as one of the main architects of the Zanzibar revolution in terms of formulating a radical agenda after the upheaval.

It is a revolution that had an impact beyond Zanzibar and the rest of East Africa. In some fundamental respects, its impact was continental in scope in terms of ideological influence and political re-alignment of allies. And as the former Zanzibar resident, Donald Petterson, whom I cited earlier and who was in the island nation during the revolution stated elsewhere in "Nine Hour Revolution":

"Zanzibar is well known for it's 'Shortest War in History.' A 19th Century battle that lasted only about 45 minutes but served to demonstrate for all time the Iron fist beneath the pre-colonial European domination of East Africa.

What is less well known is the 20th Century record Zanzibar set for similar brevity in the Zanzibar Revolution of 1964.

In this Revolution a government with over a century of continuity was toppled in less than a day. Essentially a settler society, with well-defined Arabic, Indian, Swahili,

Comorian and indigenous elements, and ruled by an hereditary sultan, the newly independent nation of Zanzibar vanished in astounding suddenness.

That night was full of suspense and surprise, courage and despair. It began at 3 a.m. on the day just before a large religious holiday.

The holiday prompted large numbers of people to congregate in and around Stone Town. They set up tents or just sleep under the palms while awaiting the opening of the festivities in the morning. Among the crowds were large numbers of young men; some of these men were followers of a minor politician named John Okello.

Just how many men actually followed Okello into revolutionary battle is of some dispute.

It is clear that by the end of that fateful day thousands had joined the revolutionaries but this was after the results were known.

It's also true that Field Marshal Okello talked of having had 4 'battalions' in the field against the government forces that night, but how men many were really there when it counted?

Okello reported that the revolution began when he marched in the dead of night on the Ziwani Police Barracks (and Armory) at the head of the 250 men of his '4th Battalion.' At 3:00 a.m. he ordered his men to cut the wire surrounding this fortified compound.

That was the first real revolutionary act and it served to 'separate the men from the boys.' Okello said of his men at the time, 'The enormity of our predicament was suddenly obvious to them: we, armed with pangas, spears and a few motor car springs were going to face the risk of close combat with men armed with automatic rifles...' All but 40 men deserted or refused to crawl through the wire.

These 40 men seized the island of Zanzibar and toppled a dynasty that had ruled the islands through 12 Sultans for over 133 years.

The revolutionaries crawled to within 25 meters of the

Barracks building. Inside, asleep were scores of paramilitary police. However like most sensible people on Zanzibar they slept on the upper floors of the building, where cooling ocean breeze could ventilate the hot tropical nights. Only two men were awake and on guard duty below.

John Okello and his men rushed at these guards. Automatic fire rang out and three of the 4th battalion men went down. However one of sentries also fell, downed by an arrow shot by a revolutionary named Albert. By then Okello had closed on the remaining sentry. It was here that the deciding moment of the revolution occurred. The two crashed together. The Field Marshall tells us that 'I got hold of the gun, we fought and I managed to hit him in the cheek with the gun butt.' The firing stopped.

His men were now at the gates of the armory where hundreds of modern weapons and thousands of rounds of ammunition were locked up. The police above, who were unarmed, (in keeping with standard peacetime practice, all weapons were locked away 'for safekeeping' when the officers were off duty), attempted to storm down the single exterior staircase and enter the fray.

However, the 4th Battalion men unleashed a rain of spears, arrows and stones on the stunned troops and they piled up upon themselves on the narrow staircase. Okello's liberated rifle, which had only three bullets left, decided the issue with a short burst of fire. The police retreated back upstairs to look for ropes to lower men out of the windows.

It was too late. The doors of the armory gave way and the 4th Battalion rushed in. Soon every man was armed with a modern automatic rifle. The 'Freedom Fighters' who had started the night armed with sharpened automobile springs now were the best equipped force on the island. They poured a fuselage of fire into the upstairs rooms and very shortly the surviving police surrendered.

The sultan's forces made one serious attempt to counter

attack the rebels. The 'flying squad' arrived on the scene about an hour after the defeat of the Ziwani garrison. These 75 or so men had only light duty firearms and were no match for the now heavily armed Battalion ensconced in the fortified Armory.

The rebels allowed the sultans' paramilitary police to approach and then poured an overwhelming storm of fire into them. The firing was so intense that the surrounding bush caught fire and the police retreated in despair.

With their new base secure, guns were distributed to the other three battalions (who had encircled but not yet attacked other key sites). In short order the few other police posts and the communications centres were overrun and captured. The most serious resistance was offered by the Malindi Police Station, where firing could still be heard in the late hours of the morning.

However, by noon, the Sultan had fled. The rest is history."[68]

There are many conflicting reports about what actually happened on that day. But there is no question that neighbouring Tanganyika supported the revolution; so did Ghana under Nkrumah according to the testimony of one of the leading figures in the Zanzibar Revolutionary Council, Sheikh Thabit Kombo, which became the government after the revolution.

Regardless of the different interpretations of what happened in Zanzibar during that period, and why the revolution took place, what is clear to black Africans in Zanzibar and to many other Africans elsewhere, and to thoughtful non-African observers, is that the revolution was not a spontaneous uprising. It was a product of cumulative suffering blacks had endured for centuries under Arab domination.

It was a powerful response to such oppression and exploitation, as clearly shown by the overwhelming support the revolution got from the vast majority of black

Africans in the island nation. The revolution was also an integral part of the nationalist tide sweeping the continent during the era of decolonisation.

A lot has been said about the Soviet Union, the People's Republic of China, East Germany, Cuba and other socialist countries and their involvement in Zanzibar during those turbulent times. What is overlooked or deliberately ignored in all this is the nationalist aspirations of the black African majority in the island nation. They wanted to be free.

And it was not just the socialist countries which got involved in Zanzibar. The United States also had a strong interest in what was going on and looked at Zanzibar from an American perspective influenced by the Cold War to secure American geopolitical interests in the region and neutralise Soviet and Chinese influence.

The policies of both ideological camps were dictated by Cold War imperatives with regard to most parts of the Third World. And Zanzibar was no exception. Before the revolution, Zanzibar was not high on the American agenda of Cold War politics. But the revolution changed all that, prompting American officials to draw up contingency plans on what to do in case they had to intervene in Zanzibar.

Unfortunately, their perception of Zanzibar was refracted through the prism of the Cold War to the exclusion of any other interpretation which would have been more rational and realistic than what they had.

Declassified documents from the US State Department that were made available in 1999 a few years after the end of the Cold War precipitated by the collapse of the Soviet Union shed some light on what American leaders thought should be done about Zanzibar because of the revolution that had taken place in the island nation.

According to those documents, on 7 February 1964, the US State Department prepared a report for President Lyndon Johnson which stated:

"The crux of the Zanzibar matter is to prevent its takeover by the Communists. The new regime is an uneasy coalition of African nationalist and pro-Communist elements, each struggling for power. We are gravely concerned that the role of the nationalists may be deteriorating.

The elements of preventing a Communist takeover include:

1. Elimination or control of 'Field Marshal' Okello and armed thugs, who represent a continuing threat to order and stability.

2. Development of an independent nationalist government probably built around President Karume, leader of the Afro-Shirazis.

3. Political containment of any pro-Communist force, including Babu and Hanga, if they are unwilling to work with Karume. Babu and Hanga have had strong ties with Peiping and Moscow. Nevertheless Nyerere believes in the showdown they are African nationalists who can be and must be worked with. This is questionable.

4. Support and strengthening of Nyerere in Tanganyika and Kenyatta in Kenya.

...The U.K. has a military capability in the area to disarm Okello and his followers and to maintain order. It would do this on its own initiative if British nationals were endangered. Otherwise, understandably, it would desire a written GOZ request from Karume. Only the British can act militarily with adequate effectiveness.

...Every effort must be made to induce the British to take effective action. Since any definitive U.S. action would be based on the extent and type of action by the British, alternative measures the U.S. might take diplomatically, covertly or through economic or technical assistance would best be considered in light of the British program.

Despite the short-term stability which the U.K. military

presence probably will insure, basic problems will remain, making British disengagement extremely difficult. Dependable African security forces cannot quickly be developed.

At the same time, East Africa's leaders will be under mounting domestic pressure to seek early U.K. withdrawal. Domestic and general African pressures could lead to a British withdrawal before internal security forces have been adequately strengthened."[69]

Because of the revolutionary nature of the Zanzibar regime which was perceived to be anti-West, the United States assumed a more active role in African affairs and did everything it could to contain the revolutionary elements in Zanzibar. When Zanzibar united with Tanganyika, American officials hoped that President Nyerere would have a moderating influence on the revolutionary government in Zanzibar.

However, he did little to please the West. Tanzania under his leadership was non-aligned and went on to establish strong ties with many countries in the socialist camp – while also maintaining ties with the West – and adopted policies for socialist transformation of the country along African lines in pursuit of African socialism; what Nyerere called *ujamaa*, a Kiswahili term meaning "familyhood," based on the traditional African communal way of life.

The revolutionaries in Zanzibar had, of course, already embraced socialism although of a more radical kind with some of them espousing Marxist principles.

Although the Zanzibar revolution had an impact beyond Zanzibar, it was not engineered, orchestrated or manipulated by external forces and elements. It was an indigenous phenomenon and a military expression of the political aspirations of the oppressed black African majority.

Arabs and other non-blacks who supported the

revolution also wanted a new society restructured along egalitarian lines in which rule by an oligarchy of whatever stripes would have no place under the new dispensation. And that is what gave the revolution its transcendent and nationalistic character as a non-racist uprising, getting full support from some Arabs like Abdulrahman Mohamed Babu who was a nationalist more than anything else.

Whatever happened in the island nation, and regardless of the different interpretations which are still being given today by many people including politicians, scholars and laymen alike, there is no question that the revolution was a momentous upheaval of cataclysmic proportions in the context of Zanzibar and changed the island nation forever. Zanzibar has never been the same again.

The revolution also played a critical role in the formation of the union of Tanganyika and Zanzibar on 26 April 1964. Both leaders, Nyerere of Tanganyika and Karume of Zanzibar, wanted their countries to unite. But the union would probably not have taken place when it did had it not been for the Zanzibar revolution.

The revolution provided an impetus towards unification for a number of reasons. Black Africans in Zanzibar were afraid that their former Arab rulers would try to come back and re-institute Arab domination of the island nation. To prevent that, they sought protection from Tanganyika, a much bigger country that was also predominantly black, by forming a union under one government.

Nyerere and other leaders of Tanganyika were also concerned that instability in Zanzibar – possibly leading to anarchy – would have a direct impact on the mainland and negative consequences which should be avoided before it was too late. Unification of the two countries would be the best way to avert such a catastrophe. It would also enable Nyerere to control some of the far more radical elements in the government of Zanzibar.

Some observers *still* contend that the union of

Tanganyika and Zanzibar was a product of the Cold War. They argue that the United States wanted to neutralise communist influence in the island nation. And a union with Tanganyika would provide such a solution.

Frank Carlucci, who was the American consul in Zanzibar during the revolution and who later became director of the CIA and US secretary of defence, said he was not sure whether motivation for the union came from Nyerere or the American government. But he admits that there was concern in the American government that if the situation in Zanzibar was not contained, the island nation would become a communist stronghold.

A number of American officials said they feared Zanzibar would become another Cuba or the Cuba of Africa. And the Zanzibari leader who was feared the most as the spearhead of such communist penetration was Abdulrahman Mohamed Babu.

Babu was a subject of discussion in many circles. For example, in Nigeria, American Ambassador Averell Harriman asked Nigerian leaders what they thought about Babu. Nigerian Foregin Minister Dr. Jaja Wachuku assured Harriman that he had known Babu for many years and that Babu was an African nationalist more than anything else.

It is true that the United States characterised Zanzibar as "the Cuba of Africa"[24] after the January 1964 revolution led by John Okello who toppled the Arab-dominated regime and transferred power to the predominantly black majority and their allies including a number of Arabs, Iranians (originally from Shiraz in Iran), and others. But it is also true that the people who led the revolution were not interested in substituting one master for another – capitalist or communist – and their uprising was not communist-inspired.

The communist threat in Zanzibar was overly exaggerated. Even the leaders who could have established communism on the isles dismissed the threat. They were explicit in their intentions and would not have shied away from acknowledging that they were going to establish communism in Zanzibar – which would have been an open secret, anyway, sooner rather than later.

They included Abdulrahman Mohammed Babu, the most prominent leader with communist leanings on the islands and whom the CIA followed closely, as it did all the other leaders including Abdullah Kassim Hanga. According to one of the declassified documents in the US Archives written from Nigeria by the American diplomat and statesman Averell Harriman (he was a trip to Nigeria as a special envoy) to President Lyndon B. Johnson and Secretary of State Dean Rusk on March 25, 1964:

"In long talks with Prime Minister Abubakar (Tafawa Balewa) and Foreign Minister (Jaja) Wachuku,...both minimized concern I expressed for Communist takeover in Zanzibar, assured me that Karume was sensible and Babu was primarily African nationalist and would not permit Communist takeover. When I pressed Wachuku, he firmly insisted he could guarantee Babu whom he had personally known a long time."[70]

The dispatch from Nigeria by Harriman was followed by other reports on the potential for communist penetration of Africa during the early years of independence in the sixties.

Ambassador Harriman himself in another report to President Johnson on 28 October 1964, about nine months after the Zanzibar revolution and just one day before the Union of Tanganyika and Zanzibar was renamed Tanzania (on October 29, 1964), conceded:

"Not a single new African nation has succumbed to Communist domination."[71]

The report is one of the declassified documents

published in *Foreign Relations of the United States 1964 – 1968*. The document has also been been cited by other people including Kevin Kelly, "How Communism Affected US Policy in East Africa," in *The East African*, Nairobi, Kenya, 6 December 1999, the same year the declassified documents from the US State Department were released.

Officials in the Johnson Administration were convinced that communists had played an active role in the Zanzibar revolution on 12 January 1964, according to released documents contained in the 850-page volume of *Foreign Relations of the United States 1964 – 1968*. As one US State Department background paper, 7 February 1964, asserted:

"There was obvious communist involvement in Zanzibar."[72]

Yet, the same officials admitted that disturbances in other parts of East Africa – the army mutinies in Tanganyika, Kenya, and Uganda in January 1964 – around the same time did not appear to be communist-inspired. In fact, President Nyerere himself resolutely maintained:

"(There was) no evidence whatsoever to suggest that the mutinies in Tanganyika were inspired by outside forces – either Communist or imperialist."[73]

The army mutinies started in Tanganyika on 20 January 1964 and spread to Kenya and Uganda within two days. The mutineers demanded higher salaries and expulsion of British army officers whom they said should be replaced by African officers. But there was also potential for a military coup in each of those mutinies.

In Tanganyika, the involvement of union labour leaders Christopher Kasanga Tumbo and Victor Mkello who had close ties to the mutineers created strong suspicion that the mutiny was an attempt to overthrow the government.

There was also a common logic that linked the mutinies to the Zanzibar revolution. The revolution was an African uprising against Arab domination and had a distinct racial component (it was also a class conflict between dispossessed blacks and the merchants and landowners who were mostly Arab and Indian), as was clearly demonstrated during the revolution in which many Arabs and Indians, as well as some Comorians, but mostly Arabs, were massacred.

The highest figures of those who were killed – 13,000 to 20,000 – come mostly come from the supporters of the old Arab regime who, even today, are still opposed to the union of Tanganyika and Zanzibar.

The army mutinies in Tanganyika and in the other two East African countries (Kenya and Uganda), partly inspired by the uprising in Zanzibar, also had a racial dimension. In addition to demanding an increase in salaries, the mutineers also demanded the replacement of British army officers with African ones to Africanise the armed forces all the way to the highest level in a true spirit of independence by eradicating the last vestiges of colonialism.

The mutiny in Tanganyika was not only the first one among the three in East Africa; it was also the most successful in terms of "usurpation" of power as the only mutiny that almost ended up in a military coup.

Reports on the mutiny in Tanganyika were published in the *Standard*, Dar es Salaam, 22 – 23 January 1964.

In spite of all the speculations about the spectre of communism looming over East Africa, especially Tanganyika and Zanzibar, we see that from all available evidence, it is clear that communism – or any form of external involvement or manipulation – was not a factor in the army mutiny in Tanganyika or those in Kenya and Uganda; three inter-related incidents in a chain reaction that almost plunged the three countries into chaos during those fateful days in January 1964.

Probably more than anything else, even more than salary demands, the mutinies were inspired by black nationalism and were a military expression of indigenous political aspirations; so was the Zanzibar revolution, although it transcended race and included some Arabs and people of Persian origin in the vanguard in the quest for racial justice.

But since the oppressive regime that was overthrown was Arab, oppressing and exploiting black people more than anybody else, the revolution assumed a racial dimension as an indigenous expression of the political and economic aspirations of the black majority – who did not need communism to wake them up to reality and show them that they were being oppressed and exploited by the Arabs because they were weak and black. Experience is the best teacher.

Although all three governments – under Nyerere in Tanganyika, Jomo Kenyatta in Kenya, and Milton Obote in Uganda – survived and remained in power, there is no doubt that the mutinies had a profound impact across the continent and helped change the course of African history during the post-colonial era.

The mutinies not only demonstrated the power of the armed forces to extract concessions from national leaders and governments; they also showed, probably more than anything else, that soldiers in any African country had the power to overthrow governments without fear of retribution or any kind of punishment against them. Governments were too weak to stop or punish them, except in cases of abortive coup attempts.

Within a few years, military coups became a continental phenomenon, although not all of them could be attributed to the mutinies in East Africa. The coup in Togo is a good example. It took place in January 1963, almost exactly one year before the army mutinies in East Africa.

But like their counterparts in the three East African countries who mutinied in January 1964, soldiers in other parts of Africa knew on their own that they could storm out of the barracks, force national leaders to bow to their demands, and even overthrow them at will.

They knew the military was the strongest institution in Africa. Civilian governments were at their mercy and remained in power because soldiers allowed them to. The people were powerless to stop such intervention even if some of the governments which were being overthrown were popular and had been democratically elected.

The army mutinies in the three East African countries not only helped inspire military coups on the continent when soldiers in other countries saw how they could use guns to extract concessions from civilian governments and even overthrow them if they wanted to; they were also some of the earliest manifestations of the intrusive power of the military in African politics as a continental phenomenon, and of what was yet to come in an even more violent way: coups and assassinations spanning four decades.

The events in Tanganyika and Zanzibar in January 1964 – the Zanzibar revolution and the army mutiny on the mainland – were soon followed by another major development unprecedented anywhere else in Africa: formation of a political union of two independent states, Tanganyika and Zanzibar, to create Tanzania on April 26th in the same year.

It is the only union of independent states ever formed on the continent. It has existed for more than 50 years. It has faced problems through the years, especially from Zanzibar where secessionist demands continue to pose a threat to the stability of the union. Greater autonomy for Zanzibar may help to neutralise those demands. And it is highly unlikely that the union will collapse in spite of the problems it continues to face.

The Union Question

WHEN people come to Tanzania, they see a peaceful country which is the envy of its neighbours where civil strife in one form or another threatens national stability.

But beneath this tranquil atmosphere, even in peaceful Tanzania, which it is comparatively speaking, are simmering tensions between a significant number of Zanzibaris and mainlanders over the union between Tanganyika and Zanzibar.

It's nothing new. There have always been murmurs and occasional outbursts through the years among many people in the former island nation of Zanzibar who resent their status in the union as "junior partners" and even as "colonial subjects" ruled by "Tanganyikans" who dominate the union government.

They feel that they are not fairly represented in the union government and don't get the benefits they are entitled to as equal partners in the merger. They believe that Zanzibar was swallowed up by Tanganyika.

There are complaints from the mainlanders as well. They feel that Zanzibar, being such a small entity and with far fewer people than the mainland does, is overly represented in the union government and plays a fa bigger role – far out of proportion to its size – in union matters than it should.

There are even some people on the mainland who say the union should be dissolved. They want an independent Tanganyika.

Also, there have been calls from both sides for three separate governments.

In the 1990s, a group of 55 members of parliament (MPs) from Tanzania mainland who came to be known as the G-55 supported a bill, introduced by one of them, calling for the establishment of a separate government for Tanganyika.

Currently, under the union constitution, the union government is also the government of Tanzania mainland. Tanganyika no longer exists. The term is not even in the nation's political vocabulary but Zanzibar is.

Zanzibar exists as a political entity, although not as an independent state despite claims to the contrary by many Zanzibaris who either don't understand the former island nation's status in the union or simply don't want to be a part of it.

And there are Zanzibaris. But there are no Tanganyikans; they ceased to exist when the two countries united in April 1964 to form Tanzania.

The most explicit demand for three separate governments to come from Zanzibar was first articulated by Aboud Jumbe when he was concurrently serving as president of Zanzibar and first vice president of the United Republic of Tanzania.

He was thwarted in his attempts to champion his cause and even lost his job as president of Zanzibar and vice president of Tanzania under Nyerere.

President Nyerere argued that restructuring the union on the basis of three governments would destroy the union. It was also Nyerere who neutralised another attempt, this time by a group of mainland parliamentarians, to establish three separate governments for the country.

But the issue did not die. It's still being discussed by a

significant number of people.

On the mainland, the most vocal proponent of a separate union government was Reverend Christopher Mtikila, the leader of one of Tanzania's opposition parties, the Democratic Party, who also called for the dissolution of the union and a return to the status quo ante, with Tanganyika reclaiming its status as a sovereign entity separate from Zanzibar.

Another opposition party, the Civic United Front (CUF) which is strongest in Zanzibar especially on Pemba Island, has also called for an end to the union. As the party's opposition leader, Seif Shariff Hamad, bluntly stated in October 2000 just before the Tanzania general election in an interview with *Time* magazine:

"If we win I see no reason to stay in the Union. Zanzibaris have not benefited from it one bit. I would go to the mainland and start talks on a programme to move toward full independence."

Yet, there is no provision in the constitution of the United Republic of Tanzania which allows secession. But that has not stopped a significant number of Zanzibaris from demanding independence from Tanganyika – mainland Tanzania – which, they claim, has colonised them.

Zanzibar's outspoken former Attorney-General and later Chief Justice Wolfgang Dourado who once was detained for more than 100 days for criticizing the union and calling for a three-government federation during Nyerere's presidency, articulated similar sentiments, echoed by many Zanzibaris, when he was also interviewed in October 2000 by *Time*:

"The millions and billions of aid and development money that comes into Tanzania, do your research into how much of it comes here. Nothing. We try to talk to them but it's a dialogue with the deaf and dumb."

Former Vice President Aboud Jumbe, who was forced to resign in 1984, even wrote a book about the problem. As I state in my book, *Nyerere and Africa: End of an Era*:

"The title of his book is *The Partnership: Tanganyika-Zanzibar Union: 30 Turbulent Years*, published in 1994, ten years after he resigned, in which he contends that Zanzibar has not benefited from the union since it was formed in 1964. As he stated at a press conference in Dar es Salaam in January 1998 on the 34th anniversary of the Zanzibar revolution, he did not understand why the government continued to maintain the rigid structure of the union and refused to have three governments in spite of the desire for such change among many people in the country:

'I don't understand why the government should cling to this stand, but I suspect it is for the same reasons that my book, *The Partnership*, has been ignored since the era of the single party system.'

On whether the union was beneficial, and if it had in any way benefited Tanzania mainland since he said it had not benefited Zanzibar, he bluntly stated:

'Ask Nyerere, because he is the one who went to Zanzibar. He is the one who wanted the union. He must have had goals. Has he achieved them? I cannot speak for mainlanders on the achievement of the union.'

He also went on to say that he believed the shortcomings of the union of Tanganyika and Zanzibar had played a major role in delaying the establishment of an East African federation.

Therefore, there are serious problems. And I don't

believe that if a referendum were held today, the majority of the people of Zanzibar would vote in favour of the union as it is now. It should be restructured to accommodate their interests and ventilate their grievances. That is why the ruling party CCM is not very popular in Zanzibar.

The union can and should be saved. The question is how.

Continue to talk to the people of Zanzibar. Listen to their demands and grievances. Give them meaningful concessions. Otherwise we are going to have an eruption which could threaten and even destroy the union.

But Zanzibaris – not all of them – are not the only people who are not satisfied with the union. Many people on the mainland, including a significant number of members of parliament, feel the same way. They also want three governments. And they feel that Zanzibar is overly represented in the union government and in parliament far out of proportion to its size.

I believe the union will continue to exist. But it is a precarious existence. Dialogue and concessions are critical to its continued existence. So is rule by consensus, including formation of coalition government which should include major opposition parties." – (Godfrey Mwakikagile, *Nyerere and Africa: End of an Era*, Third Edition, New Africa Press, Pretoria, pp. 635 – 636).

There are also many Zanzibaris who contend that Zanzibar never lost its status as a independent nation. They say it's still a country which should also have the right to enter into treaties with other nations and international organisations including becoming a member of the Organisation of the Islamic Conference (OIC).

When it attempted to become a member of OIC in the 1990s, the union government effectively blocked the move. But resentment still exists in Zanzibar against this decision by the leaders of the United Republic.

The assertion by many Zanzibaris that they are a separate sovereign entity was accentuated when one cabinet member in the government of Zanzibar warned that Zanzibar would not even share its oil wealth with Tanzania mainland if oil was discovered in the isles in commercial quantities; further complicating the nature of the relationship between the two former independent states which now constitute the United Republic.

The status of Zanzibar again became a public issue in June 2008 when a representative from Zanzibar in the union parliament said the island nation entered the union as an independent country and was therefore still a sovereign entity.

Tanzania's prime minister, Mizengo Pinda, a lawyer, said Zanzibar was no longer a sovereign state. He went on to say that both Tanganyika and Zanzibar lost their sovereignties when they united in 1964 to form one country: the United Republic of Tanzania.

But that was not the end of the debate.

Some representatives in the Zanzibar legislature also brought up the matter and wanted the Articles of Union to be clarified concerning the status of Zanzibar – whether or not it was a sovereign state and had the right to enter into agreements with other countries for its own benefit as a separate and sovereign entity.

One of the arguments the union government and Tanzania's ruling party, CCM, used against claims that Zanzibar was still an independent nation was that when some people in Zanzibar were charged with treason, the case was dismissed by the High Court because whatever they conspired to do or were accused of doing could not be classified as treason against Zanzibar because Zanzibar was not a sovereign state and treason can only be committed against an independent state.

That was the argument which was used by their lawyer. And he won the case. It is also the same argument, among others, the union government and the ruling party cited to refute claims by some Zanzibaris that Zanzibar was still a sovereign entity just as it was before it united with Tanganyika in 1964 to form Tanzania.

Disputes between the main opposition party (CUF) in Zanzibar and the ruling CCM have also marred relations between them through the years since the introduction of multi-party politics. CUF has complained of rigged elections to keep it out of power. The ruling government claims it has won all the elections, despite irregularities in the polls confirmed by many observers.

The results of the last election in 2015 were nullified by the Zanzibar Electoral Commission (ZEC) when it became obvious the Civic United Front would win.

It is clear that the ruling party, CCM, will never allow the opposition to be declared the winner even if there is indisputable proof it overwhelmingly won the election. It will never be allowed to form a government; it will never be allowed to rule Zanzibar. Presidential elections in Zanzibar for the presidency of the former island nation are meaningless.

One of the leading CCM members in Zanzibar, Ali Karume, son of Zanzibar's first president Abeid Karume, bluntly stated in 2015 that opposition parties should not even be allowed to participate in presidential elections in Zanzibar.; only CCM candidates should.

History is invoked to justify that position. Post-colonial Zanzibar, after the sultan was ousted, is a product of the 1964 revolution. Only the revolutionary party which came to power after the revolution – the Afro-Shirazi Party (ASP) which merged with the Tanganyika African National Union (TANU) in 1977 to form CCM – can legitimately claim to be the guardian of the revolution and is the only one, now as CCM, that can rule the former island nation.

Even if Zanzibar were to regain its sovereign status, CMM would never allow the Civic United Front or any other opposition party to win national elections in the island nation.

There are problems within Zanzibar itself, and there are problems in the union which must be resolved in order to have a stable union.

So, while the union continues to exist, there's no question that it also has a lot of problems mainly because of the dissatisfaction of many Zanzibaris with the merger which they say robbed them of their nationhood, freedom and independence as a people with their own identity and right to live the way they want to as they did before the two countries united in 1964 to form the macro-nation of Tanzania.

Where the union is headed is anybody's guess. But in order for it to survive, meaningful concessions must be made to satisfy Zanzibaris and assure them that they are equal members in the union and not subordinates as they always have claimed to be since the union was formed.

Accommodation must also be made to satisfy mainlanders who feel that Zanzibar is getting too much from the union, far more than it deserves.

They also feel that it has too much say in union matters at the expense of mainlanders whose interests are sometimes ignored just to satisfy Zanzibaris in order to keep them in the union.

Both sides need to compromise in order to save and strengthen the union. And that includes re-writing the constitution. It should be a constitution of the people, not of the leaders and their parties, especially the ruling party which wants to perpetuate itself in office.

Problems are not going to go away by pretending that they don't exist; nor are they going to be solved by ignoring the interests of one side or the other or both.

After travelling a long journey for 52 years since the union was formed in 1964, Tanzania is now at crossroads. As one of Tanzania's newspapers, *ThisDay*, 22 July 2008, stated in "Union Between Mainland and Zanzibar At Crossroads?":

"Serious cracks have started to appear in the 44-year-old Union between Tanzania mainland and Zanzibar, with various commentators warning that the political marriage is passing through a particularly testing period in its history.

Several members of parliament interviewed separately by *ThisDay* have cautioned that the ongoing squabbling over Zanzibar's status in the Union could revive demands for mainland Tanzania to have its own government.

The concerns follow a recent declaration by a senior minister in the Isles Revolutionary Government that there will be no sharing of oil revenues with mainland Tanzania if economically viable deposits of the natural resource are discovered in the Isles.

The minister's remarks were the latest salvo in what is seen as an increasingly heated debate over Zanzibar's sovereignty - or lack of it.

The MP for Bariadi East, John Cheyo (UDP), said if Zanzibar continues to press for greater autonomy within the current two-government Union structure, proponents of the idea for a mainland Tanzania government within the Union could also well re-ignite their argument.

He recalled the infamous group of 55 MPs from mainland Tanzania – better known as G55 – who rocked the nation in the 1990s by demanding the formation of a third government representing Tanganyika (mainland Tanzania) within the union.

The Opposition lawmaker advised Zanzibaris to uphold the Union for the interests of both sides to the equation, saying if the prevailing situation is not checked, 'we fear we may go back to the G55 issue, since the people of the former Tanganyika also need to have their own identity maintained.'

According to Cheyo, there is also significant concern in mainland Tanzania that, despite its relatively tiny population, Zanzibar has such a 'big representation and say' in the current Union government.

Only through sacrifice and mutual trust can the Union between the two countries survive the current political turbulence, he asserted, calling for the government to organize a national debate on what kind of constitutional reforms may be required to 'best suit our changing needs.'

The infamous G55 surfaced in 1993 after the then Chunya MP, Njelu Kasaka, tabled a private member's motion in Parliament calling for the formation of the government of Tanganyika after Zanzibar lawmakers demanded that the islands be allowed to join the Organization of Islamic Conference (OIC).

Another prominent member of the pro-Tanganyika government group was Phillip Marmo, who is still MP for Mbulu on a CCM ticket, and is currently a minister of state in the Prime Minister's Office.

On his part, Kondoa South legislator Paschal Degera (CCM), who was also a member of the G55 movement, has told *ThisDay* that he doesn't think the Tanganyika government issue will be revived anytime soon.

He recalled that the G55 move to form the proposed Tanganyika government was fiercely opposed at the time by the Father of the Nation, the late Mwalimu Julius Nyerere, on the grounds that it was against the two-tier Union structure policy of the ruling Chama Cha Mapinduzi.

'When we met in Dodoma, it was agreed that the ruling party's policy was that of a two-government union, and we left it at that. We find it strange that Zanzibaris now want us to discuss the issue of sovereignty,' he said.

Degera criticized the government of inaction on various recommendations on the union structure made by a number of committees.

The MP advised the government to seriously address the cracks in the Union, and push through Parliament the necessary constitutional amendments if required.

'Zanzibaris are questioning their share of revenue from

the Union government. They have their own government looking after their interests, but we mainlanders don't question them about that,' he noted.

Mpwapwa legislator George Lubeleje (CCM) said he is in support of Prime Minister Mizengo Pinda's statement in Parliament last week that the national (Union) constitution clearly says Zanzibar is not a sovereign state.

'This issue is very clear...the constitution of the United Republic (of Tanzania) states that Zanzibar is part of the Union,' said Lubeleje.

The Minister of State in the Vice-President's Office responsible for Union matters, Muhamed Seif Khatib, said the country's constitution is not written in stone and can be amended if necessary.

'The constitution is not a holy book, it can be amended...After every five years, we have a tradition of making changes through Parliament, which I believe is the competent authority to make any amendments to our constitution,' Khatibu told *ThisDay* in an interview.

The minister said there was no need for a protracted debate on the matter, noting that premier Pinda has already instructed the attorneys-general (AGs) in both the Union and Zanzibar governments to study the concerns amongst some Zanzibar legislators about Zanzibar's constitutional position in the Union set-up.

He called for patience as the two AGs look into the legal interpretations of the matter, but agreed with the assertion that Zanzibar is not a sovereign state.

In October 2006, the High Court of Zanzibar dismissed a case challenging the legality of the 1964 Act of Union, which formed Tanzania out of the islands of Zanzibar and the Mainland area formerly known as Tanganyika.

In dismissing the case, Zanzibar High Court judge Mbarouk Salim said the claim had not been properly filed. 'The applicants had no proper understanding of legal procedures,' he said.

The judge also said the time for challenging the Union

had expired. 'The proper people to have been sued in this matter were the late Mwalimu Julius Nyerere [who signed on behalf of Tanganyika] and the late Abeid Amani Karume [who signed on behalf of Zanzibar), because they are the founders,' Mbarouk said.

Ten Zanzibaris filed the case, claiming that the now 44-year-old agreement signed by the two leaders had never been properly ratified.

The claimants also said the agreement was invalid because the attorney-general's office had failed to produce an official copy of the original agreement, which therefore seemed to have been lost.

The Union agreement gave the two islands that form Zanzibar – Pemba and Unguja – semi-autonomous status. Zanzibar has its own president, government and parliament, but they must still defer to the president of the United Republic of Tanzania.

Some groups of Zanzibaris have been claiming that the Tanzanian (Union) government oppresses them economically. The Zanzibar government cannot sign agreements with international companies that want to invest in the islands.

In 2005, Zanzibar hoisted its own flag after the House of Representatives unanimously approved a Bill seeking the introduction of a Zanzibar flag.

The need for having a specific flag for the Isles was not a critical issue until the multi-party political system was ushered in, and the Opposition pressed for it. It argued that the flag was necessary to accord Zanzibar a distinct identity." – (*ThisDay*, Dar es Salaam, Tanzania, 22 July 2008).

What the union of Tanganyika and Zanzibar is going through is a cautionary tale, and an apt warning to the people of East Africa who want to unite and form a federation. It is an eye opener to what is in store for them should they ever unite.

As for Tanzania, she has yet to address the union question in a way that the matter needs to be addressed. There is a need for public debate and may be even for a referendum on this highly contentious subject.

The future of the country *can not* be decided by one party. Tanzania is a union of the people, not of the leaders alone. The people constitute the nation. They can not commit treason against themselves. Let the people decide.

Notes

1. Colin Legum, *Pan-Africanism: A Short Political Guide* (New York: Frederick A. Praeger, 1965), see texts of declarations of the Ghana-Guinea union, and the Ghana-Guinea-Mali union, appendices 6 and 12.

2. Haroub Othman, "The Union with Zanzibar," in Colin Legum and Geoffrey Mmari, editors, *Mwalimu: The Influence of Nyerere* (Trenton, New Jersey: Africa World Press, 1995), p. 173.

3. Frank Carlucci, quoted by Haroub Othman, "The Union with Zanzibar," ibid.

4. Haroub Othman, ibid., pp. 173 - 174.

5. Benjamin Mkapa, in his national broadcast on Radio Tanzania, Dar es Salaam (RTD), announcing the death of Julius Nyerere, quoted by the Associated Press (AP), October 14, 1999.

6. Benjamin Mkapa, quoted in "Tanzania: IRIN Focus on the Union," October 28, 1999.

7. Ali A. Mazrui, "Nyerere and I," in *Voices*, Africa Resource Center, 1999.

8. Julius Nyerere, in *The New York Times*, December 19, 1961; Ali A. Mazrui, *Towards A Pax Africana* (London: Weidenfeld & Nicolson, 1967), p. 77.

9. Julius K. Nyerere, "Nationalism and Pan-Africanism," in *WAY Forum*, No. 40, September 1961; and in Paul E. Sigmund, Jr., editor, *The Ideologies of the Developing Nations* (New York: Frederick A. Praeger, 1963), pp. 208, and 209.

10. Julius Nyerere, in Tanganyika *Standard*, Dar es Salaam, November 1964.

11. Julius Nyerere, in an interview with James McKinley, "Tanzania's Nyerere Looks Back: Many Failures, and One Big Success – Bringing A Nation to Life." *The New York Times*, and the *International Herald Tribune*, September 2, 1996.

12. Julius K. Nyerere, Julius Nyerere, "Freedom and Unity," *Transition, Volume 0, Issue 14, 1964*, Kampala, Uganda, pp. 40 – 45. This was a republication of what he wrote earlier in June 1960 before he led Tanganyika to independence the following year. For an analysis of cooperation among the three East African countries of Kenya, Uganda and Tanganyika, see also Donald Rothschild, *Politics of Integration: An East African Documentary*, Nairobi, Kenya: East African Publishing House, 1968.

13. *Intelligence Study: Zanzibar: The Hundred Days' Revolution (ESAU XXX)*, Directorate of Intelligence, Central Intelligence Agency, No. 18, RSS No. 0013/66, 21 February 1966, pp. xiii, xiv.

14. Helen-Luoise Hunter, *Zanzibar: The Hundred Days' Revolution*, Westport, Connecticut, USA: Greenwood Publishing Group, 2010, pp. 95, 96, 98.

15. Mohammed Ali Bakari, *The Democratisation Process in Zanzibar: A Retarded Transition*, Hamburg, Germany: Institut für Afrika-Kunde, 2001, pp. 118 – 119.

16. Nyerere, quoted by Bakari, ibid., p. 119. Nyerere also, cited by Bakari, quoted by Martin Bailey, *The Union of Tanganyika and Zanzibar: A Study in Political Integration*, Syracuse: East African Studies, 1973, p. 3.

17. Ambassador Donald Petterson interviewed by

Charles Stuart Kennedy and Lambert Heyniger, 29 –30 November 2000, *The Association for Diplomatic Studies and Training (ADST), Foreign Affairs Oral History Project*, p. 50; copyright 2002 ADST.

18. Ambassador Robert T. Hennemeyer interviewed by Charles Stuart Kennedy, February 1989, *The Association for Diplomatic Studies and Training (ADST), Foreign Affairs Oral History Project*, pp. 8 – 20; initial interview date: 15 February 1989; copyright 1998 ADST.

19. Ambassador Donald Petterson interviewed by Lambert Heyniger, 29 – 30 November 2000, *The Association for Diplomatic Studies and Training (ADST), Foreign Affairs Oral History Project*, pp. 27 – 37, 38 – 40, 42 – 48, 50 – 57; initial interview date: 13 December 1996, copyright 2002 ADST.

20. Ambassador Robert C.F. Gordon interviewed by Charles Stuart Kennedy, January 1989, *The Association for Diplomatic Studies and Training (ADST), Foreign Affairs Oral History Project*, pp. 16 – 18; initial interview date: 25 January 1989, copyright 1998 ADST.

21. Ambassador Frank Carlucci interviewed by Charles Stuart Kennedy, *The Association for Diplomatic Studies and Training (ADST), Foreign Affairs Oral History Project*, June 1997, pp. 28 – 38; initial interview date: 1 April 1997, copyright 2000, ADST.

22. Robert Henneyer, interview, *The Association for Diplomatic Studies and Training, Foreign Affairs Oral History Project*, ibid.

23. Ambassador John Howard Burns, interviewed by Charles Stuart Kennedy, May 1995, *The Association for Diplomatic Studies and Training, Foreign Affairs Oral History Project*, pp. 18 – 27, copyright ADST 1998.

24. Ambassador Claude G. Ross interviewed by Horace G. Torbert, February 1989, *The Association for Diplomatic Studies and Training, Foreign Affairs Oral History Project*, pp. 62 – 71; initial interview date: 16 February 1989, copyright 1998 ADST.

25. Julius Nyerere, in an interview with Ikaweba Bunting, "The Heart of Africa," *New Internationalist*, Issue 309, December 1998.

26. Julius K. Nyerere, "Policy on Foreign Affairs," in J.K. Nyerere, *Freedom and Socialism: A Selection from Writings and Speeches 1965 – 1967* (Dar es Salaam, Tanzania: Oxford University Press, 1968), p. 369.

27. Ann Talbot, "Nyerere's Legacy of Poverty and Repression in Zanzibar," in "World Socialist Web Site: WSWS: News & Analysis: Africa," International Committee of the Fourth Internationale (ICFI), London, November 15, 2000.

28. Abdulrahman Mohamed Babu, "The 1964 Revolution: Lumpen or Vanguard?", in Abdul Sheriff and Ed Ferguson, eds., *Zanzibar Under Colonial Rule* (Athens, Ohio: Ohio University Press, 1991). See also, A. M. Babu, *African Socialism or Socialist Africa?* (Dar es Salaam, Tanzania: Tanzania Publishing House, 1981).

29. Jorge Castañeda, *Compañero: The Life and Death of Che Guevara* (New York: Alfred A. Knopf, 1997), pp. 326 – 327, and 328.

30. Gamal Nkrumah, "The Legacy of A Great African," in *Al-Ahram Weekly*, Issue No. 452, Cairo, Egypt, 21 – 27 October 1999.

31. Jim Lobe, "Tanzania: Restiveness in Zanzibar," in *Foreign Policy Focus: Self-Determination*, 2 May 2001.

32. Averill Harriman, "Telegram from the Embassy in Nigeria to the Department of State/1/," Lagos, Nigeria, March 25, 1964, 7 p.m., in US Diplomatic Archives: Nigeria (1964 - 1968), *Foreign Relations of the United States 1964 - 1968, Vol. XXIV Africa*, US Department of State, Washington, D.C. Source: Johnson Library, National Security File, International Meetings and Travel File, Africa, Box 31, Harriman's Trip, 3/64. Confidential; Priority; Passed to the White House.

Averill Harriman, in *Foreign Relations of the United States 1964 - 1968*, op. cit.; Kevin kelly, "How

Communism Affected US Policy in East Africa," in *The East African*, Nairobi, Kenya, December 6, 1999.

33. US State Department document, 7 February 1964, in *Foreign Relations of the United States 1964 - 1968*, op. Cit.

34. Julius Nyerere, in the *East African Standard*, Nairobi, Kenya, February 13, 1964; quoted by Ali A. Mazrui, *Towards A Pax Africana*, op. cit., p. 153.

35. Ronald Aminzade, "The Politics of Race and Nation: Citizenship and Africanization in Tanganyika," Department of Sociology, University of Minnesota, December 2, 1998. See also *Tanganyika Standard*, Dar es Salaam, Tanganyika, January 22, 1964; *Tanganyika Standard*, January 23, 1964, on the mutiny.

On the incendiary debate on Africanisation in the preceding years, which led up to the mutiny in January 1964, see also, *Mwafrika*, Dar es Salaam, Tanganyika, October 4, 1960, a newspaper published in Kiswahili. The Minister of Labour Derek Bryceson, a British who settled in Tanganyika in 1951, said in parliament that Tanganyikans of Asian and European origin should also be considered as Africans, and defined as such; to which leaders of the opposition African National Congress (ANC) responded: "The meaning of Tanganyikans is Africans with black skins."

See also Tanganyika Council Debates (LEGCO – Legislative Council – Debates), speech of Bhoke Munanka, October 13, 1960: "Africanisation means Africanisation, it does not in any way suggest localisation (to include local Asian and European Tanganyikans and other non-blacks together with African Tanganyikans)"; *Ngurumo*, Dar es Salaam, Tanganyika, 3 - 4 November 1960, another Kiswahili newspaper containing reports on the heated debate on Africanization, and definition of "Africans."

Besides Zuberi Mtemvu, leader of the opposition African National Congress (ANC) and others in parliament, another ardent and uncompromising advocate of rapid Africanisation was Christopher Kasanga Tumbo, former trade union leader and member of parliament who resigned from his position as high commissioner (ambassador) to Britain and returned to Tanganyika in August 1962 to form the People's Democratic Party (PDP). The PDP's leading and founding members included several ANC activists, and the party advocated racial policies on citizenship, Africanization, and on minorities - Asians, Europeans, Arabs and other non-blacks - contrary to what TANU said, and objected to clauses of the new republican constitution, "which made the president a virtual dictator." See *Tanganyika Standard*, Dar es Salaam, Tanganyika, January 9, 1963.

In early January 1963, the PDP leaders met to discuss plans to merge with the ANC. See *Tanganyika Standard*, Dar es Salaam, Tanganyika, January 4, 1963; *Tanganyika Standard*, January 18, 1963, in which it was reported that the opposition parties, including AMNUT (All-Muslim National Union of Tanganyika), demanded a referendum on the one-party system.

See also Julius Nyerere, in a letter to all the cabinet members and their ministries, January 7, 1964, against Africanization: "The nation must use the entire reservoir of skill and experience.... The skin in which this skill is encased is completely irrelevant.... This means that discrimination in civil service employment as regards recruitment, training, and promotion must be brought to an end immediately.... We cannot allow the growth of first and second-class citizenship. Africanization is dead." In the *Tanganyika Standard*, Dar es salaam, Tanganyika, January 8, 1964.

Trade union leaders objected vehemently to this directive from President Nyerere. Teendwa Washington, leader of the Local Government Union, accused Nyerere of taking Tanganyika "back to the colonial days." See *Tanganyika Standard*, Dar es Salaam, Tanganyika, January

9, 1964.

Almost exactly two weeks later, on January 20, after Nyerere issued his policy directive against Africanisation, the army mutinied over this very policy, demanding higher salaries and the replacement of British army officers by black ones in pursuit of full Africanisation of the armed forces.

36. Kevin Kelly, "How Communism Affected US Policy in East Africa," *The East African*, Nairobi, Kenya, 10 December 1999; US State Department background paper, February 7, 1964, in *Foreign Relations of the United States 1964 - 1968*, op. Cit.

37. Ulric Haynes, in a National Security Council memo, June 8, 1966, in *Foreign Relations of the United States 1964 - 1968*, op. cit.

38. Julius Nyerere, "Principles and Development," in J.K. Nyerere, *Freedom and Socialism: A Selection from Writings and Speeches 1965 – 1967* (Dar es Salaam, Tanzania: Oxford University Press, 1968), pp. 202 – 203.

39. Julius Nyerere, "Rhodesia in the Context of Southern Africa," in *Foreign Affairs*, New York, April 1966; J.K. Nyerere, *Freedom and Socialism*, op. cit., pp. 143, 154 - 155, and 156.

40. J.K. Nyerere, on the Warsaw Pact invasion of Czechoslovakia, August 1968.

41. Colin Legum and John Drsydale, eds., *Africa Contemporary Record: Annual Survey and Documents 1968 – 1969*, London: Africa Research Limited, 1969, pp. 221, and 614.

42. J.K. Nyerere, "Policy on Foreign Affairs," in Nyerere, *Freedom and Socialism*, op. cit., pp. 370, and 371.

43. J.K. Nyerere, ibid., p. 203.

44. Ibid., p. 202.

45. Mohammed Ali Bakari, *The Democratisation Process in Zanzibar: A Retarded Transition, The Democratisation Process in Zanzibar: A Retarded*

Transition, Hamburg, Germany: Institut für Afrika-Kunde, 2001, p. 122.

46. Mwesiga Baregu, quoted by M.A. Bakari, ibid., p. 123. See also, cited by Bakari, Mwesiga Baregu, "In Defence of Closer Union and Greater African Unity," *The African Review, Vol. 22, No. 1 and 2*, 1995, p. 82.

47. Benjamin Mkapa, quoted in Benjamin Mkapa, quoted in "Tanzania: IRIN Focus on the Union," 28 October 1999; CNN, Dar es Salaam, 20 November 2000, "Tanzania's Mkapa pledges to act on Zanzibar, fight corruption."

48. Samir Amin, "The First Babu Memorial Lecture," in honour of the late Abdulrahman Mohammed Babu (22 September 1924 – 5 August 1996), London, 22 September 1997. See also Samir Amin, "The First Babu Memorial Lecture on 22 September 1997," *Pambazuka News, Issue 451*, 8 October 2009; Abdulrahman Mohammed Babu, "A New Europe: Consequences for Tanzania," in the *Review of African Political Economy*, Vol. 18, No. 50, Spring 1991, pp. 75 – 78. Mohamed Suliman and A.M. Babu, "Face to Face with A.M. Babu," in the *Review of African Political Economy*, vol. 22, No. 66, December 1995, pp. 596 – 598.

49. Ali A. Mazrui, in "Africa's Mwalimu: Ali Mazrui Pays Tribute to Julius Nyerere," in *Washington Magazine*, Washington, D.C., Vol. 12, No. 4, Fall 1999; Ali A. Mazrui, "Mwalimu Rise to Power," in the *Daily Nation*, Nairobi, Kenya, October 17, 1999; Ali A. Mazrui, "Nyerere and I," in *Voices*, Africa Resource Centre, October 1999.

50. Ali A. Mazrui, "Witness to History: Interview with Ali A. Mazrui," *The Gambia Echo*, 25 July 2008.

51. Julius K. Nyerere, in an interview with M.A. Novicki and B. Boorstein, in *Africa Report*, November 30, 1985, p. 10. See also Pal Ahluwalia and Abebe Zegeye, "Multiparty Democracy in Tanzania: Crises in the Union," in *Africa Security Review*, Vol. 10, No. 3, 2001; Martin

Bailey, *Union of Tanganyika and Zanzibar: A Study in Political Integration*, Syracuse, New York: Syracuse University, June 1973.

52. Julius Nyerere in his speech during the 40th anniversary of Ghana's independence, Accra, Ghana, March 1997.

53. Julius Nyerere, quoted by Austin Ejiet, "Kwa heri, Mtukufu Rais Julius K. Nyerere," in *The Monitor*, Kampala, Uganda, October 17, 1999. See also A. Ejiet, Ibid.:

"Three things sum up Mwalimu Julius Nyerere for me. Sometime in the mid-sixties (sic) a Swiss bank wrote offering to keep his money in a secret-coded account at extremely generous interest rates.... But far from jumping at the offer, the president published the letter in the national newspapers with the memorable declaration that he had no money to hide and that the little that he had could only be banked in Tanzania where it belonged....This action underscored the president's faith in his country and spoke volumes about the extent of his sincerity.

Shortly after this, a type of precious stone was unearthed in Tanzania. The country's parliament unanimously resolved to name this gem the 'Nyeretrite' in recognition of his stature as a statesman locally as well as internationally. The president thanked his countrymen for their kind consideration but politely declined the honour. Instead he proposed that the stone be named the 'Tanzanite.' Tanzania, he arugued, was more important than individuals.

Just one more. Mwalimu Julius Nyerere paid a visit to Ghana shortly after his retirement in 1985 and reportedly berated the leadership of that country for the shabby way in which the republic's founder, Kwame Nkrumah, had been treated."

54. Julius K. Nyerere, in "The Heart of Africa: Interview with Julius Nyerere on Anti-Colonialism," in *New Internationalist*, Issue 309, January-February 1999.

The interviewer was Ikaweba Bunting, an African-American who had lived in Tanzania for 25 years when he interviewed Nyerere. As he stated:

"In recognition of Nyerere's passing, I present his last great interview. The first issue of *The Internationalist* in 1970 had as its cover story an interview with President Julius Nyerere of Tanzania, then at the very centre of the new movement for world development. Three decades on, Nyerere is, Mandela aside, Africa's most respected elder statesperson, still active in attempts to resolve the current conflicts in Burundi and DR Congo. No one is better placed to look back on the anti-colonial century....

It has been my privilege to be associated with Mwalimu Nyerere for the past 25 years. During a visit to Harlem, New York, in the late 1960s Mwalimu extended an invitation to Africans in the Diaspora to come to Tanzania and participate in building a socialist African state. I came over through a new organization called the Pan-African Skills project and have lived in Tanzania ever since, for a quarter of the century.

Nyerere's Tanzania was a magnet for anti-colonial activists and thinkers from all over the world. Uganda's President Yoweri Museveni, for instance, was deeply influenced by his time as a student at the University of Dar es Salaam. Museveni belonged to a study group led by the Guyanan Walter Rodney, who wrote his seminal book *How Europe Underdeveloped Africa* while he was a professor there.

The University of Dar es Salaam became the centre for the guerrilla-intellectuals and activists of African liberation movements. FRELIMO of Mozambique, the ANC and PAC of South Africa, ZANU and ZAPU of Zimbabwe, the MPLA of Angola and SWAPO of Namibia all had offices and training camps in Tanzania. The country also gave safe haven to US civil-rights activists, Black Panther Party-members and Vietnam War resisters.

It was an exciting place to be. Under a head of state

who valued equal rights, justice and development more than pomp and power of office, Tanzania was at the heart of the anti-colonial struggle.

Over the years I have often been able to sit with Mwalimu and reflect on Africa's struggle for self-determination and development. Now, in December 1998, prompted by the *New Internationalist* special issue on the Radical Twentieth Century, Mwalimu Nyerere and I sat down over two days at his home in Butiama, Tanzania, and reflected on his role over the past 50 years as an activist and statesperson in the anti-colonial cause."

Nyerere's awakening started early when he was a student at Makerere University College, Kampala, Uganda, which was then and for many years the most renowned institution of higher learning in colonial Africa, attracting students from all parts of the continent. As he stated in the same interview:

"At Makerere in 1943 I started something called the Tanganyika African Welfare Association. Its main purpose was not political or anti-colonial. We wanted to improve the lives of Africans. But inside us something was happening.

I wrote an essay in 1944 called The Freedom of Women. I must be honest and say I was influenced by John Stuart Mill, who had written about the subjugation of women. My father had 22 wives and I knew how hard they had to work and what they went through as women. Here in this essay I was moving towards the idea of freedom theoretically. But I was still in the mindset of improving the lives and welfare of Africans: I went to Tabora to start teaching.

Then came Indian independence. The significance of India's independence movement was that it shook the British empire. When Gandhi succeeded I think it made the British lose the will to cling to empire. But it was events in Ghana in 1949 that fundamentally changed my attitude. When Kwame Nkrumah was released from prison this produced a transformation.... First India in 1947, then Ghana in 1949.... Under the influence of these events, while at university in Britain, I made up my mind to be a full-time political activist when I went back."

Nyerere was 27 years old in 1949, and 21 when he founded the Tanganyika African Welfare Association at Makerere University College in 1943.

55. Donald Petterson, "The Zanzibar Revolution."
56. D. Petterson, ibid.
57. Donald Petterson, "The Association for Diplomatic Studies and Training Foreign Affairs Oral History Project," interviewed by Charles Stuart Kennedy and Lambert Heyniger on 30 November 2000; initial interview date: December 13, 1996, pp. 50, and 55.
58. D. Petterson, ibid., pp. 37 – 38.
59. Ibid., pp. 40, 42.
60. Ibid., pp. 49 – 50.
61. "Declaration of Federation by the Governments of East Africa" signed by Julius Nyerere, Milton Obote, and Jomo Kenyatta, Nairobi, Kenya, 5 June 1963.
62. CIA, *Intelligence Study – Zanzibar: The Hundred Days' Revolution (ESAU XXX), No. 18, RSS No. 0013/66, 21 February 1966*, pp. 1 – 2, v, xiii – xv, 9 – 10, 63 – 64, 118 – 119, 120 – 121, 122, 123, 125, 136.
63. *Intelligence Study: Zanzibar: The Hundred Days' Revolution (ESAU XXX), Directorate of Intelligence, Central Intelligence Agency, No. 18, RSS No. 0013/66, 21 February 1966*, pp. 126 – 127.
64. Robert Conley, "Tanganyika Vote Completes Union," *The New York Times*, 26 April 1964.
65. Ronald Aminzade, *Race, Nation, and Citizenship in Post-Colonial Africa: The Case of Tanzania*, New York: Cambridge University Press, 2013, pp. 99 – 102. See also, cited by Ronald Aminzade, Amrit Wilson, *U.S. Foreign Policy and Revolution: The Creation of Tanzania*, London: Pluto Press, 1989; Anthony Clayton, The Zanzibar Revolution and its Aftermath, Hamden, Connecticut, USA:

Anchor Books, 1981, p. 70; Abdulrahman Babu, "I Saw the Future and It Works," in Haroub Othman, ed., *I Saw the Future and It Works: Essays Celebrating the Life of Comrade Abdulrahman Mohamed Babu 1934 – 1996*, Dar es Salaam, Tanzania: E&D Limited, 2001; Godfrey Mwakikagile, *The Union of Tanganyika and Zanzibar: Product of the Cold War?*, Pretoria, South Africa: New Africa Press, 2008; Julius K. Nyerere, "The Union of Tanganyika and Zanzibar," *Freedom and Unity: Uhuru na Umoja: A Selection from Writings and Speeches, 1952 – 1965, Volume 1*, Dar es Salaam, Tanzania: Oxford University Press, 1967, p. 292).

66. Julius K. Nyerere, *Freedom and Unity: Uhuru na Umoja*, Dar es Salaam, Tanzania: Oxford University Press, 1969, p. 292.

67. Andrew Nyerere, in Godfrey Mwakikagile, *Nyerere and Africa: End of an Era*, New Africa Press, Fifth Edition, Dar es Salaam, Tanzan, and Pretoria, South Africa, 2010, pp. 125 – 126.

68. Donald Petterson, "Nine Hour Revolution."

69. *Foreign Relations of the United States 1964 - 1968*, pp. 610 – 611.

70. Averell Harriman, Johnson Library, National Security File, International Meetings and Travel File, Africa, Box 31, Harriman's Trip, 3/64. Confidential; Priority; Exdis. Passed to the White House. See also, US Diplomatic Archives: Nigeria (1964 - 1968), *Foreign Relations of the United States 1964 - 1968, Vol. XXIV.*

71. Averill Harriman, in a report to President Lyndon B. Johnson, 28 October 1964. See *Foreign Relations of the United States 1964 – 1968*; Kevin Kelly, "How Communism Affected US Policy in East Africa," *The East African*, Nairobi, Kenya, 6 December 1999.

72. US State Department background paper, 7 February 1964, in *Foreign Relations of the United States 1964 – 1968.*

73. Julius Nyerere, quoted in the *East African*

Standard, Nairobi, Kenya, 13 February 1964; cited by Ali Mazrui, *Towards A Pax Africana*, op. cit., p. 153.

President Julius Nyerere mixing sand from Tanganyika and Zanzibar to symbolise the merger of the two countries when they united on 26 April 1964 to form the United Republic of Tanganyika and Zanzibar, renamed the United Republic of Tanzania on 29 October 1964.

www.ingramcontent.com/pod-product-compliance
Lightning Source LLC
LaVergne TN
LVHW051823080426
835512LV00018B/2694